THE ROYAL HORTICULTURAL SOCIETY

STEP-BY-STEP
VEG
PATCH

THE ROYAL HORTICULTURAL SOCIETY

STEP-BY-STEP
VEG
PATCH

Lucy Halsall

LONDON, NEW YORK, MUNICH, MELBOURNE, DELHI

Senior Editor Chauney Dunford   **Managing Editor** Penny Warren
Editor Becky Shackleton   **Managing Art Editor** Alison Donovan
Senior Art Editor Alison Shackleton   **Publisher** Mary Ling
Jacket Designer Nicola Powling   **Art Director** Peter Luff
Production Editor Raymond Williams   **Publishing Director** Mary-Clare Jerram

Picture Research Susie Peachey   **RHS Publisher** Rae Spencer-Jones
Photography Mark Winwood   **RHS Editor** Simon Maughan

First published in Great Britain in 2012 by Dorling Kindersley Ltd
80 Strand, London WC2R 0RL
A Penguin Company

2 4 6 8 10 9 7 5 3 1

001–183129–Mar/2012

A CIP catalogue record for this book is available from the British Library.

ISBN 978-1-4053-9443-7

To find out more about RHS membership, contact:
RHS Membership Department, PO Box 313, London SW1P 2PE
Telephone: 0845 062 1111
www.rhs.org.uk

Printed and bound by Tien Wah Press, Singapore.

Discover more at **www.dk.com**

Lucy Halsall is editor of *Grow Your Own* magazine, a dream job for her as she describes it as *The Good Life* TV series in magazine format. Before this she worked at the RHS Garden Wisley and as gardening editor at *Amateur Gardening* magazine. Lucy was raised on her family's smallholding and has been cultivating salads and vegetables since her teenage years. Lucy describes her own garden as "small, yet very productive!"

Contents

Your growing space

Planning your plot

Grow your own vegetables

Grow your own fruit

Problem solver

Your growing space

Why grow your own food?

Anyone who has ever picked fresh strawberries will know how unlikely it is that the first harvest will reach the kitchen. The urge to eat them there and then usually beats all but the strongest wills, reflecting one of the main reasons to grow your own – taste. Freshness equates to flavour, and growing your own crops allows you to pick them at their best. Compare shop-bought broad beans to your own crop and you'll never buy them again. However, there are also many other reasons to grow your own crops, whether it's for your health and that of your family, for environmental concerns, or for the pleasure of it.

Fresh and healthy

The positive effects of eating fruits and vegetables on health has long been known, but there are also direct benefits of actually growing them yourself. Vitamin and antioxidant levels are at their highest when crops are first picked, with the levels falling by half after 7–14 days of harvest. Although supermarkets sell fresh produce, you can rarely tell how long ago it was picked or how well it has been stored, especially if it has been imported or kept in refrigeration. Growing your own food means you can pick fruits and vegetables no sooner than is really necessary, ensuring they are as fresh, tasty, and nutrient-packed as possible.

Growing fitter

In addition to eating more healthily, the tasks involved in growing your own crops also provide good exercise, improving fitness, stamina and flexibility. Just one hour's digging can burn off over 300 calories, while even light pottering means being active.

Good for the environment

Local and global concerns have driven many people to assess the impact of food production on the environment, and terms such as "food miles" and "carbon footprint" have become synonymous with a responsible, ecologically-minded attitude. Producing your own food at home embraces both these concepts – food miles are zero and the carbon footprint is negligible.

Growing your own fruit and vegetables isn't just about jumping on the latest bandwagon however, it's pretty fundamental – people need food. By growing it in your own back garden or allotment, you are reducing the strain on global supplies. You will also know exactly how "green" it is or how ethically it has been produced – organically perhaps. You can also share your surpluses, helping to reduce the global impact of others.

Space to grow

Growing fruits and vegetables does require space but that doesn't mean having a large garden of your own – or even a garden at all. Allotments have surged in popularity in the last decade, with friends now commonly sharing plots to beat the waiting lists. The community spirit found at most allotment sites makes them ideal for beginners, with plot-holders freely sharing knowledge, experience, tools and produce. Many areas also have community gardens, which offer similar benefits without a waiting list.

If you have a garden, or access to one, use every inch of space. Walls, balconies and fences are all suitable for growing crops, as are containers, windowsills, windowboxes and hanging baskets. Even the smallest plot with just a few plants will give you a taste of what growing your own fruits and vegetables is all about.

Allotments and community gardens *are ideal for beginners to learn the basics and to experience growing crops for the first time.*

Greater choice

Commercial growers are motivated by yield, shelf-life and uniformity, and grow vast monocultures of just a few varieties, giving little choice in the shops. When growing your own, you can set your own priorities when deciding what to plant. There are thousands of different crops and varieties to try, many developed over generations, with qualities better suited to your own tastes.

(above) **Beetroots are quick to grow** *and require little care or experience. Try varieties you don't see in supermarkets, like ones with striped flesh.*

(above left) **Strawberries are the taste of summer** *and are very easy to grow. Plant them in patio pots or in hanging baskets, and enjoy them utterly fresh.*

You're unlikely to ever see 'Nun's Bellybutton' French beans, 'Fat Lazy Blonde' lettuce, or 'Yellow Stuffer' tomatoes in the supermarket aisles, so why not grow them instead? You can even develop your own strains.

Crops in small spaces

There's no denying that having less space limits the amount of fruit and vegetables you can grow, but by thinking laterally you can still produce enough to supplement your needs, even if you can't supply everything. Instead of planting vegetables that take up lots of space but are cheap to buy, choose more space-efficient crops, such as climbing beans, that make best use of the room you have. Prioritize what you grow and plant the crops you like to eat – think quality not quantity, and grow varieties that are expensive to buy in the supermarket.

Small but perfectly formed

Small spaces are actually brilliant for growing fruits and vegetables as they are usually enclosed by walls or fences, giving them similar growing conditions to traditional, walled gardens – just on a smaller scale. A south- or west-facing bed offers the perfect environment for chillies, peaches, aubergines, strawberries, herbs – and any other number of crops that revel in the warmth of the sun. In contrast, north- and east-facing aspects are cooler and shadier, ideal for growing tender lettuces and leafy brassica crops.

Most small plots have a full range of aspects, which means they can provide the complete spectrum of growing environments any kitchen gardener would require. In contrast, large plots are often more exposed, lacking shade, shelter from the wind, or a handy water supply. This limits the crops that can be grown to those that will tolerate everything the elements can throw at them.

Small spaces can be highly productive; *the trick is make use of every inch available, including the walls and fences. Position containers wherever there is enough room, and train growth vertically.*

(left) **Growing bags** *are designed for crops, and can be used outside as mini beds. For deep-rooted crops, cut them in half and stand them upright.*

(below) **Fewer crops means less care**, *which is ideal if you are short on time and space. Only grow as much as you can care for to avoid disappointment.*

Urban gardens

Small plots are particularly productive in towns and cities, thanks to the "urban heat island" effect. In essence, large buildings provide shelter from the wind and also absorb heat during the day, which is radiated back at night. This action, along with the heat generated by urban life raises the local temperature by a useful few degrees. This allows urban growers to extend their growing season in spring and autumn, and to benefit from higher summer temperatures than rural counterparts. In practice, it means that long-season crops, such as chillies, sweetcorn and winter squashes, give a better harvest. It can even make growing exotic crops more successful, such as figs, okra, loquat, and tomatillo.

Less space, less effort

Having a small plot also brings other advantages, besides the crops you can grow. Although larger sites can accommodate more plants, they also take a lot more looking after. The novelty of pushing a wheelbarrow to your allotment or leaving slugs in your car boot on the journey home from the plot can soon wear thin.

Small gardens are far less daunting, especially for those new to growing their own crops. You can cultivate areas in bite-sized chunks, there's little risk of being overwhelmed with weeds, and you won't be tethered to a watering can all summer. It's also easier to sneak out in your pyjamas in the morning to enjoy homegrown fruit for breakfast.

Space for creative thinking

Making the most of a small plot involves being creative with the space you have and the crops you grow – which is part of the fun. Any object that holds sufficient compost and has drainage holes can be used as a planter, so use your imagination. Certain crops grow well planted together, so try different combinations to create schemes that are both colourful and productive.

The sky's the limit

Space at ground level is the most limiting factor in small plots, as all plants need room to grow. However, a useful way around this is to plant climbing and trailing crops, and to train their growth vertically, leaving space at their base for other crops. Climbing French and runner beans, cucumbers, trailing squashes, and cordon tomatoes all produce valuable crops from minimal space. They can either be planted to grow against walls or fences, or at the base of free-standing wigwams, which can even be sited in ornamental beds.

Speedy crops

To make the most of the space you have, choose crops that can either be harvested over a long period, or those that mature quickly and can soon be replanted. One large pot sown with cut-and-come-again salad leaves will keep the average family supplied for well over two months. Once cut,

these rapid growers will yield again within three weeks. "Baby" vegetable varieties of turnip, cauliflower, beetroot, carrot, and cabbage are harvested within a couple of months of sowing. Another way to ensure maturity within minimal time is to start plants off under cover in pots and modules, or to purchase plug plants. The time saved by planting rather than sowing into the final growing positions allows you to squeeze in another crop or two before the growing season ends.

Bountiful varieties

As well as choosing crops that mature quickly or over a long period, look for varieties that are known to give a large crop. If you only have space for a few plants, it's worth making sure the ones you plant are as productive as possible. Many varieties have been bred specifically to suit compact gardens, so seek advice when deciding what to plant.

(above) **Tasty young turnips** *can be harvested a few weeks after sowing. Start early and you can enjoy several crops in the same season.*

(left) **Containers** *can be planted up under cover in spring to give the crop a head start. They can also be moved inside during autumn to grow on longer.*

(far left) **A wigwam of beans** *will crop all summer, but only takes up the same amount of space as three or four potato or cabbage plants.*

Making the most of limited space

1 Hanging baskets These offer a space-saving way to grow many different crops, including mixed summer herbs, salad leaves, tumbling tomatoes, and even chillies. They must be kept well watered and fed, and given a bright spot. Hang near the kitchen for easy picking.

2 Trailing crops Plants like squashes, can be trained along the ground, as well as vertically. Use short canes to train the stems along the edges of beds or paths so they are easy to harvest, and to free up space for planting other crops.

3 Quick spring container crops Make use of vacant planters not yet filled with summer bedding. Early Swiss chard and radish will be ready to harvest before your tender ornamentals need to be planted out in early summer.

4 Handy mini crops Sow quick crops wherever gaps develop in the garden during the year. Many mature in a matter of weeks, so can be sown direct to crop before the end of the season. Also sow between your ornamentals.

5 Wall training Use vertical surfaces to support climbing and trailing crops. Many fruits, including apples, crop very well when trained against walls and fences, freeing up useful bed space.

6 Underplanting Take advantage of the bed space beneath taller crops, like sweetcorn, by underplanting. Keep them well watered and lettuce will benefit from the light shade, while long squash stems can be trained out towards the sunlight.

Essential tools and equipment

Gardening involves many practical and strenuous techniques, but choosing the right tools for the job will make the tasks easier and more successful. For example, using secateurs to cut through very thick stems not only hurts your hands, it can also damage the tool itself. Similarly, budget tools made of poor quality materials will wear out more quickly, proving a real false economy. Buy the best you can afford, and also consider good quality second-hand tools.

Growing your own need not be expensive, *as many key pieces of equipment can be bought cheaply and re-used. Be prepared and stock up on the essentials at the beginning of the season.*

Digging

A good spade and fork are essential for digging, along with a hand trowel for excavating smaller holes. Assess your physical strength before buying a fork or spade – the smaller blade of a lady's border spade, for example, will allow you to lift a lighter weight of soil than a larger, standard model. Handle designs vary from brand to brand, so choose one that feels comfortable. For repetitive tasks such as digging these are important considerations.

Weeding

A hoe is an extremely useful tool for removing young weed seedlings from among your crops. Long-handled models are ideal or larger beds or if you find bending difficult, whereas short-handled "onion" hoes are ideal for smaller areas and raised beds. A hand fork will also help you to easily remove weeds, especially those with long tap roots, like dandelions.

Propagation

When preparing a seedbed outside, a rake is extremely handy. The fine teeth filter out clods of earth and loosen weeds and stones so that the soil takes on a fine, crumbly texture, perfect for germination. The edge of a hoe can be used to make drills.

Indoor propagation, or sowing into pots, requires a range of containers and seed compost, as well as labels, a pencil, and a dibber. If you invest in a heated propagator, you will be able to raise a wider range of crops.

Pruning

A good pair of secateurs is essential. Cutting and pruning are repetitive tasks so a well-designed handle grip will be easier on your hands – try out a selection of models before you buy. If your fruit trees need renovation then loppers and a pruning saw are also invaluable for the more sizeable branches. Telescopic loppers with extendable handles are useful if your plants have reached lofty dimensions.

Keep your tools well maintained

It is vital to keep tools clean and in good condition, otherwise the health of your plants might suffer. Clean tools such as secateurs with disinfectant between uses to prevent diseases passing from one plant to another, and keep them well oiled and tightened up to ensure that they cut as cleanly and efficiently as possible. Apply oil to tools such as spades and forks to prevent them from rusting.

The garden basics

It is best to invest in good-quality tools that will last, so make sure you only buy those you really need – a fork is essential on an allotment but may be unnecessary if you are only growing in pots on a patio.

1 Fork Excellent for working organic matter into the soil, forks are also useful for lifting crops or moving plants.

2 Spade Ideal for digging over large areas of light soil and moving mulches, a spade is a vital tool for a larger plot.

3 Dutch hoe This versatile tool is ideal for killing annual weeds: it severs the roots so that the plants then die. It is also useful for drawing soil up around crops.

4 Rake This tool is crucial in site preparation: use it to remove stones and clods of earth, level the soil, and create a fine tilth for sowing seeds.

5 Dibber Used for making holes for sowing or planting, a dibber is also useful for marking out seed drills.

6 Trowel The ideal size for creating planting holes, a trowel is an essential tool when transplanting your crops.

7 Secateurs This versatile tool can be used for harvesting crops such as peppers and asparagus as well as for pruning back fruiting bushes.

8 Cloche Useful for warming up the soil for early crops or for providing pest protection, a cloche is an easy way to get your plants off to a good start.

Deciding what to grow

It's inevitable to have the odd dearth and glut in your harvests but that's what freezers and friends are for. But with a little preparation however, you can minimize the peaks and troughs to ensure a steady flow of fresh produce. It is a good idea to begin planning your crops the previous autumn, when seed companies release their catalogues. While it's not crucial to be very organized on a small-scale plot, time spent planning is time well spent. Each crop entry in this book gives sowing times and weeks to maturity. These will vary according to where you garden but will help you plan your supply of food.

Grow what you like
Make a list of the fruit and vegetables you eat and then create two columns: "to buy" and "to grow". Although self-sufficiency is a brilliant concept, few people have enough space to actually achieve it, so select crops carefully to maximize space. Try to be fairly picky at this stage – for example, if you only have space for containers, devoting them to early, melt-in-the-mouth new potatoes is sensible; planting them with maincrops, which will take far longer to mature, may not be the best use of the space. At the top of your "to grow" list should be crops that are expensive to buy or difficult to obtain, or those that are at their very best eaten fresh. Bulkier crops, or those that are cheap and readily available should be at the bottom of this list.

Consider your space
Once you've established your "to grow" crops, calculate how much room you'll need to grow them and which month they'll mature. Compare potential gluts and dearths with the space you have available, and it should become apparent if certain crops need to migrate into the "to buy" column instead. Don't forget to consider how well certain crops store. For example a glut of chillies to dry or broad beans and blueberries to freeze is actually a godsend, as these crops preserve very well. Winter squashes and garlic are easily kept in a dry, frost-free shed or garage. In contrast, you may not have space or inclination to store more than a few pumpkins.

Staggering your harvests
It is important to consider how soon you'll be able to eat the produce that you grow, and to sow your seed accordingly. Carry out "successional sowings"– sow a pinch of seeds every few weeks, rather than all in one go, for a constant supply of fresh crops. Alternatively, swap cultivars with friends and family. These will mature at different rates and a single sowing of a selection of types can provide a more steady supply, and allow you to

Storing surpluses

If you have a glut and can't eat your fresh crops fast enough, then do not despair. There is a wide range of ways to store surplus crops, but knowing which to use is key, as not all fruits and vegetables suit every method.

1 Drying Vegetables such as onions and garlic should be dried thoroughly before storing – lay them out on racks in a dry, frost-free place. Herbs and chillies can also be dried. Consider drying slices of other crops such as apples and plums in the oven on a low heat, to completely dry them out.

2 Freezing This is a useful method for storing a wide range of crops. To prevent berries forming a solid lump when you freeze them, lay them out on trays so that none of them are touching. Vegetables will store for longer if they are blanched – quickly immersed in boiling water – before freezing. This is ideal for crops such as asparagus and sprouting broccoli.

3 Preserving Transforming crops into delicious savoury chutneys or relishes and sweet jams and jellies is an ideal way to preserve a wide range of fruits and vegetables, capturing their flavours when they are at their peak.

4 Storing Many fruits and vegetables will keep well if they are simply kept in a cool, well-ventilated, frost-free place. Wrap apples and pears in waxed paper to help maintain their juiciness; keep potatoes in paper sacks so that light cannot reach them.

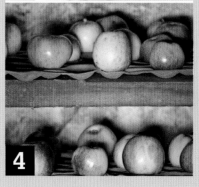

(above) **Redcurrants** *can be used very successfully in jams and jellies, or frozen for later use, so a glut need not mean that the fruits have to go to waste.*

(above left) **Salad leaves** *can be expensive to buy and are ideal for sowing successionally, as they will be ready in just a few weeks. Sow a variety of types for a constant supply of delicious, mixed leaves.*

try different flavours and textures, too. Another option is to sow some seeds under cover, and some outside. Those that are protected will get a head start. To extend the season, also consider growing crops that mature naturally over a long period.

Choosing the right spot

The microclimates that your garden creates will inevitably suit some crops better than others. For this reason don't rush in, but instead take a little time to identify the different areas within your plot and then match the crops accordingly. Draw a plan and mark on it where the sun can and can't reach, as this is the primary factor to consider when deciding what crops to grow. When given the right position, you'll find that your fruit, herbs, and vegetables will thrive, yield more heavily, and will also show greater resilience to pests and diseases.

Hot and sunny

South- and west-facing sites capture the most sunshine, so count yourself lucky if you have a fence or wall with this orientation. Many crops, such as fruits and fruiting vegetables, rely on sunlight to maximize their sugar levels, so make the most of these areas. These high-sugar crops often require a long growing season, and benefit from additional shelter.

Bright but cool

Soil and container compost dries more quickly in sunnier positions, which will affect different crops in different ways. Container-grown fruit trees, for example, produce bigger and sweeter harvests when exposed to full sunlight, but will shed fruitlets if they become dry during the crucial spring fruit-setting period. To ensure a good crop, position them in the sun but keep the roots cool and well-watered. Conversely, a potted fig will revel with hot sun on its roots, as do most Mediterranean herbs.

An open, sunny position *is ideal for a range of crops, including carrots, leeks, lettuces, and potatoes, as long as they receive adequate water and are not allowed to dry out.*

Shade and moisture

North- and east-facing sites receive less sunlight but are equally useful in the vegetable garden, providing a cool environment in which many leaf crops thrive, such as cabbages, kale, spinach, and summer salads.

The main advantage of a shadier spot is that it is easier to maintain cool roots, which allows for steady growth with less risk of premature flowering, known as "bolting". Moisture is also lost less quickly from the soil, and crops growing here may require watering less frequently as a result. If however, you find that these cooler pockets are too moist for your crops, add plenty of bulky organic matter to the soil, such as composted bark, to improve drainage. Alternatively, grow them in raised beds filled with free-draining soil or compost.

Rain shadows

One final key area requiring careful management is the base of walls and fences, especially the sides facing

(top) **Plant leafy crops** *such as colourful Swiss chard in partially shaded, north- or east-facing sites. The plants will benefit from this site as too much sun might otherwise scorch its large, lush foliage.*

(above) **Wall-trained fruit trees** *take up very little growing space and can look impressive. Ensure that they are not allowed to dry out when in flower or fruit if they are planted in a "rain shadow".*

away from the prevailing wind. These areas often suffer from "rain shadows", where rainfall cannot reach the soil. If planting here, keep the area well watered during spring and summer, especially if you are growing fruit crops, which are sensitive to even brief dry spells.

Cold and wind

Many gardens may well experience regular prolonged freezes and frosts. Sloping sites and valleys in particular are at risk of collecting cold pockets of air, known as "frost pockets", at their lowest points. A wall, fence, or thick evergreen hedge can also collect cold air if the ground slopes above it. In these cases, choose hardy, robust vegetables and, if you wish to grow fruit, choose late-flowering varieties to avoid the worst of the cold, or wrap plants with fleece during frosty spells. Cold soils are less damaging if they are dry, so add bulky organic matter to these sites to help plants overwinter.

Some garden sites may also be vulnerable to the wind. Wind has two major actions: buffeting foliage and drying out plants. While Mediterranean herbs would be quite happy in such conditions, leafy spinach or Swiss chard would fast become tattered. Use screens or other more robust plants to deflect or filter fast-moving air, and plant in large, thick-walled containers to moderate the effects.

If a late cold spell is forecast, *cover vulnerable plants over with garden fleece to protect them from frost damage.*

Preparing the soil

Whether you sow your seeds directly in the ground, or sow crops under cover first and then plant them out, preparing your soil in advance is crucial. Start by identifying your soil type and pH so you can decide whether you need to make any changes, as some crops cope better than others in certain conditions. The best time to dig over your plot is between mid-autumn and mid-spring – break up compacted soil, remove any weeds, and work in plenty of organic matter, such as well-rotted garden compost, to improve yields.

Understanding soil types

The type of soil you have plays an important role in how well your crops grow, as most plants have preferred conditions – such as warm, light, well-drained soil or one cool and moisture-retentive. The soil you have also affects how you manage it to get the best results, and how easy it is to work with. The first step is to identify the soil type you have and to check it in different parts of the garden.

Sand, silt and chalk soils

Soils that contain a high proportion of sand drain very freely and lose nutrients quickly, although warm up rapidly in spring. They are light and easy to dig, but need regular watering and feeding throughout the year. Soils rich in silt and chalk particles also drain freely but retain nutrients better, which makes them better suited to growing crops. All three types can be made more moisture- and nutrient-retentive by regularly digging in well-rotted organic matter, such as garden compost, manure, leaf mould, or composted bark chips. This organic matter will act like a sponge to help absorb moisture and whatever fertilizers you apply, while at the same time allowing the soil structure to remain airy and open.

Clay soils

Clay soils have the opposite qualities to sandy types; they are moisture-retentive and fertile, but slow to warm in spring, and are heavy to dig. They are also very sticky when wet, often becoming waterlogged, and are prone to baking solid during summer dry spells. Moderate clay soils are good for growing most crops, especially if improved by digging in well-rotted organic matter. If the soil contains a lot of clay and drains very poorly, try growing your crops in raised beds.

Loam soils

This type of soil contains an even mix of sand, silt, and clay, and is a real godsend for growers. It is ideal for most fruit and vegetable crops and needs very little improvement.

How to test your soil

Soil testing kits are commonly available and are a quick, easy way to find out the pH of your soil (from very acidic (1) to very alkaline (14), with 7 being neutral). Simply shake up a sample of your soil with the testing solution and then judge the colour against the kit's pH chart. Perform the test in several places around your garden, as the pH may vary greatly, even within one site.

An easy way to check your soil type is to roll some between your fingers. Clay soils can be easily moulded into balls due to their clinging, sticky texture. Sandy soils are far more crumbly and will not hold together (see image, left). Loamy soils feel silky and mould quite well. Your soil is likely to be a mixture of all three types, but performing this test will help you to tell which is dominant.

Soil cultivation

A final consideration is whether to dig the soil over extensively or not. There are two schools of thought, known as the "dig" and "no-dig" approaches. The argument for digging is that it breaks up compacted soil, removes pernicious weeds, incorporates soil improvers, and encourages the deep rooting of crops. A winter dig also exposes pests to predators and cold conditions, and helps to break up heavy clods of earth. Most garden soils will benefit from an initial dig.

However, there is also an argument for fewer cultivations after the initial dig. This encourages natural fertility to rise and soil structure to stabilize. Weed seeds aren't repeatedly brought to the surface and worms and other beneficial fauna are undisturbed. Mulches are simply laid on the surface for worms to draw down into the soil.

Ultimately, a combined approach is often best. It may be necessary to dig if compacted areas of soil form or if perennial weeds begin to encroach.

Acid and alkaline soils

Even if your soil is fertile, the crops growing may not be able to absorb all the nutrients they need, which leads to deficiencies (see. p.246). A common cause for this is soil acidity, or pH, which can restrict the availability of certain nutrients to the plants growing there. While it is possible to alter soil pH to suit the crops you'd like to grow, it is a difficult and endless task that is rarely worth the hard work involved.

Instead, check the pH of your soil (see left) and grow those crops that grow best in the conditions you have. Brassicas, for example, crop better in alkaline soil, while blueberries must have acid conditions. Alternatively, if you want to grow crops that don't suit your soil pH, plant them into raised beds or containers filled with suitable soil or compost.

(top) **Digging in well-rotted organic matter** *helps to improve the structure of your soil, as well as the nutrient content. Apply it at least once a year in spring or autumn for long-term benefits.*

(above) **Raised beds or containers** *offer the ideal solution to problematic, hard-to-manage soils as they give you the opportunity to start afresh. Fill with a loamy, rich, free-draining soil.*

For a "no-dig" mulch, *lay a thick layer of organic matter such as compost on the soil surface and simply leave it to be broken down.*

Sowing and planting

Raising plants from seed is an easy and inexpensive way of growing many vegetables and herbs, and it opens the door to a vast array of delicious home-grown food. If you only have limited space, consider which crops can be sown directly outside and which should be started indoors. Don't waste valuable indoor space on crops that thrive when sown outside, such as beetroots. Instead, save it for crops like chillies that benefit from a longer growing season.

Sowing under cover

Sowing seed under cover allows you to get off to an early start and extend your growing season – seed can be sown indoors at times of year when it would otherwise perish outdoors. This is also especially useful for long-season plants such as aubergines and peppers, as it gives them sufficient time to mature and set their fruits. Heated propagators are readily available and are useful for starting off crops over winter. Generally, set a temperature of 12°C (54°F) for hardy crops and 18°C (64°F) for tender ones.

Light levels

If you sow your seed too early, when light levels are low, your seedlings will struggle and produce stretched, leggy growth, even if you provide them with additional heat. Early spring is sufficiently early to sow most crops. However, if providing enough light is problematic, consider sowing hardier crops directly outdoors and buy plug plants of those that require a longer growing season. While plug plants are more costly, they are excellent if you want just a few plants for a small plot, and the variety on offer is increasing annually.

Pots, trays, and compost

Crops that have large seeds, such as runner beans and squashes, can be sown singly in pots. Module trays are ideal for medium-sized seeds such as cabbage and beetroot, while small-seeded lettuces and celery should be sown in seed trays – once the seeds germinate, transfer or "prick out" into pots or modules. Use seed compost as this is finely milled to remove lumps and contains few nutrients.

Hardening off

Young plants grown under cover will not have been exposed to the weather or to outside temperatures and will need to be acclimatized to outdoor conditions before being planted out – a process termed "hardening off". Place crops in a shady, sheltered spot outside during the day and then bring them back indoors at night, to gradually make the plants more robust. Do this for seven to ten days,

(above) **Tender plants such as cucumbers** *should be started off under cover as they need a minimum temperature of 20°C (68°F) to germinate.*

(right) **Use the cut-off tops of bottles** *to serve as homemade cloches. These will keep plants warm in cold, frosty weather, and will also deter pests.*

depending on the hardiness of your crop. If you are pricking out or planting on into another container or growing bag, water this well and then leave it in a warm spot overnight. The aim of this is to prevent the compost from becoming too cold, as this can cause a transplant shock.

Direct sowing

If given sufficient protection, hardy crops can be sown directly into the ground, which can be useful if you do not have the indoor space to dedicate to a propagation area. Some crops, such as calabrese, resent having their roots disturbed, so benefit from not being transplanted, and most root crops will thrive if sown direct. Ensure that you prepare the soil thoroughly in advance – you may need to warm the soil using a cloche or cold frame if the weather is cold.

Plant buying options

If you don't have the space or time to grow plants from seed there is a range of other options for you to choose from. Plants are available to buy at varying stages of growth and will provide a faster and easier alternative to growing from seed. Bear in mind however, that the range of varieties is not as great as is available for seeds, and that the process is invariably more expensive.

1 Plug plants Available from garden centres or via mail order, plug plants are crops that are purchased when they are mature enough to plant out. They offer a faster and easier, but more expensive, alternative to growing crops from seed and are ideal if you have a small space and only want a few plants.

2 Tray packs If you are looking to fill a whole row of plants, or want to buy in bulk, trays of plants will be more cost-effective than buying individually grown plants. Buy them while they are still relatively young.

3 Pot-grown plants Crops can also be purchased at a more advanced stage of growth, grown on in individual pots. This method is relatively expensive but it is a good way to buy crops that need a long growing season, such as chillies, peppers, and sweetcorn.

4 Bare-root Plants such as brassica seedlings (shown) are sown in seed beds and then dug up and sold "bare-root". Fruit trees and bushes are also available to buy from autumn to spring and should be planted straight away.

Getting an early start

When growing crops in a limited space you want it to be as productive as possible. While you can't make the plot itself any bigger, you can at least prolong the growing season as much as possible, so that your crops mature sooner and continue later into autumn. This involves protecting your plants from spring frosts and autumn chills, allowing you to start them off earlier and to keep them growing as long as possible. This is simple to achieve, especially if you grow hardier crops and those that reach a harvestable size quickly.

Sowing under cover

A greenhouse or conservatory offers the ideal conditions to sow seeds early and to grow plants on before planting out. They are not essential however, and you can easily start seeds on your windowsills, where they will germinate quickly at room temperatures. Seedlings can also be grown on here but turn them every few days to prevent them growing towards the light and becoming crooked. Shade hot windows to avoid scorching the young soft growth.

Simple covers

Cold frames and mini-greenhouses offer similar benefits to full-size greenhouses, and can be used to raise hardier crops in spring, or for later sowings of more tender seeds – remember that plants must be kept well ventilated or they may dry out. They are also ideal for acclimatizing seedlings raised on windowsills to outdoor temperatures. Both are good for smaller plots as they can be taken apart and stored when not in use. Unlike cold frames, mini-greenhouses are often tall enough to grow mature crops, such as tomatoes and peppers.

Garden cloches

Cloches are temporary covers that trap heat and protect plants from cold, and can be used to warm the soil before sowing outside and to encourage early growth. They are usually made from glass, rigid plastic, or polythene, and there are many different types available, including tunnel cloches to cover rows, or dome cloches for single plants. Place them over seeds sown directly outside to promote quick germination or to protect newly planted crops from the cold weather. Alternatively, you can also use them to protect late-sown summer crops during autumn.

Protective fleece

Garden fleece is lightweight fabric, used to protect tender seedlings and plants from frost damage. It is useful for spreading across larger areas, such as whole beds or drills, but can also be wrapped around individual plants. To be effective however, the

(above) **In late summer** *use cloches to cover more delicate plants like basil to keep them cropping longer, especially as the nights cool down.*

(above left) **Starting plants under cover** *gives them a valuable head start. Peas and broad beans can be sown in autumn to plant out in spring.*

fleece needs to be held away from the leaves using canes or wire hoops. Fleece should also be held firmly in place, as it can easily blow away. For extra protection, use several layers but remove them once the risk of frost has passed.

DIY protection

Although you can buy cloche and cold frame kits, it's often just as easy to make your own. That way, you can tailor them exactly to your site and the crops you grow. It will also be cheaper, especially if you reuse materials or objects you already have.

1 Windowsill growing Group seedlings together in trays on your windowsill to keep them warm and moist. If you want to provide more light, make a reflector using cardboard and tin foil. This will encourage seedlings to grow straight and promote stronger stems.

2 Cold frames These are easy to make using old window frames. Use bricks or blocks to build up the sides, or make a simple wooden base, placing the window on top. These can be permanent or temporary features.

3 Simple shelters Small squares of glass, Perspex, or clear plastic make excellent cloches, and can be leant together at the top or propped up on canes to form more open shelters. Any clear glass will do, such as that from old windows. Take care with sharp edges or wear gloves.

4 Bottle cloches Cut-off clear plastic bottles make excellent cloches, especially larger ones, and can be used to protect individual plants. Remove the tops to provide good air flow and protect the plants growing inside with a light sprinkling of slug pellets. With the base removed, the cloches stack and store easily.

Growing in raised beds

If you have enough space outside, raised beds are excellent for growing fruit, vegetables, and herbs, and can make an attractive addition to the garden. Their raised level allows you to easily and comfortably reach your crops for weeding, maintenance, and harvesting, while the additional height also helps the soil to warm up rapidly in spring, naturally extending the growing season by a precious few weeks. Many raised beds are quick and simple to build, and can be constructed from a variety of materials such as wooden sleepers or slate tiles.

Long-lasting brick-built structures *can look attractive and will stand the test of time. To give low-growing crops extra shelter from the wind, fill the bed leaving a 20cm (8in) gap at the top.*

The benefits of beds

Growing in raised beds rather than in the open ground allows you greater control over the growing conditions of your crops. When creating a new bed or renovating an old one, you can fill it with fresh, rich soil but even in subsequent years it will be easy to improve the soil to suit your crops.

It is far easier to control the pH of a contained area of soil, so crops such as brassicas, which require a slightly alkaline environment, can be easily accommodated. The raised height of the bed also makes it easier to dig it over and remove stones, which is ideal for root crops such as carrots that will suffer in stony, compacted soil. Organic matter can be applied as necessary and there will be little wastage, unlike on a larger plot, where it may be added to an area that later becomes a path between beds.

The elevated soil level will provide good drainage, so if your ground is usually waterlogged then this is a great way to provide a space for herbs and other warm-season plants that revel in a well-aerated plot.

Bed management

However, raised beds are not without their drawbacks: the soil drains more quickly than in a ground-level bed, so they will need watering more often. Ants like free-draining soil, although regular cultivation will stop them establishing, and snails may like to gather on the bed edges – however, this means that they're easy to find.

Temporary raised beds

An attractive temporary option, although only suitable for crops with shallower root systems, is to surround growing bags or wide containers with an edging frame, made from a material such as wicker, shown here. These raised beds can be "constructed" in different locations year-on-year, and once you have harvested your crops they can be taken down and packed away to save space.

Different materials and designs

It's simple to create your own raised beds, but there are many kits available if your DIY skills aren't particularly polished. Think creatively when choosing your edging, and invest in good-quality, sturdy, durable materials.

1 DIY kits Ready-prepared kits, available in a variety of materials, can be easily assembled for a neat, stylish effect.

2 Wood Invest in some good-quality timber and ensure that it is properly treated to prevent it from rotting. Be creative: decking, for example, makes excellent edging, while chunky pieces of wood give a more modern feel.

3 Metal Raised beds made from metal suit a contemporary design. However, keep the soil well watered as it will be vulnerable to temperature changes.

4 Brick Use new or recycled bricks, breeze blocks, or stone to create sturdy, long-lasting raised beds. These structures could be used to create some informal seating around the growing area, and can suit a cottage garden design.

5 Recycled materials Think creatively, as materials such as used tyres can make a striking design statement. Bear in mind that old railway sleepers, which were once very popular, ooze tar in hot weather, so are used less widely now.

6 Slate pieces Tiles of slate are very attractive and can be used to edge a shallow bed. They will not support a lot of weight though, so do not overfill.

Growing in containers

Growing crops in pots is second nature to many gardeners. As well as providing extra growing space, it offers many benefits, such as easier weeding and the option to move your crops under cover for protection or to extend their cropping season. It can also give you a wider choice of crops to grow as you can choose the soil type, meaning you are not limited to growing only those plants that will thrive in your garden soil. However, feeding and frequent watering are vital, so you may wish to invest in an automatic irrigation system. To help conserve moisture, add water-retaining gel to the compost and mulch the surface to prevent evaporation.

Mix and match *crops in containers of different sizes and colours. Integrate the pots with ornamental plants to add colour and interest to the display while the edible plants are developing.*

Choosing the right container

All containers should have drainage holes in the base to allow excess water to drain away, but the material they are made of will determine how quickly they will dry out. Unglazed terracotta pots are extremely porous and so will readily lose water through their sides, especially if positioned in a sunny spot. Conversely, thick-walled concrete tubs are very moisture-retentive. Wooden barrels are best lined with plastic to reduce water loss.

Match the container to the crop you'll be growing in it. The shallow roots of radishes and salad leaves, for example, means that container choice for these crops is virtually limitless – from windowboxes to old boots and tea pots, you can really have fun with the way you grow them. Just bear in mind the smaller the pot, the more frequently it will need watering. Large crops, such as cabbages and potatoes, will require tubs with a minimum depth and diameter of 30cm (12in).

Fruit in containers

It's crucial to pick a container that is deep and wide enough for long-term fruit crops. Opt for a minimum depth of 30cm (12in) and a width at least 10cm (4in) larger than the existing pot. Re-pot annually in early to mid-spring when your tree or bush is still young and its growth rate is rapid. As the plant matures, its growth rate slows – check the roots – if they're not yet filling the compost then don't re-pot until the following year. When the container is large enough to make re-potting unnecessary, simply "top-dress" each spring by replacing the top 10cm (4in) of compost. Stand your pot on "feet" in winter to aid drainage.

Quirky containers

Think creatively when choosing where to sow or plant your crops. Experiment with unexploited growing areas and unusual containers, such as these cress-sown egg shells, which would make a fantastic family project. Plant breeders are latching onto the trend for all things small by developing some hugely productive yet very compact varieties, so look out for these.

Different types of containers

With the wide range of container types available, you will easily be able to find one that fits your garden design. Try to make the most of all of your available space – many pots can be fastened onto walls or fences, so can be incorporated into even the smallest garden.

1 Hanging baskets Suitable for tumbling crops such as tomatoes and strawberries, hanging baskets can look incredibly striking when planted up with a mix of colourful edible and ornamental plants.

2 Terracotta pots Available in a range of sizes and shapes, these rustic-looking containers make an lovely addition to a patio, and will support a variety of crops.

3 Windowboxes Ideal for crops with shallow roots such as salad leaves, windowboxes are best sited close to the kitchen for easy access during cooking.

4 Fabric bags The depth of these bags makes them a great choice for potatoes, which can be easily earthed up during growth. They can then be folded up after your crops have been harvested.

5 Wall pouches These attractive, space-saving devices allow you to make the most of an unused vertical surface. They are ideal for herbs or salad leaves, but will need frequent watering.

6 Wall planters These large containers must be securely fastened as they will need to support the weight of relatively large plants. Keep them well watered, and ensure that fruits are supported.

Watering and feeding

Keeping your fruit and vegetable plants well-watered and fed is essential for a good harvest, especially in smaller plots where every plant matters. Regular care also promotes strong, healthy growth, which is better able to fend off pests and diseases. Crops in pots and raised beds are almost totally reliant on you, so keep a watering can handy.

How and when to water

Growing fruits, herbs, and vegetables closely together in a small space, especially in containers, limits the amount of root space these plants have. This high concentration of roots needs continual access to moisture if it is to grow well. The ideal would be to install a drip irrigation system set at a level that ensures your soil or compost is evenly and consistently moist, but this is a luxury. Watering cans and hosepipes are more the norm; a thorough soak of beds every few days will ensure water penetrates to the deepest of roots, not just those near the surface (pots may require a daily drench). Do this in the evening or morning, not during the heat of the day, to reduce evaporation. Keep all plants well-watered when they are in flower or setting fruit. Dry spells now will cause flowers and young fruits to wither, reducing the harvest.

Make the most of moisture

To help your soil retain moisture better, especially if it is light, regularly dig in well-rotted organic matter, which acts like a sponge. If you grow

(above) **Mulching plants** helps to retain moisture in the soil by preventing evaporation. Organic mulches will also feed your plants.

(left) **Automatic micro-irrigation** is a worthwhile investment if you grow lots of crops in containers but have limited time to water them.

(far left) **Young plants** are especially vulnerable to drying out. Water them regularly, at least until they are planted out and fully established.

crops in containers, add water-retaining granules before planting. Set up water butts in your garden to collect rainwater, and consider recycling some household water, such as that which has been used to wash and prepare vegetables and salads. If you are going on holiday, group potted crops together in a shady spot and stand them in trays – or ask a neighbour to water while you are away. Doing this is actually better than an automatic watering system, as crops can be harvested at the same time to ensure repeated cropping. (It also serves as a great reward for the temporary waterer.)

Feeding your crops

Growing crops takes a lot of nutrients from the soil or compost, which can become exhausted, so it is essential to replenish them regularly. There are three main nutrients that plants need most; nitrogen for leaf growth; phosphorus for healthy roots; and potassium (potash) for flowers and fruits. In addition, they also require small amounts of "trace" elements for overall health, including magnesium, iron and boron. When feeding your crops, choose a feed that meets your crops' needs. Root crops benefit from fertilizer high in phosphorus to encourage root growth; leaf crops require feeds rich in nitrogen; and fruiting crops, such as tomatoes, require lots of potash. The wrong type of fertilizer can encourage the wrong type of plant growth. Soil type will affect how often you should feed – sandy soils lose nutrients quickly, clay holds on to them.

Fertilizer types

There are two types of garden fertilizer to use: natural feeds based on organic plant and animal matter, and artificial ones made from chemicals. Both can be applied in various ways and each offers its own advantages. Most are allocated an "N:P:K" value, which is the general ratio of nitrogen (N), phosphorus (P) and potassium (K) within a fertilizer, to help you choose the right feed for your crop. Whichever you use, avoid over-feeding in the hope of bigger harvests as you are more likely to damage plant roots.

1 Granular fertilizers This type of fertilizer breaks down slowly in the soil and provides plants with long-term nutrition, often lasting all season. They are easy to handle and apply, and are available as natural or artificial feeds.

2 Liquid fertilizers These are quick-acting feeds, ideal for giving crops a boost. Natural and artificial types are available, sold as soluble powders or liquid concentrates. Dilute them according to the instructions given.

3 Compound fertilizers Rather than supplying a balanced feed, these chemical or natural fertilizers are used to supply specific nutrients, such as iron sulphate to increase iron in the soil, or bone meal to add phosphorus.

4 Well-rotted organic matter This is used to add natural nutrients to the soil, as well as to improve its structure. There are many types to use, such as garden compost and horse manure.

Planning your plot

Making a start

A three-metre square plot is a good size for most first-time fruit and vegetable growers, and provides ample space for a useful selection of crops, yet is small enough to look after easily. To illustrate this, we created, planted, and harvested the plot featured throughout this chapter in a single growing season, showing what you can achieve. To help you get started and decide what to grow, follow the planting guides (pp.44–49) for different summer combinations to suit different needs; easy-to-grow, the family plot, and a scheme for gourmet crops. Although these plans are for a 3x3m (10x10ft) square plot, you can adapt them to whatever space you have, whether it's a smaller bed, or a collection of pots and growing bags on the patio.

Preparing your plot

Before sowing or planting, the most important task is to prepare the area first, between autumn and early spring (see pp.20–21). Exactly what this will involve depends on your soil and site, but it's worth spending time now to ensure a good harvest and to prevent problems later. Provide the best conditions you can by enriching the soil with nutrients, and by resolving problems, such as poor drainage, perennial weeds, or areas of compaction.

If you are growing in containers or growing bags, place them in the sunniest position possible before sowing or planting (see pp.28–29).

Dig the soil well, *breaking up large clumps and removing any weed roots. Avoid treading on newly dug areas.*

Add well-rotted organic matter, *such as garden compost, to the soil to improve fertility and moisture retention.*

Rake the surface *to leave it fine and level, which is ideal for sowing seeds directly. Remove any weed seedlings.*

Use fabric membrane *to help control weeds if you are unable to sow seeds straightaway.*

Our planting plan

This combination of vegetables is aimed at beginners, growing their own crops for the first time. It includes reliable crops that are quick to grow and can be picked over several weeks. Speedy salad leaves and herbs can be picked a few weeks after sowing, either as cut-and-come-again leaves or as whole plants. The beans will last through summer and the potatoes and kale will provide a welcome harvest in autumn.

TOP ROW: ■ sweetcorn x 9 ■ summer squash x 1 ■ runner beans x 8 ■ French beans x 6 ■ maincrop potatoes x 4

MIDDLE ROW: ■ dwarf bush tomatoes x 5 ■ cucumbers x 3 ■ kale x 4 ■ courgettes x 2

BOTTOM ROW: ■ beetroots x 20 ■ carrots x 40 ■ radishes x 40 ■ Swiss chard x 8 ■ kohl rabi x 12 ■ oriental greens x 20 ■ lettuces x 20 ■ coriander x 6 ■ parsley x 4

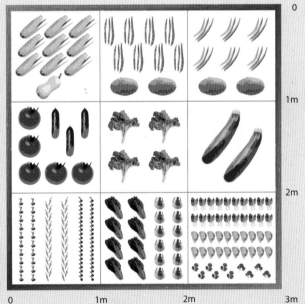

Warm the soil with cloches *so your seeds germinate more quickly. Use them to protect young plants.*

Insert garden canes *to mark out your planting plan, indicate where to sow, and to support plants.*

OTHER JOBS TO DO

- Weed regularly to prevent weeds competing with your seedlings
- Fork in granular fertilizer before sowing seeds directly
- Keep the soil free from plant debris, which can harbour diseases
- Start sowing seeds under cover to plant out in spring
- Chit early seed potatoes (see p.146) to give them a head start

Planting the bed

Once the soil is prepared you can turn your attention to sowing and planting. Hard frosts are likely in early spring, making it too soon to plant tender crops which could be damaged. Instead, sow hardier vegetables now, such as carrots, peas, beetroots, and radishes, directly in the soil. These will germinate more quickly in soil that has been warmed first with cloches and plastic sheeting. To encourage stronger growth, protect the seedlings with cloches, and thin them as they develop to ensure good air flow and to prevent competition between the young plants.

Frosts become fewer and less severe in late spring, when you can start to acclimatize tender crops sown under cover or bought in, such as sweetcorn, French and runner beans, tomatoes, and courgettes. This involves standing seedlings outside in the day and bringing them in at night for about ten days. Plant out in early summer when the risk of frost has passed.

Plants grow rapidly as the weather warms, *making this a busy time on your plot. Keep on top of maintenance at this stage to ensure your plants get the best start. Weak or dead plants can easily be replaced if replanted soon.*

French and runner beans *twine up their supports once established. Tie in any young, wayward shoots.*

Water seedlings well *when planting out to encourage deep rooting, making them more resilient.*

Some hardy seeds *can be sown directly in spring. Prepare your soil well first and keep it evenly moist.*

Thin direct-sown crops *as soon as they develop so that the remaining plants grow unhindered.*

Biodegradable pots *mean less root disturbance when planting out. Keep them moist to help them rot away.*

Keep garden fleece handy *in case the weather turns cold. Cloches can also be used.*

OTHER EARLY-SEASON JOBS

- Be vigilant against slugs and snails – use pellets around seedlings
- Encourage germination by temporarily covering drills with newspaper
- Sink upturned bottles next to squashes for easy watering
- Hoe between crops to keep on top of weed control

Tending the crops

Growth rates will increase as temperatures rise in early summer, so it's important to keep on top of crop developments. Quick-maturing crops such as radishes, salad leaves, and herbs may begin to provide you with early harvests, while fruits and vegetables that take longer to mature will benefit from continued care and maintenance – tie in tomatoes and cucumbers to their stakes and remove any yellowing leaves from plants.

Earthing up potatoes will ensure that the developing tubers don't become exposed to any light, which would turn them green and inedible; keeping on top of weeds will discourage unwanted competition; while erecting insect-proof barriers will prevent carrot root flies from attacking and boring holes in crops. Be sure to keep up with these jobs now as the results will pay dividends.

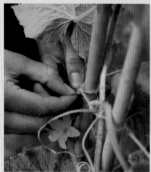

Regularly tie in *developing cucumber stems to their supports using soft twine. They grow quickly.*

Radish sowings *will mature in as little as five weeks. Pick them young, before they become woody.*

Keep carrots well weeded *as competition from unwanted growth can cause reduced yields.*

Erect insect netting*, 60cm (24in) high, around your carrots to prevent carrot flies (p.238) laying their eggs.*

To ensure strong roots *that will sustain plenty of pods, keep French and runner beans well watered.*

Regularly earth up *soil around your developing potato plants to prevent light reaching the tubers.*

Check plants *for signs of pests and diseases. Remove any diseased growth and control pests promptly.*

Salad crops *will be developing quickly, so harvest leaves from individual plants as needed.*

Young growth *is a magnet for slugs and snails. Make sure appropriate controls are in place, such as pellets.*

Remove yellowing foliage *from plants such as kale, kohl rabi, and courgettes, to ensure good hygiene.*

OTHER MID-SEASON JOBS

- Thin out Swiss chard plants, using the thinnings as a baby salad leaf
- Attach individual tomato plants to a stout bamboo cane
- Regularly harvest basil and coriander to encourage further growth
- Feed fruiting vegetables weekly with liquid tomato fertilizer

Plenty to pick

Mid- to late summer is the most productive time on the plot, when spring sowings and plantings are ready to harvest. Pick crops such as French beans, courgettes, salad leaves, and herbs regularly as their individual pods, fruits, and leaves mature in succession, giving you a continuous harvest. Other crops, such as carrots, and beetroot, yield one-off harvests, and once picked, the area they occupied can be re-used. Making further sowings or plantings at this time will ensure that your plot's productivity doesn't fizzle out, and if watered well, new crops will quickly establish.

Remember that certain long-season crops, such as sweetcorn, tomatoes, and runner beans, will begin to mature in late summer. Make sure you look after them well to encourage good harvests into the autumn.

Train wayward squash stems *as they'll be putting on plenty of strong stem growth now.*

Cucumbers reach their peak *over a few days. Check regularly and cut them as soon as they are ready.*

Sow seeds direct *in bare patches of soil for a continuous supply. Keep the drills well watered in hot spells.*

Pull up individual carrots *as soon as they reach a harvestable size, selecting the largest roots first.*

Harvest courgettes regularly *or they will soon grow into marrows. Check plants every few days.*

Pull up whole lettuce plants *or leave the cut stalk in the ground to re-sprout fresh loose leaves.*

Keep sweetcorn well watered *after the silks and tassels emerge, to encourage the greatest yields.*

OTHER PEAK-SEASON JOBS

- Pull up baby beetroot regularly
- Check for pests and diseases
- Water crops thoroughly
- Apply liquid feeds routinely

Ending the season

Now is the time for late crops to come into their own. Sweetcorn, winter squashes and tomatoes require ample growing time and sunshine to reach their sweetest, and will reach their best in autumn. Maincrop potatoes are also ready for harvesting, as their skins will have formed, preparing them for storage.

Bare patches will become more common as spent crops are pulled up. Sow these with quick-growing microgreens or hardy salad leaves for a late crop, or start preparing the area for next year – cover it with mulch to prevent weed growth, or leave it bare to the elements so that frost can penetrate and expose pests. Your compost heap will be getting full now, as crops are cleared. Turn the contents once or twice during autumn, moving material on the outside to the centre.

Focus your watering *on crops that are still maturing, such as late pumpkins and salad leaves.*

Cut winter squashes *before the first frosts and lay them in a sunny position so that the skins harden.*

Mulch bare soil *with organic matter, which will break down in time for spring planting.*

Squeeze in late sowings *of hardy crops, such as salad leaves, which can be covered with cloches.*

French and runner beans *will keep on bearing pods until the first frosts if plants are picked over.*

Gently pull back *the outer leaves of sweetcorn cobs to check if the kernels are mature enough to pick.*

Leave maincrop potato tubers *on the soil surface for a few hours to dry before placing them in storage.*

Courgette plants *will be coming to the end of their life now – make a final harvest then compost them.*

Harvest the leaves *and seed pods of coriander. Dry the seeds and freeze any surplus leaves until required.*

Pull up spent crops *and place on the compost heap. Chop them into pieces to speed up decomposition.*

OTHER LATE-SEASON JOBS

- Continue to harvest Swiss chard through the winter
- Cover over any new sowings with bell or tunnel cloches
- Stop watering tomato plants to encourage fruit ripening
- Store surplus root crops in a frost-free shed or garage

The easy-to-grow plot

If you are new to growing your own food, this mix of vegetables, along with strawberries, will provide a steady supply for your kitchen. Many crops are ideal for beginners, either because they are easy to care for, suffer from few pest and disease problems, or yield reliable harvests with little input. By growing just one or two different crops per square metre, you can easily get to grips with their cultivation. As your confidence and experience grow, try adding more of the crops listed below to the overall plan and tailor the plot to supply your own specific needs.

Growing in containers

Low-maintenance vegetables are ideal for containers, windowboxes, and even hanging baskets. You can also grow a wall of summer strawberries by planting one per 20cm (8in) pot and fixing each to a fence or trelliswork in a sunny spot. Shallow-rooted salad crops are perfect for smaller containers, whereas onions and French beans need pots with a minimum depth of 25cm (10in). Choose large tubs or even sacks for potatoes and courgettes.

Alternative easy-to-grow crops

Tomatoes
pages 54–57

Garlic
pages 162–163

Runner beans
pages 70–71

Sweetcorn
pages 166–169

Broad beans
pages 76–77

Winter squashes
pages 86–89

Carrots
pages 138–139

Turnips
pages 140–141

Easy-to-grow mix

This combination of crops will provide you with all the basics, giving quick results and high yields if grown on a well-prepared, fertile soil. The large patch of strawberries will ensure a bumper crop throughout the summer months; easy-to-grow French beans will crop reliably right through to autumn; and just two courgette plants will supply more than you can eat. Sow fast-growing radishes in regular batches for a steady supply, sowing your next crop as soon as a row has been cleared.

TOP ROW: ■ maincrop potatoes x 4
■ new potatoes x 6 ■ onions x 60

MIDDLE ROW: ■ spinach x 16
■ beetroot x 30 ■ courgettes x 2
■ French beans x 12

BOTTOM ROW: ■ radish x 40
■ lettuce x 8 ■ radish x 40
■ strawberries x 12

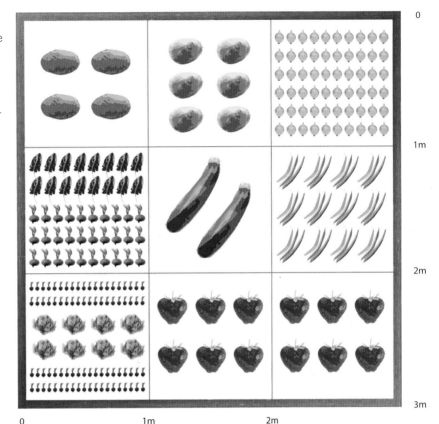

Swiss chard
pages 124–125

Oriental greens
pages 120–121

Autumn raspberries
pages 202–203

Lettuces
pages 112–115

Shallots
pages 156–157

Plums
pages 218–219

Also consider growing:
■ Chillies (pp.60–63)
■ Endive (pp.128–129)
■ Kohl rabi (pp.170–171)
■ Rhubarb (pp.186–187)
■ Coriander (pp.190–191)
■ Parsley (pp.190–191)
■ Mint (pp.192–195)
■ Chives (pp.192–195)
■ Cabbage (pp.94–99)
■ Blackcurrants (pp.208–209)
■ Blueberries (pp.212–213)
■ Plums (pp.218–219)

The family plot

There are plenty of delicious fruits and vegetables on the family shopping list that can easily be grown in the garden: a 3x3m (10x10ft) plot can provide you with a range of fresh crops, and many will grow in containers too, if space is tight. Consider giving each family member responsibility for a specific section or crop, as this will encourage friendly rivalry that may result in a better-maintained garden. Sharing the growing experience and passing tips and techniques down the generations will ensure that growing fruit and vegetables becomes second nature to all involved.

Growing in containers

If you don't have a lot of space, or you simply fancy growing in containers, choose large pots and fill them with high-yielding family favourites. Baby parsnips and carrots can be sown in deep containers, while lettuce and beetroot will thrive in shallower pots. Blueberries, strawberries, and apples are also ideal. Ensure that crops such as French beans, tomatoes, squashes, courgettes, and sweetcorn are given a warm, sunny spot to encourage their pods and fruits to develop.

Alternative family crops

Peas
pages 68–69

Cabbages
pages 94–99

Pumpkins
pages 90–91

Cucumbers
pages 80–81

Radishes
pages 134–135

Brussels sprouts
pages 106–107

Swiss chard
pages 124–125

Kohl rabi
pages 170–171

Family mix

Designed for maximum productivity, this planting scheme includes the most popular crops that will be ready to harvest in summer, autumn, and early winter. Make full use of the space by underplanting a triangle of slower-growing sweetcorn with a fast-growing squash, which will cover the ground under the sweetcorn. Winter crops like calabrese and purple-sprouting broccoli occupy the ground for a long period and so are planted together where they won't be disturbed.

TOP ROW: ■ early potatoes x 6
■ beetroot x 30 ■ lettuce x 8
■ bush tomatoes x 4

MIDDLE ROW: ■ calabrese x 8
■ sprouting broccoli x 2 ■ squash x 1
■ sweetcorn x 9 ■ French beans x 12

BOTTOM ROW: ■ carrots x 45
■ parsnips x 8 ■ onions x 30
■ leeks x 10 ■ courgettes x 2

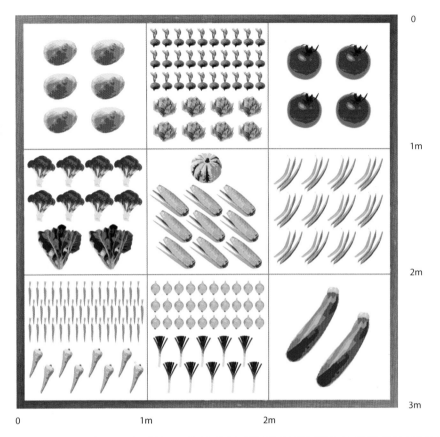

Chicory
pages 126–127

Peppers
pages 58–59

Strawberries
pages 200–201

Annual herbs
pages 190–191

Aubergines
pages 64–65

Redcurrants
pages 206–207

Also consider growing:
■ Chillies (pp.60–63)
■ Runner beans (pp.70–71)
■ Broad beans (pp.76–77)
■ Cut-and-come-again salads (pp.116–117)
■ Spinach (pp.122–123)
■ Turnips (pp.140–141)
■ Garlic (pp.162–163)
■ Rhubarb (pp.186–187)
■ Raspberries (pp.202–203)
■ Blueberries (pp.212–213)
■ Apples (pp.214–215)
■ Cherries (pp.220–221)

The gourmet plot

The vegetable and fruit world is a diverse one, and brilliant for adventurous cooks. Many crops, such as globe artichokes and chicory, or unusual varieties of fruit and vegetables, like purple carrots or red gooseberries, add excitement and interest to the garden, so why not embrace them – they're not likely to be found in many shops. These crops are also colourful characters, allowing you to create an eye-catching garden, as well as a highly productive one. The saying that you "eat with your eyes as well as your mouth" has never been more appropriate.

Growing in containers

This plot features a mixture of textures and colours, meaning you can create moveable combinations of pick-and-mix crops. Unusual salad leaves, herbs, edible flowers, and the feathery foliage of fennel and asparagus are just a few contrasting examples. Some bush fruits and perennial vegetables are included here and require loam-based compost to boost health and longevity. Thirsty crops, such as fennel and celeriac, will need regular watering.

Alternative gourmet crops

Kale 'Black Tuscan'

Carrot 'Purple Haze'
page 138

Cabbage 'Siberia'

Tomato 'Tigerella'
page 56

Sprouting broccoli 'Claret'
page 104

Watercress
pages 130–131

Kohl rabi 'Kolibri'
page 170

Swiss chard 'Ruby'

Gourmet mix

The aim here is to fill your plot, no matter how large or small, with produce that is expensive to buy or rarely seen in your local supermarket. Asparagus and redcurrants are luxury crops that are relatively easy to grow. Broad beans, picked young and sweet, are a revelation compared with any you can buy in the shops; and rows of fresh oriental greens will supply enough leaves and stems for your stir-fries and salads all summer.

TOP ROW: ■ salad potatoes x 6
■ broad beans x 20 ■ asparagus x 4

MIDDLE ROW: ■ celeriac x 9
■ strawberries x 8 ■ redcurrant x 1
■ Florence fennel x 10 ■ garlic x 14

BOTTOM ROW: ■ squash x 1
■ chicory x 6 ■ shallots x 8
■ loose-leaf lettuce x 8 ■ oriental
greens x 10 ■ loose-leaf lettuce x 8
■ oriental greens x 10

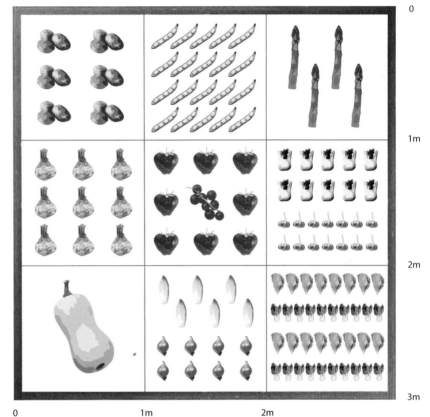

Also consider growing:
■ Pepper 'Yellow Stuffer'
■ Chilli 'Ancho'
■ Pea 'Purple Podded'
■ French bean 'Lingua di Fuoco'
■ Winter squash 'Uchiki Kuri' (p.88)
■ Pumpkin 'Rouge Vif d'Etampes' (p.90)
■ Jerusalem artichokes (pp.184–185)
■ Coriander (pp.190–191)
■ Gooseberry 'Lancashire Lad' (p.210)
■ Gage 'Coe's Golden Drop'

Beetroot 'Chioggia Pink'
page 136

Peppermint
pages 194–195

Peach 'Garden Lady'
page 222

Globe artichokes
pages 182–183

Calabrese 'Romanesco'
page 102

Blueberries
pages 212–213

GROW YOUR OWN Vegetables

Fruiting crops

Although commonly regarded as vegetables, these crops are actually fruits because this is the part of the plant you eat, unlike root or leaf crops. They are among the most exciting vegetables to grow, coming in a range of shapes, sizes, and colours to suit all tastes. Requiring a sunny, warm spot and high-potash feed, tomatoes, peppers, chillies, and aubergines will reward you with produce that is sweet (and in some cases hot) as well as delicious. Many varieties have been bred to be compact and heavy cropping, so they are perfect for those who don't want their vegetables to take up too much space in the garden.

STEP-BY-STEP Tomatoes

Tomatoes are easy to grow under cover or outside in a sunny spot, and produce a reliable harvest all summer. There are many varieties to choose from, producing fruit in a wide array of colours, flavours, and sizes. These fall into two main types: cordon tomatoes that are usually trained up tall canes or strings, and bush varieties that are grown more freely. There are also dwarf varieties to grow in containers, and tumbling tomatoes for hanging baskets.

	SPRING	SUMMER	AUTUMN	WINTER
SOW				
HARVEST				

TIME TO HARVEST: 16–18 WEEKS

SUITABLE FOR: BEDS, CONTAINERS, AND GROWING BAGS – UNDER COVER OR OUTSIDE

11 plants

3M (10FT) ROWS
Plant 30cm (12in) apart, depending on variety

GROWING BAGS
3 plants in each

1 Sowing seeds

Sow tomatoes under cover in mid-spring. Fill a pot or tray with compost, water well, then sow the seeds on top, spacing them about 1cm (½in) apart. Cover lightly with compost and place the tray in a heated propagator set at 18°C (72°F) for a week or two, or until they germinate. Prick the seedlings out into individual pots when they develop their first pair of leaves. Grow them on under cover for a few weeks until ready to plant into their final growing positions.

Sowing seeds individually *into modules removes the need to prick them out as seedlings. This minimizes root disturbance of young plants.*

Grow the seedlings on *until roots appear at the base of the modules. They can then be potted on into larger pots or planted out if conditions allow.*

To conserve moisture, *make the planting holes in your growing bags just large enough to plant into but leave room so you can water easily.*

Support tomato plants *as they grow, especially those trained as cordons. Vertical strings are very practical for indoor crops, and are very flexible.*

2 Growing indoors

Tomatoes crop best when grown under cover in greenhouses or growing frames, and can be planted into beds, growing bags, or containers. They need a bright spot, shaded from hot sun, with good airflow, and should be watered daily in warm spells and fed regularly. Cordon varieties, trained as a single stem with the sideshoots removed are best for growing this way as they require less space than bush-types.

TIP *Hang sticky yellow traps near indoor crops to control whitefly (see p.238).*

3 Growing outside

To grow tomatoes outside, choose a sunny site and prepare the soil by digging in well-rotted organic matter. Alternatively, plant into growing bags or containers. Water plants during dry spells and regularly feed with tomato fertilizer. Bush tomatoes have more room to spread outside, and should be supported with several canes per plant.

Plant out tomatoes *at the same depth as they were in their pots and firm them in gently.*

Insert canes *near the plants after planting. Outdoor cordons require only a single support.*

Tie in the tomato stems *as they grow to help support the developing trusses of fruit.*

Use your fingers to pinch out *sideshoots as soon as they appear on cordon tomatoes. Use a sharp knife to remove older, thicker shoots.*

Tomato plants are especially thirsty *when they are in flower or fruit. It is important to keep plants in growing bags constantly moist.*

4 Training

Cordon tomatoes are grown as single stems trained up a cane or string. Regularly check your plants for sideshoots in the leaf joints and pinch them out. The sideshoots on bush-types can be left to grow. Once cordon plants have formed four or five flower trusses, cut out the tops to stop further growth.

5 Routine care

Water all plants regularly (possibly daily for under cover crops) and feed them every week with a high-potash tomato fertilizer once the first flowers appear. Avoid letting plants dry out, which can cause the fruit to split and may lead to the nutrient disorder, blossom end rot (see p.247).

6 Harvesting

Tomatoes ripen from midsummer onwards; for the best flavour, wait until each fruit is evenly coloured. Smaller tomatoes ripen quickly but larger fruits, like those from beefsteak-types, can take several days. Picked tomatoes keep for a few days but if you can't use them soon, cook and freeze surpluses. Underripe fruits will ripen indoors if kept in the sun near a banana.

To harvest fruit, *place your thumb on the stalk "knuckle" and bend the tomato upwards.*

Tomatoes

1 'Totem' This dwarf bush variety should be planted in a growing bag or windowbox, and won't need pinching out. The cherry-sized red fruits are produced in abundance.

2 'Tumbling Tom Yellow' This compact, cascading bush tomato is ideal for growing in sunny hanging baskets. Pick the cherry-sized, golden fruits throughout summer.

3 'Tumbler' This cascading bush tomato is an excellent choice to grow in hanging baskets, windowboxes and containers. It is particularly well suited to smaller gardens.

4 'Marmande' This beefsteak variety bears large, deep red fruits with few seeds. Grow this cordon-type outdoors; support it with a stake and remove any sideshoots.

5 'Sungold' One of the sweetest-tasting, this hybrid bears cherry-sized, deep-orange fruits. It is suitable for growing indoors or out, and should be trained as a cordon.

6 'Gardener's Delight' A well-known cherry variety, it bears long trusses of sweet, red fruits. It can be grown under cover or outside and should be trained as a cordon.

7 'Sweet Olive' A hybrid "baby plum" tomato, it yields oblong-shaped red fruits, each about 4cm (1½in) long. It is suitable for growing inside or out, but should be staked for support.

8 'Moneymaker' A traditional cordon variety that can be grown indoors or out, it bears red, medium-sized tomatoes. Remove sideshoots and train the stem up a cane or vertical strings.

9 'Tigerella' This unusual, early variety bears medium-sized, red fruits with distinctive yellow stripes. It can be grown under cover or outside, and should be trained as a single cordon.

Other varieties
'Gartenperle'
'Roma VF'
'Ferline'
'Green Sausage'
'Yellow Stuffer'
'Black Russian'

STEP-BY-STEP Peppers

Ideal for growing in containers, just two or three plants will supply you with plenty of sweet, delicious fruits, particularly if they are grown under cover. There are many different varieties to choose from, with fruits in a range of shapes and colours – including purple, orange, and black. Either harvest while the fruits are green to encourage others to form, or leave them to colour up and mature so they develop their full sweet flavour.

	SPRING	SUMMER	AUTUMN	WINTER
SOW				
HARVEST				

TIME TO HARVEST: 20–26 WEEKS

SUITABLE FOR: BEDS, CONTAINERS, AND GROWING BAGS – UNDER COVER OR OUTSIDE

8 plants

3M (10FT) ROWS
Plant out 40cm (16in) apart

GROWING BAGS
3 plants in each

1 Getting started

Peppers are tender plants that require a long growing season, so it's important to sow them under cover early in the year to give them time to mature and produce fruit. Plants will happily grow in large containers as long as you provide them with fertile compost and enough space to develop.

'California Wonder' *bears large, blocky, glossy red fruits with a very sweet flavour.*

'Marconi' *fruits are long, thin, and tapered. They mature to a rich, glossy red colour.*

'Gourmet' *is a compact plant that bears good yields of sweet, bright orange peppers.*

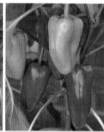
'Gypsy' *peppers are borne prolifically. The compact fruits are fleshy and very flavourful.*

Seed can be sown *individually in smaller pots. Cover each seed with a thin layer of soil and place in a heated propagator.*

Plant strong seedlings *into 9cm (3½in) pots and continue to grow them on under cover. Keep the young plants well watered.*

Once the plants' roots fill their pots *they can be planted on again. Choose a large pot so the pepper has space to grow.*

2 Sowing seeds

Fill pots with seed compost, firm gently, water well, and allow to drain. Sow seeds 1cm (½in) apart on the top, pressing them gently into the surface. Cover with a 5mm (¼in) layer of compost, water lightly, and place on a sunny windowsill. Once germinated and large enough to handle, remove from the propagator and prick out the seedlings into individual pots. When plants reach 20cm (8in) in height, start feeding them regularly with a liquid tomato fertilizer.

TIP *At about 30cm (12in) tall, pinch out the growing tips to promote bushy growth.*

3 Planting out

If you plan to position peppers outside, harden them off in early summer by placing them outside during the day and inside at night for two weeks. Plant in a sunny, sheltered site, spacing plants 40cm (16in) apart in each direction, or into containers of multi-purpose compost with a minimum diameter of 30cm (12in). Water in well.

Pepper plants will be ready to transplant *in early summer. Only plant them out once all risk of frost has passed, in a warm, sheltered site.*

Firm the plants in well *as they will become quite heavy over time. Water thoroughly, and keep the plants moist during all stages of growth.*

Insert a stout bamboo cane *60cm (24in) in height next to each plant and tie it in. The large fruits become heavy as they develop.*

When the first fruits appear, *feed the plants every two weeks. Feeding and regular watering will deter the fruit skins from splitting.*

4 Growing indoors

Peppers can also be grown on a sunny windowsill indoors or in a bright spot under cover. You will need to hand-pollinate indoor flowers. Simply insert a cotton bud or soft paintbrush into the centre of each flower once it is fully open, then transfer the attached pollen to a similarly open bloom.

5 Routine care

Keep plants well watered and feed regularly with a high potash liquid fertilizer such as tomato feed, to encourage flowers and fruit to form. Often plants will produce one large fruit before then developing others; it is best to pick this while green so that subsequent fruits are given the chance to mature.

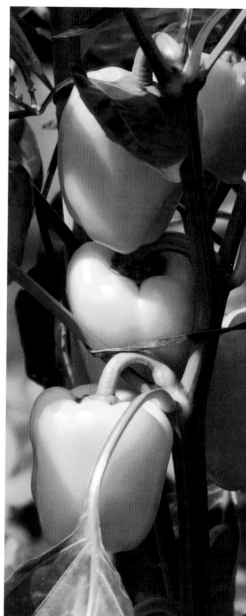

6 Harvesting

Individual fruits will begin to colour up from green, through to either yellow, orange, red, or purple, depending on the variety. Either harvest them while green, or wait for them to mature when their flavour becomes sweeter. Cut individual fruits off with a pair of secateurs rather than pulling them, as this can damage the plant. Cover outdoor plants with a cloche in autumn to help speed up ripening.

Cut the peppers *leaving a small portion of stem attached – this will help them store for longer.*

STEP-BY-STEP Chillies

These tiny peppers add real colour to the plot and are very easy to grow. All they need is a bright, sunny position and they will crop well in the smallest garden, even on a windowsill. Available in red, green, yellow, orange, and purple, and with a huge array of "heats" – from mild to atomic – it's easy to select a variety to suit your taste. Many are also excellent for drying, meaning that one plant can provide you with a whole year's supply of chillies.

	SPRING	SUMMER	AUTUMN	WINTER
SOW				
HARVEST				

TIME TO HARVEST: 20–26 WEEKS

SUITABLE FOR: BEDS, CONTAINERS, AND GROWING BAGS – UNDER COVER OR OUTSIDE

11 plants

3M (10FT) ROWS
Plant out 30cm (12in) apart

GROWING BAGS
3 plants in each

Chilli seeds *are quite large and easy to handle. Sow 5mm (¼in) deep, and if sowing into trays, space the seeds roughly 2cm (¾in) apart.*

Thin the seedlings *as they grow to one per pot. If using biodegradable pots (as above), the plants can be planted out in them; the pot will soon rot away.*

1 Sowing under cover

Chillies need a long growing season and should be sown under cover in early spring. Fill small pots or module trays with seed compost, water well and allow to drain. Sow the seed, water again, and place the trays or pots in a heated propagator set at 20–24°C (68–75°F). Once seedlings appear after a week or two, take them from the propagator and grow them on under cover in a warm position.

TIP *You can place sowings in an airing cupboard if you check them daily.*

2 Growing on

Grow the seedlings on under cover in a bright position, keeping them no cooler than 18°C (64°F), even at night. Pot up module-raised plants into 10cm (4in) pots as soon as their roots fill the cells. When seedlings reach 10cm (4in) tall, start feeding them using a high-potash liquid fertilizer, such as tomato feed. To encourage plenty of fruiting stems, pinch out the plants when 20cm (8in) tall, unless they branch out naturally.

Pot on plants *as they grow to prevent them becoming pot-bound, which will check their growth. Use a multipurpose compost.*

Grow on under cover *until frosts have passed and plants can be planted out. Pot indoor crops into their final containers once large enough.*

3 Planting out

If you plan to grow your chilli plants outside, begin hardening them off in early summer. Once they are ready they can be potted up into containers or a growing bag, or planted into free-draining soil in a sunny spot. If you are growing your plants on under cover, ensure that you pot them up into containers at least 25cm (10in) wide.

Plant chillies out *at the same depth as they were in their pots and water them in well. Protect them from slugs with a scattering of pellets.*

Support the plants *by inserting a sturdy cane next to each one and tie it in with soft string. Use several canes to support large-fruited varieties.*

Keep plants well watered *all summer to encourage a good crop. Dry spells can result in lower yields, and smaller, hotter chillies.*

Chillies crop over many weeks *and surplus fruits can be frozen as well as dried. Take care not to touch your eyes after handling them.*

4 Routine care

Water plants regularly during the growing season, especially those under cover or in containers, and feed often with a liquid tomato fertilizer. If the weather is cool or windy, or if the plants are growing under cover, hand-pollinate the flowers using a soft brush or cotton bud to encourage fruit set.

5 Harvesting

Chillies mature over several weeks and can be harvested as soon as they are large enough, whether still green or fully coloured. At the end of the season, outdoor plants can either be covered with cloches or pulled from the soil and hung in a warm dry spot for any remaining fruits to ripen.

Drying the fruit

Chillies can be dried green or fully ripe, although you'll need varieties with thin skins – fleshier types tend to decay. Lay the fruits out under cover on wire racks in a warm, dry, well-ventilated spot. Fruits can also be strung together and hung up. Chillies dry in about a week and can be stored on strings or in jars.

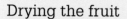

Chillies

1 'Apache' This compact variety is ideal for patio containers and windowboxes as it only reaches 45cm (18in) tall. The red fruits have a medium heat and grow to 4cm (1½in) long.

2 'Alma Paprika' A mild-tasting variety, this chilli is suitable for cooler areas. The rounded fruit grow to 5cm (2in) long, and can be sliced and used in salads. The fruits are best used fresh.

3 'Hungarian Hot Wax' This is a good choice for cooler areas, producing large, pointed, mild-tasting fruits. They ripen from pale yellow to red, and can be harvested once large enough.

4 'Prairie Fire' This is a prolific variety, and gives a steady crop of small, brightly coloured fruits throughout summer – they are very hot. Suitable for containers and for drying.

5 'Aji Amarillo' Bearing long, slender fruits that are particularly hot-tasting, this variety needs a warm position to grow well and does best under cover. The fruit can be picked green or red.

6 'Padron' This chilli produces a good crop of 5cm (2in) long fruits over several weeks that can be picked when mild and green, or left to ripen fully and heat up. It is suitable for drying.

7 Cayenne This is a type of chilli, rather than a distinct variety, and bears long curling fruit, up to 30cm (12in) long. It has thin skin, making it ideal for drying, and a hot, fiery flavour.

8 'Cherry Bomb' Producing masses of tiny, berry-like fruit that are very hot, this chilli has a compact habit and is suitable for pots. It is also attractive enough to grow as an ornamental.

9 'Demon Red' This variety gives a large crop of small red fruit that are thin-skinned and very hot. It is a compact plant, suitable for containers, and grows well in cooler areas.

Other varieties
'Heatwave'
'Hot Mexican'
'Inferno'
'Ring of Fire'
'Tabasco'

STEP-BY-STEP Aubergines

Aubergines ideally need a warm, sheltered spot but the introduction of modern hybrids and grafted plants means that they can crop well in cooler climates. A plant can produce between four and eight fruits – they do best in well-enriched soil and given a sunny site in a greenhouse. There are many different types of aubergine available, from the classic large-fruited purple-skinned varieties to tiny, green- or white-skinned types used in Asian cooking.

	SPRING	SUMMER	AUTUMN	WINTER
SOW				
HARVEST				

TIME TO HARVEST: 24–28 WEEKS

SUITABLE FOR: BEDS, CONTAINERS, AND GROWING BAGS, UNDER COVER OR OUTSIDE

3M (10FT) ROWS
Plant 30cm (12in) apart

11 plants

GROWING BAGS
3 plants in each

1 Getting started

Aubergines are commonly raised from seed but they can also be bought as young plants in spring. Grafted plants crop very heavily, and consist of a named fruiting variety grafted onto the vigorous root system of another. These plants are available from mail order seed suppliers and nurseries.

'Moneymaker' *is a reliable, large-fruited variety to grow under cover or outside.*

'Calliope' *produces a good yield of small rounded fruit. It is a good choice for pots.*

'Black Enorma' *is grown for its very large, dark, glossy fruit. It crops heavily and reliably.*

White-fruiting *plants are not widely sold but gave rise to the American common name, eggplant.*

Fill small pots or modules *with seed compost. Firm it in gently, water well and leave it to drain before sowing.*

Sow one seed *in each pot and put them in a warm propagator. Germination takes about a week but check the pots every day.*

Remove from the propagator *and grow the seedlings on. They don't need pricking out, just pot them on as they grow.*

2 Sowing seeds

Start seed under cover in early spring. Fill small pots with seed compost, firm gently, water well and allow to drain. Sow seeds on the surface, spacing them 2cm (¾in) apart (or sow individually – see left) and lightly press them into the surface using a pencil or dibber. Cover the seed with a little more compost, water them in, and place the pots in a heated propagator. Once seedlings are large enough to handle, prick them out into individual 10cm (4in) pots of multi-purpose compost and grow them on under cover. Feed regularly with a balanced liquid fertilizer to encourage healthy growth.

3 Growing indoors

When roots appear through the base of the pots, repot the plants individually into containers at least 30cm (12in) wide, filled with multi-purpose compost. If you have several aubergines, plant three plants per standard-sized growing bag. Grow them in a bright sunny position under cover, such as in a greenhouse or mini greenhouse.

Root disturbance checks growth *so keep the root ball intact when potting on plants. Also avoid letting young plants become pot-bound.*

Outdoor plants should be hardened off *fully before being planted out. Gradually acclimatize them to outdoor conditions over a few weeks.*

Aubergine fruits become heavy *as they develop. Support fruiting plants with canes and string to prevent the stems snapping.*

4 Growing outside

Once all risk of frost has passed, plant aubergines out in a sunny, sheltered spot. Plant directly into the soil or grow outside in containers. Support all plants with canes and pinch out the main shoot when they reach 30cm (12in) tall to promote bushier growth.

5 Routine care

Keep plants well watered, and as soon as the first flowers appear, switch from a general purpose liquid feed to one high in potash to encourage fruiting. The flowers require pollination so open greenhouse doors on sunny days if growing plants under cover.

6 Harvesting

Harvest fruits as soon as they are large enough. The skins should still be shiny; if they are dull then the aubergines are over-ripe. Pick regularly to encourage fruiting and remove small fruits at the end of the season to help those that remain to develop fully.

TIP	*Aubergines don't keep well so use them shortly after picking.*

Cut ripe aubergines *from the plants using secateurs. The stems can be tough and woody.*

Podded crops

Harvested while still young and eaten within the hour, the taste of peas and beans is absolutely sublime. One of the secrets to a good harvest is encouraging a strong root system to ensure the continued production of flowers and pods – a cool, moist root zone is ideal. Continual picking also encourages a prolonged harvest of peas and beans, giving a steady supply of tender pods throughout summer. The ability of some crops, such as peas and beans, to absorb nitrogen from the air and lock it into the soil also increases soil fertility.

STEP-BY-STEP Peas

All vegetables taste better when picked fresh but that is especially so with peas, which are almost like a different crop from shop-bought pods. Peas are very easy to grow, with dwarf and climbing forms, and are ideal for smaller plots. Sown little and often, you can enjoy fresh peas from late spring to mid-autumn. As well as traditional podded peas, try your hand at premium types like sugar snaps and mangetout, which are expensive to sow.

	SPRING	SUMMER	AUTUMN	WINTER
SOW				
HARVEST				

TIME TO HARVEST: 12–14 WEEKS

SUITABLE FOR: BEDS AND CONTAINERS

60 plants

3M (10FT) ROWS
Sow or plant out 5cm (2in) apart

CONTAINERS
20 plants in each

1 Getting started

Peas are raised from seed and come in two forms, those with smooth or wrinkly seeds. Smooth-seeded varieties are hardier, and are suitable for sowing early. Those with wrinkly seeds are sweeter tasting, and are best sown in late spring and summer. Check the packet before deciding which to plant.

'Oregon Sugar Pod' *is a sugar snap variety that should be harvested as whole pods when young.*

'Douce Provence' *bears a good harvest of traditional podded peas on dwarf plants.*

'Meteor' *produces a generous crop of sweet-tasting peas on compact plants. It is good in pots.*

'Feltham First' *is a dwarf, early-cropping variety, suitable for growing in containers.*

In small pots, *sow three seeds in each but don't thin them; in "growing tubes", sow seed singly. Seeds should be sown 5cm (2in) deep.*

Keep seedlings cool and well watered *until planted out to encourage a strong root system. Their growth can be checked by poor care, reducing yield.*

2 Sowing under cover

Peas can be sown in spring to plant out when the weather warms. Alternatively, for an earlier crop, they can also be sown in autumn and kept under cover to plant out as larger plants in spring. Sow into cardboard "growing tubes" or deep pots filled with seed compost. Water the seeds in and they will germinate without additional heat within two weeks. Grow them on, harden them off, and plant out when the plants reach about 20cm (8in) tall.

TIP *Make your own "growing tubes" using old newspaper or rolls of cardboard.*

3 Sowing outside

When the soil starts to warm up in spring, make a drill 10cm (4in) wide and 5cm (2in) deep. Water it well then space seeds 5cm (2in) apart along its length. Cover the seeds with soil, firm in gently, and water. If you are sowing in summer, water the soil well in the two days beforehand, and sow seed deeper than normal, at 8cm (3in).

Pea seeds need warm soil, *around 10°C (50°F), in order to germinate and may fail to grow or rot off if it is too cold or wet. Space the seed evenly.*

Thin any seedlings *growing closer than 5cm (2in) apart. These plants can be cropped as tasty pea shoots rather than composted.*

Insert canes or pea sticks *next to the seedlings for support, or stretch a length of pea netting along the length of the row.*

Water pea plants thoroughly, *especially when the flowers appear, as this well help the developing pods to swell more quickly.*

4 Providing support

Most peas are climbing plants and need support as they grow. Just after sowing or planting out, insert twiggy sticks along the row, tall enough to suit the variety you are growing (check the packet). You can also use pea netting or chicken wire held upright using sturdy canes.

5 Routine care

Keep the plants well watered throughout summer, especially when in flower or pod. Pigeons adore pea foliage and pods, and can quickly strip plants bare. If they are a problem in your area, cover young plants with fine netting, held taut to prevent birds becoming snagged. Check for gaps.

6 Harvesting

Tender young peas should be ready to harvest from early summer onwards. Pick them as they mature and eat them as soon as possible to enjoy them at their sweetest. If your plants produce a glut, it is better to pick and freeze them regularly, as peas store particularly well this way. Leave a few pods to dry on the plants and turn yellow at the end of summer if you want to collect your own seed.

If picked regularly, *plants will crop for several weeks. Check your plants every few days.*

STEP-BY-STEP Runner beans

This is one of the most productive crops you can grow, and will supply a ready harvest of tender pods throughout summer; the more you pick, the more will grow. Most runner beans are climbing plants and take up little bed space, making them a good choice for smaller plots. The easiest way to grow them is up a wigwam of canes, which can easily be incorporated into flowering borders. This also makes efficient use of your vertical growing spaces.

	SPRING	SUMMER	AUTUMN	WINTER
SOW				
HARVEST				

TIME TO HARVEST: 12–16 WEEKS

SUITABLE FOR: BEDS AND CONTAINERS

15 plants

3M (10FT) ROWS
Sow direct or plant out 20cm (8in) apart

CONTAINERS
4 plants in each

1 Getting started

For larger crops it's cheaper to grow your own plants from seed, sowing them under cover or directly outside. Runner beans are also sold as plants in spring, which is ideal if you only want a few. As well as climbing varieties, there are also dwarf bush-types that are ideal for growing in patio containers.

'Desiree' is a tasty and productive variety that gives a prolonged harvest during summer.

'White Lady' has white flowers that are less attractive to birds, which may eat them.

'Lady Di' produces long, stringless pods during summer. It is a reliable variety for beginners.

'Polestar' is a stringless variety, bearing large pods, 25cm (10in) long, throughout summer.

Prepare the soil by digging in well-rotted organic matter before sowing – this is ideal for beans, which prefer rich, moist soil.

Insert canes either in two rows to join at the top, which can then be linked as a row, or in circles of four or five to create wigwams.

Wait until the soil is warm enough before sowing directly. It needs to be at least 12°C (54°F) for them to germinate.

2 Sowing outside

Runner beans are tender plants and should only be sown outside once the risk of frost has passed. Before sowing, prepare the soil well by digging a trench or large circle (for wigwams) in spring, and fill it with well-rotted organic matter, such as compost or manure. Insert canes where the plants are to grow, and sow one or two seeds at the base of each, 5cm (2in) deep. Cover the seeds with soil, firm in gently and water well. The seeds will take a couple of weeks to germinate, after which they should be thinned to the healthiest one per cane. Protect the seedlings from slugs with a light sprinkling of pellets.

3 Sowing inside

In cooler areas, start seeds off under cover – seed will germinate earlier and more reliably. Sow the seeds individually into pots or "growing tubes" filled with seed compost and water them well. Grow them on under cover in a bright position for a few weeks. Plant out once all risk of frost has passed. Keep them well watered.

Sow the seeds *5cm (2in) deep and water well. It's worth sowing more than you need in case some fail to come up.*

Harden off the seedlings *by standing them outside during the day and bringing them in at night for about two weeks.*

Plant out seedlings *at the base of your canes, one per support. Water the plants in well and twist the stem up the cane.*

Mulch plants *with plenty of well-rotted manure or garden compost. This will help to keep the root area moist and encourage the best crop.*

Runner bean roots *grow deep into the soil. Ensure you give your plants a good soaking so the water penetrates right down to them.*

4 Mulching

Runner beans are hungry and thirsty plants. To help conserve moisture and to help feed your crop, mulch the plants in summer with well-rotted organic matter, such as garden compost. This is particularly worthwhile for crops growing in containers.

5 Routine care

Plants must be kept well watered once the flowers appear in order to produce beans; dry spells can cause the flowers or beans to wither and fall. Pinch out the growing tips when the stems reach the top of the canes to promote new cropping sideshoots.

6 Harvesting

Pick the pods as soon as they are large enough, and check plants every two or three days; regular picking promotes a prolonged harvest. Beans left to grow for too long become tough, so pick regularly when they are young and tender, and freeze surpluses.

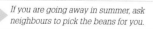

TIP *If you are going away in summer, ask neighbours to pick the beans for you.*

To save your own seed, *leave a few pods to develop fully on the plants at the end of summer.*

STEP-BY-STEP French beans

Otherwise known as filet or snap beans, French beans are an easy crop for beginners and can be harvested for their plump pods or for the beans themselves. They are also a good choice for smaller plots, with climbing varieties that can be trained up space-saving rows of wigwams, and dwarf varieties that can be grown in containers. If you have access to a warm greenhouse you can even grow them under cover for an extra-early spring crop.

	SPRING	SUMMER	AUTUMN	WINTER
SOW				
HARVEST				

TIME TO HARVEST: 12–16 WEEKS

SUITABLE FOR: BEDS, CONTAINERS, AND GROWING BAGS

12 plants

3M (10FT) ROWS
Sow or plant out 25cm (10in) apart

CONTAINERS
4 plants in each

1 Sowing outside

The simplest way to grow French beans is to sow seed in the soil in late spring. Prepare the site by digging in well-rotted organic matter, such as garden compost (this can also be done in the autumn), and remove any weeds. Firm the soil and rake it level. Insert canes where climbing plants are to grow, 25cm (10in) apart, and sow two seeds at the base of each, 5cm (2in) deep. Thin the seedlings to one per cane.

French beans are hungry plants and need moist soil, rich in organic matter to crop well.

Sow seed directly only once the soil has warmed up in spring. Use cloches to hasten this process.

2 Sowing under cover

For an early start in cooler areas, sow seed under cover, 3cm (1¼in) deep, two per pot or "growing tube" filled with seed compost. Keep them moist and germination will take about one weeks at 15–18°C (59–64°F).

Paper "growing tubes" are easy to make and ideal for bean plants, accommodating their deep roots.

Seedlings grow quickly so don't sow them too early as they can't be planted out until after the last frost.

3 Growing on

Grow the seedlings on under cover in a bright position until the risk of frost has passed. As they grow, thin those plants sown in pots to leave the strongest seedling per pot. Once the plants reach 8cm (3in) tall, harden them off by standing them outside during the day and bringing them in at night. Any seedlings sown directly outside should be kept well watered and protected from slugs. Use bottle cloches to encourage strong growth.

Seedlings become tangled unless they are thinned early. The roots will also be hard to separate.

4 Planting out

Plant out indoor-raised seedlings of climbing types at the base of their canes, water in well, and gently twine the main stem around its cane. If space is limited, insert the canes after planting. Dwarf beans can also be planted in large containers (offering at least 25cm (10in) space per plant), or plant three beans to a growing bag.

Carefully ease pot-raised beans *from their pots. Plants raised in "growing tubes" are planted tube-and-all; the paper tube will quickly rot away.*

Plant at the same depth *as the plants were in their pots, firm gently and water well. Twine the young stem around the cane after planting.*

Use canes at least 2.5m (8ft) tall *for climbing varieties, pushing 30cm (12in) into the soil. Use soft string, such as natural jute, to tie in growth.*

Weeds attract pests *and slow down growth, so keep them under control. Remove weeds between plants by hand or carefully use a hoe.*

5 Providing support

Climbing beans are self-clinging once established and will wrap themselves around their supports, although new growth and the occasional wayward stem may need tying in. Dwarf varieties have a bushy habit and do not require additional support or tying in.

6 Routine care

Once the plants start to flower, keep them well watered and feed regularly with a balanced liquid fertilizer. Dry spells may cause the flowers and young beans to drop. Protect young plants from slugs and snails with a light scattering of pellets.

7 Harvesting

Tender young pods can be picked as soon as they are large enough. Check plants every few days to pick them at their best; picking often also encourages a larger crop. If growing them for the bean seeds, leave the pods on the plant until fully mature.

TIP	*Leave a few pods to mature fully at the end of the season to collect the seeds.*

Pinch the young pods *from the stem using your fingers before they become old and tough.*

French beans

1 'Selma Zebra' An heirloom climbing variety, it matures early, bearing green pods that are heavily streaked. The distinctive purple colour disappears during cooking.

2 'Borlotto' This dwarf variety produces flat pods that are heavily speckled with red. The beans can be used fresh or dried. Support the plants to keep the pods off the soil.

3 'Rocquencourt' A dwarf variety that freely bears vivid yellow pods. It is cold-tolerant and matures quickly, so is ideal for early and late sowings, if given protection.

4 'Purple Teepee' This dwarf variety bears pods that are held above the foliage, making harvesting easier. Early and profuse, the stringless pods turn deep green on cooking.

5 'The Prince' Widely grown, this is a productive dwarf variety. The uniform green pods are borne steadily over a long season, which is unusual for a dwarf variety.

6 'Speedy' Incredibly quick to mature, this variety only takes approximately 60 days to produce green pods on stocky, dwarf plants. It is a good choice for early or late crops.

7 'Cobra' This climbing bean bears a long succession of tender, stringless, green pods. It also produces attractive purple flowers, making it a good choice to grow in an ornamental bed.

8 'Amethyst' Ideal for patio pots, this dwarf variety is especially compact. The purple pods are slender and stringless, and are borne over a long harvesting period.

9 'Delinel' This popular dwarf, green-podded variety bears tender pods that are totally stringless and have an excellent flavour. It is suitable for containers if watered well.

Other varieties
'Cornetti Meraviglia di Venezia'
'Yin Yang'
'Barlotto Lingua di Fuoco'
'Cannellino'
'Neckargold'

STEP-BY-STEP Broad beans

These small, tender beans are a must-grow crop and shop-bought pods just don't compare to those picked fresh from the plant. They are one of the first vegetables to harvest in spring, which makes them a good choice for smaller plots, as they can soon be replaced with other summer crops. If space is very limited, they can also be grown in containers. As well as the mature beans, the young tips and pods are also edible, so make the most of their versatility.

	SPRING	SUMMER	AUTUMN	WINTER
SOW				
HARVEST				

TIME TO HARVEST: 12–28 WEEKS

SUITABLE FOR: BEDS AND CONTAINERS

12 plants

3M (10FT) ROWS
Sow direct or plant out 25cm (10in) apart

CONTAINERS
16 plants in each

1 Getting started

Broad beans are usually raised from seed, although you may see young plants for sale in spring. They can be grown in most soil types, although those sown directly outside in autumn need good drainage to prevent them rotting off in the cold and wet. Check the packets for varieties suitable for autumn sowing.

'The Sutton' can be sown in autumn or spring, and crops early on sturdy dwarf plants.

'Super Aquadulce' gives an early crop of flavoursome beans. Sow autumn or spring.

'Stereo' is best sown in spring and can be picked as whole young pods, or as mature beans.

'Jubilee Hysor' bears large pods, each packed with 6–8 beans. Sow in autumn or spring.

2 Sow inside

In cooler areas, seeds can also be started off under cover in autumn or spring to plant out later, but don't give them too much warmth. Broad beans have long tap roots, so sow the seeds individually into taller pots or "growing tubes". Germination takes a week; grow them on in a cool, light spot, keeping them frost-free.

TIP Plants grown in blocks help hold each other up.

Tall "growing tubes", which you can buy or make, are ideal for sowing beans under cover.

3 Sowing outside

Broad beans can be sown directly into the soil during autumn or early spring. Fork the soil over first to remove any weeds and large lumps, and either sow into drills or into a grid pattern of individual holes, 25cm (10in) apart.

Broad beans absorb nitrogen from the air and fix it in the soil. They don't require additional feeding.

Sow the seed 5cm (2in) deep directly into beds or pots. Cover with soil, firm gently, and water in well.

4 Planting out

Once indoor-sown plants show strong growth, harden them off for a week or two to acclimatize them to outdoor temperatures. Dig over the site thoroughly to remove weeds and break up lumps, and plant out 25cm (10in) apart each way. If planted in blocks, additional support is not necessary, except on more exposed sites.

Harden off plants *before planting them out in autumn or spring. Stand them outside in the day, bringing them in at night.*

Seedlings raised *in "growing tubes" can be planted still in the tube as the roots will penetrate through. The tube will rot away.*

Protect seedlings *with fleece if hard frosts are due straight after planting. Direct-sown plants don't require protection.*

Young plants *should be well-watered at first but soon develop a deep tap root. On lighter soils, mulch plants with compost to retain moisture.*

Pinching out tips *encourages the bean pods to develop, and also provides an early crop of tasty leaves, which are delicious when steamed.*

5 Routine care

Broad beans require little care once they are growing strongly, and need only watering in summer when plants are flowering. Plants should be kept well weeded until they establish. Those grown in blocks crowd out most weeds anyway, but check occasionally.

6 Pinching out

When the first flowers begin to set pods, pinch out the soft growing tip of each plant. This causes the plants to focus on developing pods rather than leafy growth, and also deters blackfly (see p.240), which feed on the shoots during late spring and summer.

7 Harvesting

Crops sown in autumn are ready to harvest in late spring. These early crops are best harvested before the developing beans create visible swellings in the pods. All broad beans are best picked while young, so pick and freeze any you can't use straightaway. After harvesting, cut the plants to the ground but leave the roots in the soil to break down. They will release their stored nitrogen for the next crop to use.

Broad beans *are best eaten fresh but will keep well in their pods in the fridge for a few days.*

Cucurbits

This group of plants, which includes courgettes, marrows, summer and winter squashes, pumpkins, and cucumbers, is one of the most generous, especially summer varieties that produce crop after crop of melt-in-the-mouth, colourful fruits. Pumpkins and winter squashes are invaluable for storing, allowing you to savour their sweet, nutty flesh throughout autumn and winter (and beyond in many cases). The fruits of some varieties can be gargantuan, too. Vigorous growth and a hungry appetite demand fertile soil and ample moisture, with plenty of warmth to speed up fruit development. Get these conditions right and the rewards will be huge.

STEP-BY-STEP Cucumbers

These summer salad stalwarts are easy to grow in any garden, and although some varieties require a greenhouse to crop well, "ridge" varieties are perfectly happy outside. These can be left to sprawl over the ground, or where space is limited, they can be trained up stout canes, making good use of your vertical surfaces. Small-fruited "snacking" cucumbers are particularly productive and convenient, with fruit just large enough for a lunch box.

	SPRING	SUMMER	AUTUMN	WINTER
SOW				
HARVEST				

TIME TO HARVEST: 16–20 WEEKS

SUITABLE FOR: BEDS, CONTAINERS, AND GROWING BAGS, UNDER COVER OR OUTSIDE

11 plants

3M (10FT) ROWS
Plant 30cm (12in) apart

GROWING BAGS
3 plants in each

1 Getting started

Cucumbers can be raised from seed, which is ideal if you want several plants. They can also be bought as seedlings in spring, which may be a better choice if you only want a few. Cucumbers are productive, and depending on variety, just two or three plants will satisfy most families all summer.

'**Burpless Tasty**' is an outdoor variety that freely produces long, glossy green fruit.

'**Passandra**' grows indoors and gives a large crop of small, single-serving fruits.

'**Masterpiece**' is an outdoor "ridge" variety. The fruits have small prickles on their skins.

'**Crystal Apple**' bears a good crop of small, round, juicy fruits. It is easy to grow outside.

Cucumber seed can be expensive. Sow one seed per pot and keep them warm, 22-25°C (72–77°F), to encourage good germination.

Check the seed regularly until they germinate, which should take a week or two. Remove them from the propagator and grow them on indoors.

2 Sowing seeds

Cucumber seeds should be started off under cover, as plants need a long growing season to fruit well and are very sensitive to the cold. Hybrid seeds may be more expensive but they result in more vigorous, productive plants, so are worth the extra expense. Fill 10cm (4in) diameter pots with seed compost, water well and allow to drain. Sow one seed per pot, 2cm (¾in) deep, water lightly, and place them in a heated propagator until they germinate.

TIP Cucumbers require constantly high temperatures, so don't sow too early.

3 Planting out

Once they are large enough, plant cucumbers out in early summer – enrich the soil thoroughly in advance. Outdoor "ridge" varieties can be planted directly into the soil in a sunny spot and left to trail across the surface, or can be trained up canes. Greenhouse-types can be planted one per 30cm (12in) pot, or three per standard-size growing bag.

Outdoor varieties *should be hardened off for a few weeks before planting to acclimatize them to outdoor conditions.*

Insert canes to train *plants upwards where space is limited. This also keeps the fruit clean and away from crawling pests.*

Growing bags are ideal *for greenhouse crops but they can also be used outside. Allow the bag to warm up before planting.*

Female flowers *have an embryonic fruit behind the petals. These must be pollinated unless the variety is "all female". Check before you buy.*

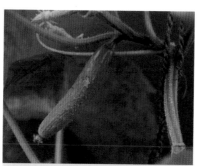

Swelling cucumbers *become heavy so make sure the stems are attached to their supports, especially mature plants with several fruits.*

4 Pollination

Outdoor varieties have both male and female flowers; the latter must be pollinated to set fruit. Many modern greenhouse varieties are "all female" and must not be pollinated – they will bear bitter-tasting fruits if they are. Grow these well away from varieties that produce male flowers.

5 Routine care

Keep plants well watered, and regularly apply tomato fertilizer, as directed by the bottle. Indoor plants thrive in high humidity, which you can achieve by watering the ground around plants. This also helps deter red spider mite and powdery mildew (see p.240 and p.244), which are both common.

6 Harvesting

As soon as individual fruits are big enough, cut them from the plants using secateurs. Cucumbers grow quickly and their quality declines if they are left too long on the plant. To enjoy them at their best, check plants daily and harvest them as soon as they are ready. The fruit can be stored in the fridge until needed, if necessary. If you expect a surplus, very young fruits can be harvested as gherkins for pickling.

Some cucumbers *are smooth-skinned, others have small prickles but they taste the same.*

STEP-BY-STEP Courgettes and marrows

Courgettes are notoriously productive and just two or three plants are all you need to be self-sufficient in them throughout the summer. They require a rich soil and are extremely easy to grow in containers and growing bags, as well as direct in the ground. There are many varieties to choose from, with green or yellow fruits, that can be either round or elongated. Leave them to mature, and your courgettes will develop into marrows, ideal for autumn stews.

	SPRING	SUMMER	AUTUMN	WINTER
SOW				
HARVEST				

TIME TO HARVEST: 14 WEEKS

SUITABLE FOR: BEDS, CONTAINERS, AND GROWING BAGS – UNDER COVER OR OUTSIDE

4 plants

3M (10FT) ROWS
Plant 90cm (36in) apart

GROWING BAGS
2 plants in each

1 Getting started

Courgettes are very easy to raise from seed, which is the best choice if you want to grow a particular variety. Alternatively, young plants are widely available to buy during spring. Courgettes crop very quickly, so consider yellow-fruited varieties as the fruits are much easier to spot among the dense foliage.

'Zucchini' crops earlier than most varieties and bears green fruit, best cut at 15cm (6in) long.

'Defender' is resistant to cucumber mosaic virus (see p.242) and crops very heavily.

'Jemmer' produces attractive yellow fruits that stand out clearly among the dense leaves.

'Parador' fruits are a striking bright yellow, and keep their colour well when cooked.

Sow seeds into 10cm (4in) wide pots part-filled with compost. Place the seeds on their sides to discourage decay, then cover with more compost.

Direct sow seeds in pairs 3cm deep (1¼in), 90cm (36in) apart, in early summer. Water well, cover with mini cloches, then thin each pair to one seedling.

2 Sowing seeds

Courgettes are tender plants, and it is useful to sow seeds under cover to give them a head start for when the frosts pass. Sow seed singly in pots, 2.5cm deep (1in), and place them in a heated propagator until germinated. Seed can also be sown directly outside during early summer, and provide a useful second flush of crops after indoor-raised plants. Choose a sunny and sheltered site, and improve the soil with organic matter before sowing.

TIP Young plants are prone to slug and snail damage; protect plants with pellets.

3 Growing on

Grow the plants on under cover at a temperature of 18°C (64°F). Keep well watered and begin feeding them with a balanced liquid fertilizer after two weeks. Plants will grow quickly and may need potting on if roots appear at the base of the pots. Harden them off and plant out in beds or growing bags (see left), or one per 30cm (12in) pot.

Seedlings sown early *may need to be potted on if they outgrow their original pots before the frosts have passed.*

Plants sown in later spring *can be hardened off as soon as the risk of frost has passed to acclimatize them to life outside.*

After planting out *you can cover plants with cloches or cut-off clear plastic bottles to help plants establish quickly.*

Mature plants *develop a broad canopy of leaves. A funnel (see below) makes watering easier; mark its position with a short cane.*

Powdery mildew *(see p.244) can develop on the foliage and weaken plants. Remove heavily affected leaves and water more regularly.*

4 Watering

Courgettes are quick growing and fruiting, and should be kept well-watered throughout summer. To make this easier, create a well around individual plants for water to collect in, or plunge a funnel (an upturned bottle with the base cut off works well) next to each plant for direct watering.

5 Routine care

Young plants need weeding until established when their dense canopy of leaves will smother other competing plants. Most courgettes form a large rosette of leaves but some newer varieties have a trailing habit and can be trained up canes. On older plants, regularly remove any yellowing leaves.

6 Harvesting

Using a sharp knife, harvest traditional courgettes when they measure between 8–15cm (3–6in) long; round-fruited varieties should be picked when 7–12cm (3–5in) across. Check over the plants daily as the fruit develop very quickly in summer. Alternatively, leave the fruits on one or two plants to develop fully. These plants will then give a smaller crop of thick-skinned marrows to harvest in late summer.

Keep harvesting young fruits – *if they are allowed to grow on, fewer fruit will be produced.*

STEP-BY-STEP Summer squashes

A close relative of courgettes, summer squash are very easy to grow and some can be trained upwards, making them ideal for smaller plots. They come in a wide selection of shapes and sizes, including scallop-edged "patty pans" and crook-necked vase-shaped varieties, and all are extremely free-fruiting. The fruits are either harvested when small and thin-skinned to eat whole, or can be allowed to grow large enough to stuff and roast whole.

	SPRING	SUMMER	AUTUMN	WINTER
SOW				
HARVEST				

TIME TO HARVEST: 14–20 WEEKS

SUITABLE FOR: BEDS, CONTAINERS, AND GROWING BAGS

2–3 plants

3M (10FT) ROWS
Plant 1–1.5m (3–5ft) apart, depending on variety

GROWING BAGS
2 plants in each

1 Getting started

Only a few varieties of summer squash are commonly sold as young plants, so they are best raised from seed. The plants crop heavily and two or three will give a good supply of fruit all summer, so don't grow more than you need. The fruits can be harvested while young to help keep on top of summer gluts.

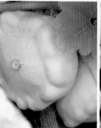

Patty pan is a type not a variety, and there are yellow, green, and white forms to grow.

'Sunburst' can be picked as young fruit or left to grow on. It crops freely if harvested often.

'Tromboncino' is best harvested when 30cm (12in) long, but can reach 1m (3ft) if left to grow on.

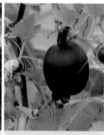

'Rolet' gives a good crop of round, cricket ball-sized fruits, that have sweet-tasting flesh.

Sow seed under cover into 10cm (4in) wide pots, 2cm (¾in) deep and cover with compost. Water them in and place the pots in a propagator.

To sow direct, first prepare a seedbed and sow the seeds 2cm (¾in) deep, 90cm (36in) apart. Position each seed on its side to help prevent it rotting.

2 Sowing seeds

For an early start, sow seeds under cover into individual pots and place them in a heated propagator until they germinate. Once the seedlings emerge, grow them on under cover at 18°C (64°F) in a bright spot. After about a fortnight start feeding weekly with liquid fertilizer. Seeds can also be sown directly into the soil in early summer. Sow seed in pairs, water them in, and cover with a cloche or cut-off plastic bottles. Thin each pair to leave the stronger.

TIP   *Summer squash prefer rich soil, so dig in organic matter well before planting.*

Growing on

3 Grow on plants raised under cover until the risk of frost has passed, then harden them off ready to grow outside. Plant them out 1–1.5m (3–5ft) apart, and water in well. To make watering easier, bury an upturned bottle with the base cut off next to each plant to act as a funnel. Plants can also be grown one per 30cm (12in) container.

Harden off seedlings *for a few weeks before planting out, placing them outside during the day but bringing them back under cover at night.*

Trailing summer squash varieties *can be planted beneath taller crops, such as sweetcorn or tomatoes, or near rows of climbing beans.*

Mulch to help maintain moisture *– if plants are allowed to dry out, or are watered irregularly, the skins of the fruits may split.*

Train trailing squash stems *along the edges of beds or paths so the fruits are easy to pick. This will also free up bed space for other crops.*

Routine care

4 Summer squashes are vigorous plants, and should be watered well and regularly fed with tomato fertilizer. To help conserve soil moisture, mulch around plants with a thick layer of compost or similar organic material. The mulch will gradually break down, steadily releasing nutrients to the plants.

Training

5 Most varieties are trailing plants and can be left to creep across the soil. To make harvesting easier, gradually remove the lower leaves as they grow, to provide access to the fruit. If space is limited, the stems can also be looped into circles on the ground or trained vertically up cane wigwams.

Harvesting

6 Squashes produce separate male and female flowers on the same plant but it is only the females that fruit. The flowers wither as soon as they are pollinated and the fruit begins to develop. Young, tender squash will be ready to harvest after four to seven days, depending on the weather. They can be left to grow longer for larger fruit that are ideal for stuffing and roasting.

Squash that develop a thick skin *before harvesting will keep longer in storage.*

STEP-BY-STEP Winter squashes

Winter squashes are available in a huge range of shapes and colours, and provide a delicious feast in late autumn and winter, especially when roasted or in soups. Easy to grow, they can be left to trail across the ground and make good use of the space between your other crops. They can also be grown in containers, with the stems trained to make a feature of the decorative fruit. If you have space, the fruits store and last well into the winter months.

	SPRING	SUMMER	AUTUMN	WINTER
SOW				
HARVEST				

TIME TO HARVEST: 18–20 WEEKS

SUITABLE FOR: BEDS AND CONTAINERS

3M (10FT) ROWS
Sow or plant 1–1.5m (3–5ft) apart
2–3 plants

CONTAINERS
1 plant in each

1 Sowing under cover

Winter squash are tender but can be sown under cover in spring to plant out when any danger of frosts has passed. Fill 10cm (4in) pots with seed compost, water them well, and then leave them to drain. Sow one seed per pot at a depth of 3cm (1¼in). Place the pots in a heated propagator set at 15–18°C (59–64°F) for a week or two. Once the seedlings emerge, grow them on in a warm, bright position.

Sow the seeds on their edge, *thin-side down, so moisture doesn't collect on the top of the seed when it is watered, running the risk of decay.*

Winter squash seedlings *grow quickly but can only be planted out after the frosts have passed, so don't sow them too early. Pot them on if necessary.*

Direct-sow seed *at the base of a sturdy support if you plan to train your squash plants as climbers. Seed can also be sown beneath tall crops.*

Thin surplus seedlings *to leave the strongest. If you have unwanted gaps, carefully move spare plants to where they are needed. Water in well.*

2 Sowing outside

Sow seeds direct in late spring. First, prepare the soil by digging in plenty of well-rotted manure or compost, and remove weeds. Then firm and rake level. For an earlier crop, warm the soil first with cloches. Sow seeds in pairs, 3cm (1¼in) deep and 1m (3ft) apart, water well, and cover with a bottle cloche. Once each group of seedlings emerges, thin to leave only the strongest. Protect plants from slugs and snails.

TIP	*Cut the base off clear plastic bottles to make your own mini cloches.*

3 Planting out

Plants sown under cover can be planted out into their final positions in early summer. Before doing so, harden them off first to acclimatize them to outdoor conditions. Place them outside during the day but bring them back in each night for two weeks. Plant out at 1m (3ft) apart and water them in well. Protect young plants from slugs.

Water the plants well *before planting them out to help their roots establish successfully.*

Plant out at the same depth *as the plants were in their pots and firm them in gently.*

Water in well *and keep plants moist until they are growing well, especially on lighter soils.*

Mulch plants with well-rotted compost *to help retain moisture, especially on lighter soils. The mulch will break down, feeding your plants.*

Trailing stems *can be looped around canes to form circles, or trained up supports. Both methods will contain the plants' spread in smaller gardens.*

4 Routine care

Plants require plenty of water during the summer months, so to make watering easier, bury an upturned plastic bottle with the base removed next to each plant (see p.91). Also feed plants well by regularly applying a general-purpose liquid fertilizer, as directed by the instructions.

5 Training

Winter squash are either bushy, or trailing. Bush-types form neat clumps of leaves, whereas trailing plants send out long, winding stems. These can be trained into loops if space is limited, or allowed to ramble among other plants. You can also train smaller-fruited varieties up trellis work or canes.

6 Harvesting

In mid-autumn the leaves will start to die back and the fruits should be colouring up well. These need to be harvested before the first frosts. Cut them from the plant, leaving a short length of stem attached to act as a handle. Leave the fruits in a warm, sunny spot for two weeks to harden the skins – a windowsill is ideal. The fruits can then be stored until needed.

Colourful fruits *can be used for temporary seasonal decoration until needed in the kitchen.*

Winter squashes

1 'Sweet Dumpling' This trailing variety bears slightly ribbed, white-skinned fruits with green vertical stripes. Each fruit grows 12–15cm (5–6in) in diameter, with yellow flesh.

2 'Uchiki Kuri' Also known as the "onion squash", this trailing variety bears delicious fruits with intense orange flesh. Expect to harvest five or six fruits per plant.

3 'Queensland Blue' This heirloom Australian variety bears heavily-ribbed grey-blue fruits. They reach 25cm (10in) in diameter, and have intensely nutty, orange flesh.

4 'Butternut' These classically shaped squashes are borne on trailing plants. With deep orange flesh and few seeds, they are ideal for roasting or stuffing. They also store well.

5 'Cream of the Crop' This variety produces large acorn-shaped fruits with cream skins and nutty-flavoured, golden flesh. The compact plants will yield three or four fruits each.

6 Turk's Turban A trailing-type with sweet flesh, it bears unusually shaped orange fruits with bold green and white stripes. The fruits grow to 20–25cm (8–10in) in diameter.

7 'Crown Prince' This trailing plant bears round, squat, grey-blue fruits, 20–25cm (8–10in) in diameter. The deep orange flesh has a very good nutty flavour when cooked.

8 'Harlequin' With its highly coloured fruit, this is an attractive variety to grow where space is limited and plants need to look, as well as produce a good harvest.

9 Vegetable spaghetti When steamed, the mild-tasting flesh of this trailing crop separates into spaghetti-like strands. Expect three or four large fruits per plant.

Other varieties
'Blue Hubbard'
'Butternut Harrier'
'Celebration'
'Sunshine'

STEP-BY-STEP Pumpkins

Mammoth pumpkins take up a lot of space in the garden, but there are plenty of varieties with smaller fruits that are ideal where space is limited – some can even be planted in containers. Pumpkins are reliable and easy to grow. They just need a good supply of water and fertile soil, with some protection against slugs and snails. Although best known for carving at Halloween, the fruits have tasty sweet flesh and store well into winter.

	SPRING	SUMMER	AUTUMN	WINTER
SOW				
HARVEST				

TIME TO HARVEST: 18–22 WEEKS

SUITABLE FOR: BEDS AND CONTAINERS

2–3 plants

3M (10FT) ROWS
Plant 1–1.5m (3–5ft) apart, depending on variety

CONTAINERS
1 plant in each

1 Getting started

Pumpkins may be sold as plants in spring but they are usually grown from seed and there are many varieties to choose from. If you want large fruits for carving, pick a suitable variety and thin the fruits to one or two per plant. For edible fruits, pick your variety and let each plant develop four or five fruits each.

'Atlantic Giant' *is one of the largest fruiting varieties and can be eaten if picked early.*

'Jack be Little' *bears small, brightly coloured fruits that are tasty as well as decorative.*

'Rouge Vif d'Etampes' *is an heirloom variety, with large fruits, good for eating or decoration.*

'Baby Bear' *is a compact variety with thin-skinned fruits, each the size of a football.*

Sow seed individually *2cm (¾in) deep into 10cm (4in) wide pots and place them in a warm propagator set at 20–25°C (68–77°F).*

Check the seeds daily *until they germinate, which takes between one and two weeks. Remove the pots from the propagator and grow them on under cover.*

2 Sowing under cover

Pumpkins need a long growing season to develop full-size fruits. Start them off under cover in spring, especially in cold areas, and then harden them off and plant outside when the frosts have passed. Part-fill small pots with seed compost, sow one seed per pot, water well, and allow to drain. Place pots in a heated propagator and keep the compost moist. When seeds germinate, grow seedlings on under cover for a few weeks in a bright spot.

TIP *Sow the seeds on their sides to prevent them decaying in the moist compost.*

3 Sowing outside

In late spring, seeds can also be sown directly into the soil. Well before sowing, improve the soil with well-rotted organic matter, such as garden compost, then sow the seeds 3cm (1¼in) deep and 1m (3ft) apart. Water them well and cover with a cloche or a large, cut-off clear plastic bottle. Keep well-watered as they grow on.

Sow outdoor seed *in groups of two or three in case any fail to grow. You can then thin to the strongest seedling as they start to develop.*

Carefully transplant *stronger spare seedlings if they are needed elsewhere on the bed. Lift them with a trowel and water well once planted.*

Mulching plants *with well-rotted organic matter, such as garden compost, will help retain moisture in summer. It will also feed your plants.*

Where space is limited, *train pumpkin plants vertically, using old nets to support the swelling fruit. Tie the stems in as they grow.*

4 Routine care

Pumpkins are hungry plants and will benefit from regular feeding with a liquid general-purpose fertilizer. Young plants need weeding until they establish fully. To keep the fruits clean and off the soil, place a short plank of wood under each one.

5 Training

Most pumpkins produce trailing stems and can be left to ramble over the ground among other plants. Where space is limited, tie the stems to canes set out in a circle and pushed into the soil. Small-fruited varieties can also be trained up sturdy supports.

6 Harvesting

In mid-autumn your fruits will be ready for harvest. Cut them with a short length of stalk attached to prevent the stem from rotting back into the fruit, and to provide a handy carrying handle. Unless you plan to use them straightaway, dry or "cure" the skins by leaving them in a sunny spot outside for at least a week. If rain is predicted, move them to a bright position under cover. The fruit will store well for months.

Small pumpkins *can be cooked whole, larger fruits should be cut into manageable pieces.*

Brassicas

Delicious and versatile, brassicas
are a must for any vegetable garden.
Robust crops like sprouting broccoli,
Brussels sprouts, and kale provide
vitamin-rich green vegetables in
the depths of winter when crops
are scarce, while cabbages and
cauliflowers have been bred for
harvesting all year round. Calabrese,
more commonly known as broccoli,
also offers tender summer-season
crops. Provide brassicas with fertile,
well-drained soil, and cover plants
to prevent damage from pests, such
as cabbage white butterfly
caterpillars, and you can enjoy a
range of tasty, nutritious green
vegetables every month of the year.

STEP-BY-STEP Summer and autumn cabbages

Whether you eat cabbage leaves as part of your Sunday roast or use them in more exotic dishes, such as stir-fries, they are an essential vegetable. They can be grown throughout the year (also see p.104), with summer and autumn varieties producing a large, reliable harvest if kept well-watered and covered with nets. Once harvested, the stumps can be left in the ground to re-sprout, giving a second crop of loose leaves and making best use of your plot.

	SPRING	SUMMER	AUTUMN	WINTER
SOW				
HARVEST				

TIME TO HARVEST: 18–24 WEEKS

SUITABLE FOR: BEDS

0	1m	2m	3m

8 plants

3M (10FT) ROWS
Plant 40cm (16in) apart

Sow the seeds thinly *and check them daily until seedlings emerge. They don't need additional heat.*

Thin seedlings *as they develop in their trays; those left can be pricked out into small pots.*

1 Sowing under cover

For an early harvest, sow summer varieties under cover in spring. Fill trays or modules with seed compost, water well, allow to drain, then sow the seeds 2cm (¾in) deep. When the seedlings appear, thin them out to leave the strongest, then prick the remaining seedlings out into small pots. Grow the young plants on indoors in a cool, bright spot for a few weeks longer.

TIP *Cabbages, like most brassicas, are prone to club root (see p.242).*

2 Sowing outside

Although cabbage can be sown under cover, the main season crop is sown outside directly into the soil. A few weeks before sowing, dig over the soil, remove any weeds, firm it, and then rake the surface level. Excavate a drill 2cm (¾in) deep, water it well, and then sow the seeds thinly along the base. Cover over with soil, firm gently, and water lightly. When the seedlings have a few leaves, thin them out, leaving the strongest. Water regularly and protect plants from slugs and snails.

Carefully tip seeds, *directly from the packet or use your fingers to sow them in pinches.*

Thin the seedling *to their final spacings or transplant them once they reach 15cm (6in) tall.*

3 Planting out

Once large enough, move the young plants, whether raised indoors or out, to their final positions. Prepare the area first by digging it over, removing weeds, and applying some high-nitrogen granular fertilizer. Water the young plants well and lift them from the seedbed, or from their trays or pots, and plant them out 40cm (16in) apart.

Transplant young plants carefully *to help minimize root loss or disturbance, which can check growth. Water plants in well after planting.*

Young plants are vulnerable to attack *from many different pests, including aphids (above, see p.240). Check for damage and infestations.*

Cover with fine netting *to prevent cabbage white butterflies from laying eggs on your plants. Use canes to hold it clear of the leaves.*

Water well *directing the flow at the base of the plants. On lighter soils, mulch around plants to help retain moisture or lay pieces of cardboard.*

5 Routine care

Keep beds weeded until plants are well established, by which time their foliage will suppress weeds. Water regularly, especially during hot or dry spells, and apply a balanced liquid feed, as directed by the manufacturers, to promote strong, leafy growth.

4 Protecting plants

Fit brassica collars around each plant to deter cabbage root fly (see p.240). At the same time, cover plants with fine netting to protect against cabbage white caterpillars (see p.238) and pigeons. Keep the netting pulled taut and check regularly for holes.

6 Harvesting

The plants are ready to harvest from late summer onwards, once they have fully-formed, leafy heads. To harvest, either cut through the tough stalk with a sharp knife or lift the roots using a fork. Mature plants can be left in the ground for a few weeks until needed but will gradually deteriorate. Trim off the outer, tougher leaves and use only the tender heart; cut heads can be stored in a fridge for about a week.

Harvest young cabbages, *picking every other one in a row, to allow others space to fully mature.*

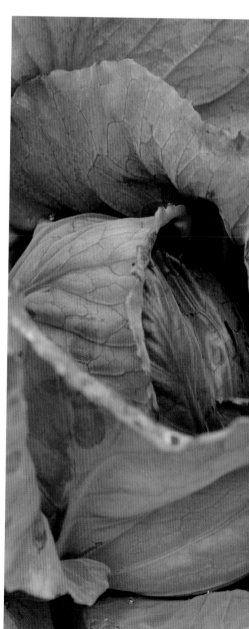

Summer cabbages

1 'Greyhound' This reliable, fast-maturing variety forms loose leafy heads with few tough stalks. If sown in spring, the first heads can be harvested in early summer.

2 'Derby Day' An early summer variety, this cabbage produces rounded heads, tightly packed with tender leaves. It is the earliest "ball" cabbage to mature during the season.

3 'Hotspur' Forming large tasty heads that are ready to harvest from late summer onwards, this variety has a short stem and few tough stalks, meaning there is little waste when cooking.

4 'Red Jewel' This variety produces dense, round heads, tightly packed with dark red leaves that retain their colour well when cooked. It is good for storing and also keeps well in the soil.

5 'Duncan' This quick-maturing variety forms loose, pointed heads. It is a versatile choice that can be sown in spring to harvest in autumn, or sown in autumn to crop in spring.

6 'Marner Early Red' Forming large heads of reddish leaves that are ready to harvest from mid-autumn, this cabbage keeps its colour when cooked and can be finely sliced and used raw.

7 'Stonehead' These mid-size, compact plants can be grown closely together, making best use of smaller plots. The heads will last well in the soil during autumn until needed.

8 'Kalibos' This heirloom variety develops small, pointed heads, packed with deep red leaves. It can be used raw in salads if chopped finely, or eat it lightly boiled instead.

9 'Hispi' This cabbage is very quick to mature, and can also be sown in autumn to harvest in spring. It forms neat, pointed heads of tasty leaves, and is a good choice for smaller gardens.

Other varieties
'Elisa'
'Kilaton'
'Primo'
'Redcap'
'Ruby Ball'
'Surprise'

STEP-BY-STEP Winter and spring cabbages

From deep green, crinkle-leaved savoys to pointed, dense-hearted spring cabbages, these hardy brassicas are invaluable during the leaner months of the year. Spring-cropping plants can be packed tightly together, making efficient use of small plots. They also give a useful secondary crop of loose leaves in spring if the cut stumps are left to grow back. Always cover your crops with netting to protect them from pests like pigeons and caterpillars.

	SPRING	SUMMER	AUTUMN	WINTER
SOW				
HARVEST				

TIME TO HARVEST: 26–28 WEEKS

SUITABLE FOR: BEDS

0   1m   2m   3m

7–11 plants

3M (10FT) ROWS
Plant out 30–50cm (12–20in) apart, depending on variety

1 Getting started

The best way to raise cabbages is from seed, sown either under cover in late spring, or inside or outdoors in summer for both winter and spring cabbages. Alternatively, if you are planning to grow just a few crops, you can buy young plants in summer, which is an easier but more costly option.

'Tundra' *is a winter variety that can be left in the ground for several weeks until needed.*

'Jewel' *produces loose heads of smooth leaves that keep well in the soil through winter.*

'January King' *can be cropped in autumn as young heads, or left to mature through winter.*

'Tarvoy' *is a slow maturing, winter savoy cabbage with sweet-tasting, crinkled leaves.*

Cabbage seeds are reliable *but sow two to a cell, just in case one fails. They are large and easy to handle, allowing you to sow them accurately.*

Grow the seedlings on *in a bright position under cover for two or three weeks, until they can be planted out into beds. Keep them cool but frost-free.*

2 Sowing under cover

Raising plants under cover helps reduce the effects of club root disease on your plants (see p.242). Fill module trays with seed compost, water well and allow to drain. Make holes 1cm (½in) deep in each cell, sow one seed in each, then thin to leave the strongest seedling once they emerge. Grow the young plants on under cover until 15cm (6in) tall. Prepare them for outdoor conditions by moving them outside during the day, then back in at night.

TIP	*Acclimatize plants to outdoor temperatures for about two weeks.*

3 Sowing outdoors

These cabbages can be sown outside in summer when the soil is warm. Prepare a seedbed by digging over the soil, removing weeds, and raking it level. Make drills, 2cm (¾in) deep, water the base well, then thinly sow the seed. Fill the drill with soil, firm gently, and lightly water again. The seeds will germinate in a week or two.

Prepare the soil before planting *out your seedlings. Digging in some well-rotted organic matter will help encourage plenty of leafy growth.*

Make drills long enough *to suit the size of your plot. To retain moisture during dry spells, cover with newspaper until the seeds germinate.*

Young cabbage plants *are ready to plant out when they are about 15cm (6in) tall. If much larger or smaller, they may be slow to establish.*

Cabbages develop a crown of leaves *so aim the water directly at the base to ensure it reaches the roots. Use a watering can with a long spout.*

4 Planting out

Winter cabbages are planted out in summer, spring cabbage in autumn. Prepare the site by digging it over to remove weeds and fork in some high-nitrogen granular fertilizer. Plant out or transplant winter cabbages 50cm (20in) apart, spring-types 30cm (12in).

5 Routine care

Water plants regularly, especially during dry spells. To encourage strong growth before winter, apply high-nitrogen liquid feed in late summer, as directed by the packet. Weed the beds regularly, and remove any yellowing leaves from the plants.

6 Harvesting

Using a sharp knife to cut through the stalk, harvest during winter and spring when individual heads are large enough to use. Mature plants can be left in the ground for a few weeks until needed but may deteriorate the longer they are left. Leave the stumps of spring cabbages in the soil and make a cross in the cut end. This will encourage them to produce a crop of loose leaves, which you can harvest a few weeks later.

Loose spring leaves *make a useful bonus crop after the cabbage heads have been harvested.*

STEP-BY-STEP Cauliflowers

It is possible to grow and harvest delicious fresh cauliflowers all year round as there is a wide range of varieties to choose from. As well as conventional white-headed types you can also grow cauliflowers with striking purple, orange, or green heads. Space the plants widely so that the heads can grow to full size, or densely in containers to produce "mini" cauliflowers. They can produce very high yields if given enough food and water.

	SPRING	SUMMER	AUTUMN	WINTER
SOW				
HARVEST				

TIME TO HARVEST: 20–26 WEEKS

SUITABLE FOR: BEDS AND CONTAINERS

5–6 plants

3M (10FT) ROWS
Plant 60–70cm (24–28in) apart

CONTAINERS
8 plants in each

1 Getting started

Cauliflowers that mature from autumn to spring are sown when conditions are warm; sowing direct into warm soils in mid-autumn is very successful. On the other hand, summer-maturing varieties are sown from mid- to late spring, and in such cases sowing in modules under cover is the best method.

'Snowball' *is sown in spring for an autumn harvest; the medium-sized heads keep well.*

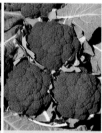

'Violet Queen' *bears purple heads in late summer that turn green when cooked.*

'Walcheren Winter Pilgrim' *is a hardy variety that is ready to harvest in spring.*

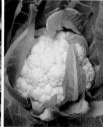

'Mayflower' *is an early variety that can be sown in mid-winter to harvest from midsummer.*

2 Sowing under cover

Fill module trays or pots with compost, water well, and allow to drain. Make a hole 1cm (½in) deep in each cell and sow two seeds into it. Firm over with compost and water in. Once emerged, thin to leave the stronger seedling.

Summer and autumn varieties *should be sown in midwinter and then placed in a propagator.*

Keep seedlings well watered *– cauliflowers are thirsty plants and require a lot of water at all stages.*

3 Sow outside

For winter and spring cauliflowers, sow the seed direct in late spring. Prepare a seedbed by digging over the ground, incorporating plenty of organic matter. Then excavate a short drill, 2cm (¾in) deep. Water the base thoroughly, sow your seeds, and then cover with soil to level and water in lightly. To prevent a build-up of soil diseases, ensure that you do not plant cauliflowers where other brassica crops have grown in the past three years.

Sow seed thinly *along the drill – once the seedlings develop they can be thinned if necessary.*

3 Planting out

Harden off module-raised seedlings when they are 15cm (6in) tall. Place them outdoors during the day and inside at night for a week. Once seedbed-raised plants reach this height, water them well and then lift gently from the soil. Summer varieties should be spaced 60cm (24in) apart each way; winter types 70cm (28in).

Hardened-off cauliflowers *should be planted promptly. You risk encouraging the plants to bolt if they become too large.*

Plant both module-grown *and seedbed-raised seedlings in soil that has had a high nitrogen granular feed incorporated.*

Firm the plants in well, *as the heads will become very heavy as they grow and will need to be well supported.*

Ensure that netting *reaches the ground, leaving no gaps for pests to crawl underneath – peg the netting down or bury it in the soil.*

Covering the cauliflower head *with its leaves will prevent white varieties from yellowing in the sun. Hold the leaves in place using garden string.*

4 Protecting plants

Water in your transplants, and fit a brassica collar around the base of each. Place netting with a maximum mesh diameter of 1cm (½in) around plants. This will deter cabbage white butterflies and pigeons. Hoe between young plants – established cauliflowers will smother any competing plants.

5 Routine care

It's especially important to keep cauliflowers well watered during the summer months to obtain a good-sized curd. As these develop, bend a few leaves in over the head – this protects summer varieties from being "burnt" by the sun, and offers winter types some frost protection.

6 Harvesting

As soon as the curds reach a harvestable size, cut them from the plant. The heads are best eaten fresh but can be stored in the fridge for a few days; they will keep better if you cut them with a few leaves attached. Blanch and freeze surplus heads.

TIP	Grow in pots for "mini" 6cm (2½in) wide curds. Space 15cm (6in) apart.

Make sure you harvest *cauliflowers while the heads are still tight, when they are at their best.*

STEP-BY-STEP Calabrese

It's well worth growing your own calabrese as homegrown crops are much more tender and flavourful than shop-bought types. The plants produce one main central head and then numerous smaller sideshoots, which prolong the harvest period; the florets also freeze well, so any gluts can be preserved for later. Don't worry if you don't have space to start plants off indoors as direct sowings outdoors in summer perform extremely well.

	SPRING	SUMMER	AUTUMN	WINTER
SOW				
HARVEST				

TIME TO HARVEST: 12–16 WEEKS

SUITABLE FOR: BEDS

0   1m   2m   3m

15 plants

3M (10FT) ROWS
Plant out 20cm (8in) apart

1 Getting started

Calabrese prefer rich, well-drained soil, so dig in plenty of organic matter such as well-rotted manure or compost in the season before planting. Ensure that no other members of the brassica family have been planted in the same location in the past three years, to help prevent the build-up of soil diseases.

'Romanesco' *has lime-green curds that are both highly ornamental and full of flavour.*

'Fiesta' *produces large, well-rounded heads and a good crop of secondary sideshoots.*

'Corvet' *is a high-yielding variety that is renowned for its large, grey-green heads.*

'Belstar' *keeps well once cut and is worth growing for its tasty blue-green heads.*

Calabrese can be overwintered *in a frost-free greenhouse for harvests in early spring. Sow in pots in late summer or early autumn.*

Seedlings will need to be thinned *to one per pot or module as they develop. Close spacing will encourage the plants to produce smaller shoots.*

2 Sowing seeds

Calabrese can be sown under cover in pots or large modules to transplant later. Fill the container with seed compost, firm gently, water well, and make two holes per pot or module, 1cm (½in) deep. Drop a seed into each hole, cover with compost, and water in lightly. Once emerged, thin to leave the stronger seedling. Alternatively, seed can be sown directly into the final position outside. Create a seedbed, mark out rows 30cm (12in) apart and sow a cluster of three seeds every 20cm (8in), into holes 2cm (¾in) deep. Thin the seedlings to the strongest and protect them from slugs using pellets.

3 Planting out

Once indoor-sown plants are 15cm (6in) tall, harden them off and plant out 20cm (8in) apart, in rows 30cm (12in) apart – do not let them become root-bound as this can cause the premature formation of small heads. Keep the plants well watered and well weeded. Place a brassica collar around each plant to deter cabbage root fly.

Divide up your plot *using bamboo canes and string – this will help you work out your plant spacings and will also act as a support for netting.*

Young plants *should be hardened off and planted out as soon as possible in spring, as they cope best with being moved if the weather is not too warm.*

Tall varieties may need staking *if earthing up does not provide sufficient support. Tie the plants in to sturdy bamboo canes as necessary.*

Mealy cabbage aphids *target brassica crops and can swarm plants, disfiguring the leaves. Aim to protect crops from an early age.*

4 Routine care

As the heads of the plants begin to develop, draw soil around the base of the stems to stabilize them – this is called "earthing up". At this point a granular high-nitrogen fertilizer can be applied to boost the main head size and to encourage the production of sideshoots for subsequent harvests.

5 Protecting plants

Erect a frame of netting over your plants to deter birds – especially pigeons – and cabbage white butterflies. Ensure the net is fine, with a maximum mesh diameter of 1cm (½in) to stop the adult butterflies reaching your plants. It is important to keep the netting taut so that birds don't become entangled in it.

6 Harvesting

The first cutting can be expected approximately 3–4 months after sowing, depending on the variety and time of year. Cut the main head off first and then, once the smaller sideshoots appear, harvest these. The younger leaves of calabrese can also be eaten.

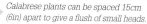

TIP *Calabrese plants can be spaced 15cm (6in) apart to give a flush of small heads.*

Use a knife *to cut the heads whole before the flower buds open. This encourages a second crop.*

STEP-BY-STEP Sprouting broccoli

This hardy crop is one of the most eagerly awaited in winter and spring, and bears a profusion of tender stems tipped with tasty white or purple florets when few other crops are available. Traditional varieties form large plants that mature slowly, and are best suited to bigger gardens. If you enjoy broccoli but have a smaller plot, there are now summer varieties that can be harvested within weeks of sowing, freeing up space for other crops.

	SPRING	SUMMER	AUTUMN	WINTER
SOW				
HARVEST				

TIME TO HARVEST: 16–36 WEEKS

SUITABLE FOR: BEDS

0   1m   2m   3m

6 plants

3M (10FT) ROWS
Plant out 60cm (24in) apart

1 Getting started

Traditional broccoli is easy to raise from seed, or can be bought as young plants, plugs, or as bare-root transplants in spring. Summer-maturing broccoli is less widely available, and is best raised from seed. Sow in batches, from late winter to mid-spring, and harvest florets early summer to mid-autumn.

'Claret' *is a reliable variety that produces succulent heads from mid-spring onwards.*

'Purple Sprouting' *is very hardy and bears an abundance of dark shoots in early spring.*

'White Star' *crops in late spring, producing attractive white heads that can be eaten raw.*

'Bordeaux' *matures in summer from a spring sowing, giving a quick crop of tasty florets.*

Sowing into modules *means the seedlings don't need to be pricked out, reducing root disturbance. They can also be sown in trays.*

Thin the seedlings, *leaving only the strongest one per module. If you have gaps, carefully replant stronger thinned seedlings into vacant cells.*

2 Sowing under cover

Broccoli is hardy and most varieties need a long growing season; give crops a head start by sowing under cover in spring. Fill module trays with seed compost, water well, then leave to drain. Make one hole per cell, 2cm (¾in) deep, and sow two seeds in each. Cover with compost and water in lightly. The seeds won't need additional heat and will germinate within two weeks. Grow the seedlings on under cover until planted out.

TIP *Raising plants under cover reduces the effects of club root disease (see p.242).*

3 Sowing outdoors

Seed can either be sown into seedbeds, with the seedlings transplanted when large enough, or directly in their final growing positions. For seedbed sowing, dig the soil over, and rake it fine and level, then sow into drills 2cm (¾in) deep. Alternatively, sow pinches of seeds at 60cm (24in) intervals, and thin to the strongest per station.

To sow longer rows, *carefully pour the seeds directly from the packet, tapping the top so they drop out at regular intervals.*

Sowing direct in clusters *takes away the need to transplant your seedlings, and means less root disturbance for the crop.*

Fit brassica collars snugly *around the base of each plant soon after planting to stop cabbage root flies from laying their eggs at soil level.*

Net plants against pigeons *and cabbage white butterflies. Keep the netting taut to avoid snaring birds and check it regularly for gaps.*

4 Planting out

Harden off indoor-raised plants before planting them out and water seedbeds well so that outdoor-sown plants are easy to lift. Prepare the soil by forking in granular high-nitrogen fertilizer, as per the instructions on the seed packet. Plant out seedlings 60cm (24in) apart and water well.

5 Routine care

Water and weed plants regularly to ensure steady growth and, as the plants become taller, earth soil up around the base of their stems to help stabilize them. If your garden is in an exposed area you might want to insert a stout cane at the base of each plant for support during autumn gales.

6 Harvesting

Once plants mature in winter and spring, and begin to develop their florets, pick them over daily to ensure you harvest the heads while still tightly closed. Cut them with a length of stem attached, roughly 10cm (4in), as this and the leaves are extremely tender to eat. Continual picking promotes new sideshoots to grow, leading to a longer harvest. The florets are best eaten soon after picking but can also be frozen.

Tender florets *should be picked before the tiny flower buds open. Cut them with a sharp knife.*

STEP-BY-STEP Brussels sprouts

A winter plot would be incomplete without Brussels sprouts, so choose from varieties that will crop from mid-autumn right through until early spring. Individual "buttons" develop over a long period, meaning that two or three plants can provide a steady supply over the winter months. In addition to the tasty sprouts, a further treat is the sprout "top" – a loose rosette of leaves that has a deliciously mild flavour, high in quality if not quantity.

	SPRING	SUMMER	AUTUMN	WINTER
SOW				
HARVEST				

TIME TO HARVEST: 30–36 WEEKS

SUITABLE FOR: BEDS

```
0            1m           2m           3m
```
6 plants

3M (10FT) ROWS
Thin out or plant to 60cm (24in) apart

1 Getting started

Brussels sprouts are worth raising from seed to give you large crop, although they can also be bought as plants in spring. Prepare your site by digging in plenty of well-rotted manure or compost during the season before planting. Brussels sprouts prefer a pH of at least 6.8, so apply lime to the soil if necessary.

'Bosworth' *is a popular variety – its firm, even, sweet sprouts should be harvested in early winter.*

'Red Delicious' *keeps its colour well during cooking; harvest the sprouts in winter.*

'Trafalgar' *bears heavy crops of reliable, firm, flavourful sprouts from midwinter to early spring.*

'Maximus' *is a high-yielding variety, bearing sweet green sprouts over a long season.*

Sprinkle the seed evenly *along the base of a short drill, with a view to transplanting them later. This makes best use of limited space.*

If you are sowing under cover, *sow the seed into holes spaced 5cm (2in) apart. Prick the seedlings out when they are strong enough to handle.*

2 Sowing seeds

To sow seed in the ground, dig over the soil to remove any weeds, firm it well, and rake it level. Either sow a short drill, 2cm (¾in) deep, from which seedlings will be moved to their final position, or sow clusters of seed at 60x60cm (24x24in) apart – this allows you to thin each cluster to the strongest seedling, minimizing root disturbance. You can also start plants off in modules under cover. Fill a module tray with seed compost, firm gently, and water well. Sow two seeds per cell, 2cm (¾in) deep, and cover with compost. Water lightly and, once germinated, thin out to leave the strongest seedling per module.

3 Planting out

Once tray-grown plants reach 10–12cm (4–5in) in height, harden them off ready for life outside. Prepare seedbed-raised sprouts for transplanting by watering the bed thoroughly. Dig over the soil ready for planting, rake it level, and firm well. Space the seedlings 60x60cm (24x24in) apart, and water in well.

Transplant the healthiest of your seedlings once they have reached 10–12cm (4–5in) tall and have four or five true leaves.

Ensure that the seedlings are planted 60cm (24in) apart so that the plants remain well ventilated. Plant Brussels sprouts in firmly.

Use brassica collars to deter cabbage root fly, which is a common brassica pest that can cause the young plants to die.

Bird netting should be pulled taut to prevent birds becoming snagged. Regularly check for gaps at the base where birds could sneak under.

Older leaves near the base of the stems naturally yellow and die; it is not a sign of poor health. They should snap off easily.

4 Protecting plants

Fit brassica collars around the base of each seedling to prevent attack from cabbage root fly (see p.240), and erect a frame of netting over plants to deter pigeons and cabbage white butterflies. Brussels sprouts can grow to around 80cm (32in) in height, so ensure the frame is tall enough.

5 Routine care

Keep the top-heavy plants stable by earthing up soil around their bases or stake them with canes. The lower leaves will yellow as they age, and should be picked off to encourage good air flow around the developing buttons. Keep plants well watered and fed using a high-nitrogen liquid fertilizer.

6 Harvesting

Harvest sprouts when large enough by firmly twisting them off; older cultivars mature from the bottom of the stem upwards. Newer hybrids mature more evenly, and can be cut as whole stems; stand them indoors in water in the cool to harvest as needed.

TIP Harvest the delicious leafy "top" before picking the sprouts themselves.

Sprouts taste especially sweet from late winter, once they have been frosted a few times.

STEP-BY-STEP Kale

Packed with vitamins, kales are very robust plants and stand extremely well over winter, providing a generous harvest in otherwise lean times. The plants are highly ornamental and are also less prone to the common pests and diseases that affect other members of the brassica family. Leaves should be harvested little and often to ensure they remain tender; two or three plants can provide ample pickings if used as cut-and-come-again crops.

	SPRING	SUMMER	AUTUMN	WINTER
SOW				
HARVEST				

TIME TO HARVEST: 24–28 WEEKS

SUITABLE FOR: BEDS

7 plants

3M (10FT) ROWS
Plant out 50cm (20in) apart

1 Getting started

Kale plants prefer a rich, well-drained, firm soil and must be given sufficient space to develop. There is a good variety to choose from: there are crinkled and savoy-leaved types, dwarf forms are available, and some types have striking purple stems. All are highly ornamental and look great in a border.

'Cavolo Nero' *has a rich flavour and its dark green, savoyed leaves are tender when cooked.*

'Nero di Toscana' *is a traditional "black" kale, with flavourful, dark green savoyed leaves.*

'Redbor' *makes an attractive border plant thanks to its purple-stemmed frilly leaves.*

'Starbor' *has heavily frilled leaves that are best harvested while young and tender.*

Seeds can also be sown into pots *– use a dibber or pencil to make holes in the compost. Sow two seeds into each planting hole.*

Sow clusters of two or three seeds *in a grid pattern, then thin the seedlings to the strongest. Protect the young plants against slugs using pellets.*

2 Sowing seeds

Crops can be sown under cover in mid-spring. Fill module trays with seed compost, water well, allow to drain, and then make holes, 1cm (½in) deep, in each cell. Drop two seeds in each cell, cover with compost and water in lightly. Thin to leave the stronger seedling per cell and grow on under cover. Kale can also be sown outside. Dig over a seedbed, removing any weeds, and work in some high nitrogen granular fertilizer. Firm the soil gently and rake it level. You can either sow a short drill to transplant later, or sow two or three seeds at their final spacings: 50x50cm (20x20in) apart.

3 Planting out

Plant out or transplant the kale seedlings at 50x50cm (20x20in) spacing during summer. Water plants in well and place cabbage root fly collars around the base of each plant. These small discs prevent the adult female fly laying her eggs next to the stem at soil level (see p.240). Hoe between plants regularly to keep weeds at bay.

Once the seedlings' roots *fill their module cells or pots, begin hardening them off ready for transplanting outside.*

Seedlings should be *firmed in well when they are planted, as the soil will help to support the eventual weight of the plants.*

Kale plants *can become quite large so it is vital to plant them with enough space to develop: around 50cm (20in) is ideal.*

Keep plants well weeded, *especially when they are young and vulnerable to competition. Pull out weeds by hand where possible.*

Cabbage white butterflies *(see p.238) lay tiny yellow eggs on the underside of leaves. Grow the plants under fine mesh netting to deter attacks.*

4 Protecting plants

Keep seedlings fed and well watered to help them recover from flea beetle attack, which can check their growth. If cabbage white butterflies (see p.238) or pigeons are a problem, use canes to erect some taut netting over the plants – use a maximum mesh size of 1x1cm (½x½in). Check for gaps.

5 Routine care

As plants continue to grow they can become quite top-heavy and tall – some cultivars can reach up to 1m (3ft) high – so you might find it necessary to stake the plants individually using stout canes or sticks. Remove and compost any older leaves that begin to turn yellow.

6 Harvesting

The inner leaves of each rosette are the most tender and the outer ones slightly tougher. Harvest the leaves when they are large enough but bear in mind that removing all the young leaves will weaken plants. Pick over the plants every few days to ensure a steady supply.

TIP *Pull up plants and compost them once they develop flowers in spring.*

Kales develop one main rosette *of leaves, and then occasionally offsets of smaller rosettes.*

Salads and leaves

Some crops don't require a lot of time, attention or space – welcome to the world of salads and leaves. This is a hugely diverse group that extends from tiny seedlings picked days after germination, and cut-and-come-again crops that harvest repeatedly, to robust Swiss chard that will crop throughout winter. Flavours vary significantly too, from crisp, buttery mildness through to a hot, peppery bite. Some of these crops can be grown in no more than a patio container or hanging basket, which means that room can be found for them in any garden.

STEP-BY-STEP Lettuces

Fast-growing and attractive, lettuces are ideal for pots, windowboxes, or growing bags if you don't have space elsewhere. Choose from dense-headed "hearting" types and frilly loose-leaf varieties – they can be harvested as cut-and-come-again crops (see pp.122–123) or allowed to develop to full size and cut whole. You never need to be short of this excellent salad staple, as sowing under cover allows you to harvest fresh leaves all year round.

	SPRING	SUMMER	AUTUMN	WINTER
SOW				
HARVEST				

TIME TO HARVEST: 6–8 WEEKS

SUITABLE FOR: BEDS, CONTAINERS, AND GROWING BAGS

9–20 plants

3M (10FT) ROWS
Plant 15–35cm (6–14in) apart

GROWING BAGS
4 plants in each

1 Sowing under cover

Early sowings can first be made under cover between late winter and early spring, to be planted outside once weather conditions are suitable. Fill modules or trays with seed compost, firm gently, water well, and allow to drain. Make a 1cm (½in) deep hole in each pot or module cell and drop two seeds into each, alternatively, sow seed in larger trays at the same depth. Cover the seeds over with compost, then water in lightly. Place in a warm, light place.

Sow two or three seeds *per pot or module and then once they emerge, thin them out leaving the strongest to grow on for planting out.*

Sow seed thinly *in larger seed trays and then prick the seedlings out once they develop. Plant them into individual pots or modules for growing on.*

Lettuce seed *can prove difficult to germinate, so sow seed in clusters in case some fail to germinate, every 10cm (4in) along the drill.*

As seedlings develop, *thin to leave the strongest per cluster, then later to 30cm (12in) between plants. The thinnings can be eaten.*

2 Sowing outside

Outdoor sowings of summer varieties can be made from early spring until midsummer; winter-hardy lettuces should be sown in late summer. Dig over the soil to remove any weeds, firm it gently, and rake it level. Create drills 1cm (½in) deep and 30cm (12in) apart, and sow seeds in clusters of four or five every 10cm (4in). Cover the seeds over with soil and water lightly. Protect the seedlings against slugs.

TIP *Leave cut stumps in the soil as they will form a second crop of smaller leaves.*

3 Planting out

Once indoor-raised seedlings are large enough to handle, gradually harden them off by placing them outside during the day and inside at night for seven to ten days. Prepare the soil by digging it over to remove any weeds. Plant the seedlings out 15–35cm (6–14in) apart and cover them with a cloche or cold frame in cool weather.

Module-raised seedlings *are ready to be hardened off and planted out once their roots fill their cell. Water them well before planting out.*

Firm the soil in well *around the heads after planting. Ensure that the lettuces have adequate room by spacing the rows 30cm (12in) apart.*

Regularly weed lettuces *used as a cut-and-come-again crop to avoid harvesting unwanted growth by mistake. Weed by hand or with a hoe.*

Lay a sand or grit ring *around the plants to keep slugs away. Check it regularly to ensure that the line has not been broken.*

4 Routine care

Keep plants well watered in warm weather so that they bulk up quickly – ensure that they do not dry out in the last weeks before harvesting, as this can cause them to bolt. Weeding between rows regularly will also be beneficial as it reduces competition for light, nutrients, and moisture.

5 Protecting plants

Slugs and snails (see p.240) are the most common pest, especially during periods of warm, wet weather. Lay bait traps or organic pellets for them, or use grit to create a barrier around your crops. Aphids can also be problematic, so check over plants regularly for signs of damage.

6 Harvesting

Cut individual leaves from loose-leaf lettuces when they mature, or harvest them all at once. Varieties that form a dense head of leaves, or "heart", can be cut whole once mature. Sow seeds little and often for a regular supply of fresh leaves. Although some types will mature faster than others, a good rule of thumb is to sow a new batch when the previous one is ready to be planted out or thinned for a second time.

Harvest lettuces whole *as soon as they are large enough, or cut the leaves individually.*

Lettuces

1 'Pinocchio' This semi-cos lettuce has upright leaves and sweet, yellow hearts. It is cold tolerant, so is good for early sowings. Its compact habit makes it ideal for containers.

2 'Tom Thumb' A butterhead variety, it produces tender green leaves, which are sweet, with little bitterness. Compact, it is useful for windowboxes or containers.

3 'Freckles' This cos lettuce is unusual as its deep green, glossy leaves are splashed with burgundy. The upright plants have sturdy growth and are slow to bolt.

4 'Winter Density' Widely-grown, this gem lettuce is popular for it hardiness and its dense hearts. It also has good heat tolerance, and is ideal for early or late crops.

5 'Sioux' An iceberg-type, its crisp, green leaves flush an attractive red as they mature, especially in sunny sites. It has good mildew resistance; sow it repeatedly in summer.

6 'Lollo Rosso' Well-known, this loose-leaf variety has red-flushed, crinkled leaves that can be harvested as and when needed. Alternatively, whole heads can also be cut.

7 'Mottistone' This variety has wavy-edged leaves that are mid-green and flecked with burgundy. The leaves can be harvested individually, or crop the loose heads whole.

8 'Little Gem' A popular semi-cos variety, it produces small, dense hearts, and is ideal for sowing in containers. It is slow to bolt in summer, and is cold resistant.

9 'Nymans' This eye-catching, semi-cos lettuce has glossy burgundy leaves and a yellow heart; it can be harvested as a baby leaf. It is slow to bolt and has good mildew resistance.

Other varieties
'Arctic King'
'Red Salad Bowl'
'Cocarde'
'Lobjoits Green'
'Marvel of Four Seasons'

STEP-BY-STEP Cut-and-come-again salad

This term describes a method of growing salad leaves, rather than an actual vegetable, and is extremely quick and productive. It is ideal for containers and allows you to make use of bare patches for short periods, making it a good choice for smaller plots. Useful crops can even be raised on windowsills. Often these salad leaves are sold in blends, such as a hot and spicy mix, or stir-fry mix, but you can make up your own mixtures to suit your taste.

	SPRING	SUMMER	AUTUMN	WINTER
SOW				
HARVEST				

TIME TO HARVEST: 4–6 WEEKS

SUITABLE FOR: BEDS, GROWING BAGS, AND CONTAINERS – UNDER COVER OR OUTSIDE

30 plants

3M (10FT) ROWS
Sow and thin to 10cm (4in) apart

GROWING BAGS
12 plants in each

1 Getting started

These salad plants are raised from seed and can be sown in batches through the year. Lettuce is commonly used but most salad crops can be grown this way. They are mainly grown outside in summer but you can also grow smaller crops under cover, even on the windowsill, to harvest in spring or autumn.

Corn salad is a useful leaf crop to grow during winter. It is very hardy and crops regularly.

Lettuce crops reliably as young leaves and there are many good varieties to grow.

Land cress has a spicy flavour. It is a good choice to grow under cover for an early crop.

Rocket has a peppery flavour and combines well with milder-tasting leaves like lettuce.

Sow the seed according to the spacings given on the packet. Some salads are sown deeper or more thickly than others.

Pick leaves individually as soon as they are large enough to use. The plants will continue growing and produce more.

Cutting the plants off checks their growth and they will take a week or two to recover. Water them well to promote re-growth.

2 Under cover crops

If you don't have outdoor space, or just want an extra early or late harvest, grow plants under cover. Use growing bags or fill pots or seed trays with compost, water well, and leave to drain. Sow seeds on the surface and cover lightly with compost. Keep moist until the seeds emerge in a week or so, then harvest the leaves once large enough, leaving the bases to re-grow. Expect two or three similar harvests before the plants run out of steam.

TIP Feed indoor crops with balanced liquid fertilizer to encourage new growth.

3 Sowing outside

For larger crops sow direct into the soil in summer. First dig it over to remove weeds, firm it gently, then rake it level. Mark out drills 1–2cm (½–¾in) deep and water the base well. Sow the seeds, cover with soil, then water again. If sowing in warm weather, temporarily cover the soil with sheets of newspaper to help retain moisture.

Sow into drills *to help you tell any weeds apart from your crop. On smaller plots, you can also sow directly into containers or growing bags.*

Crops in containers or growing bags *will dry out more quickly than those grown directly in the soil and will need more regular watering.*

Plants picked for individual leaves *will continue to grow until they wear out. They are longer-lived than plants harvested to the base.*

4 Routine care

Seedlings will emerge in a few days (if your drills are covered with newspaper, check underneath every day and remove as soon as the seeds germinate). Keep the rows well weeded, and water regularly to promote quick growth. Protect your plants against slugs with a light sprinkling of pellets.

5 Harvesting

These salad crops can be ready for harvest in as little as three weeks in the height of summer. You can either pick individual leaves as they become large enough to eat, or you can cut back whole rows using scissors. Use the salad leaves fresh and only pick them when you intend to use them.

Growing on

Salad plants that are cut to the base should be given time to recover and encouraged back into growth. Water them well, adding a dilute liquid fertilizer to the water, and they should be ready to harvest again within two weeks. The plants will wear out after a few crops, so sow new batches to provide healthy replacements.

STEP-BY-STEP Microgreens

This tasty, trendy crop often features on fine restaurant menus, and is amazingly easy to grow. Harvested as tiny seedlings, the plants are ready to crop in little more than a week. There are dozens of vegetables that can be grown this way, and you can sow them together for different flavour combinations. You don't need a garden or any outdoor space – they grow well in pots on bright windowsills, and can even be sown on damp cotton wool.

	SPRING	SUMMER	AUTUMN	WINTER
SOW				
HARVEST				

TIME TO HARVEST: 7–10 DAYS

SUITABLE FOR: BEDS AND CONTAINERS, UNDER COVER OR OUTSIDE

3,000 plants

3M (10FT) ROWS
Sow and thin to 1cm (⅓in) apart

CONTAINERS
300 plants in each

1 Getting started

Microgreens are raised from seed and there are many types. Ready-mixed combinations are also available or you can mix your own. Most of the vegetables grown as microgreens are the same as those you sow for conventional crops, they are just harvested as seedlings instead. If you have spare seeds left over from sowing garden crops, try sowing them as microgreens rather than storing them until next year.

Basil *Like many culinary herbs, the young seedlings have a rich, sweet taste.*

Beetroot *Although normally grown as a root crop, the tasty leaves are also edible.*

Cabbage *All brassica seedlings are edible, and have a delicious nutty flavour.*

Coriander *Full-grown plants often bolt, so use it as a fresh-tasting seedling instead.*

Swiss chard *These soft-leaved seedlings have a delicate, earthy flavour, good for salads.*

Celery *Enjoy the delicious taste of this late-season stem crop throughout the year.*

Lettuce *Use the tasty seedlings as a garnish, or as an alternative to traditional cress.*

Pak choi *This useful crop can be harvested at almost any stage, including as seedlings.*

Chives *These tender leaves have a sweeter flavour than full-grown plants. Use as garnish.*

Pea shoots *These have the familiar pea flavour and are ideal in salads and stir-fries.*

2 Sowing under cover

Fill seed trays with moist compost and sow the seeds on top. Cover them lightly with more compost and water lightly. The seeds will germinate in a few days and should be grown on in a bright position until large enough to harvest. Seeds can also be sown uncovered on trays of moist kitchen paper or cotton wool.

Sow seeds thickly *to give a good crop, and sow more every few days for a constant supply. Keep them handy on your kitchen windowsill.*

Seed can be sown outside *directly in the soil, although you can also sow small batches in containers, growing bags, or even windowboxes.*

If you have trouble differentiating weed *seedlings from your crop, sow in drills rather than blocks to make them easier to spot.*

3 Sowing outside

Before sowing outside, prepare the area by weeding it well and rake the soil level and fine. Water the soil, sow the seed 5mm (¼in) deep in blocks or rows, cover lightly and water again. Protect plants from slug damage with a light sprinkling of pellets.

4 Routine care

Crops grown under cover need little care, other than watering them once or twice until harvested. If sown outside, weed seedlings may also come up among your microgreens. Remove weeds early in case they are harvested by mistake.

5 Harvesting

Depending on the temperature and light levels, seedlings can be ready for harvest in as little as a week. Ensure they are kept well-watered during this period. Pinch off individual leaves with your fingers, or cut whole clumps of seedlings with scissors.

| TIP | *Use cut seedlings before they have a chance to wilt; within the hour ideally.* |

Harvest microgreens *when the seedlings develop their first pair of "true" leaves.*

STEP-BY-STEP Oriental greens

The majority of Oriental greens are leafy brassicas that are brilliant in stir-fries or for use in salads. There is a plethora of crops in this group, and even pak choi, just one member, ranges from large, tall types grown for their crunchy stems, to those that remain squat with disc-like leaves. Oriental greens are ideal for filling summer gaps in the vegetable garden as they benefit from a mid- to late summer sowing and will grow extremely quickly.

	SPRING	SUMMER	AUTUMN	WINTER
SOW				
HARVEST				

TIME TO HARVEST: 6–8 WEEKS

SUITABLE FOR: BEDS, CONTAINERS, AND GROWING BAGS

15–20 plants

3M (10FT) ROWS
Plant 10–20cm (4–8in) apart

GROWING BAGS
5 plants in each

1 Getting started

It is important not to sow Oriental greens too early in the year as the cold temperatures and increasing day length make these crops very prone to bolting (quickly running to seed) – waiting until midsummer will discourage this. High temperatures and dry spells can also cause plants to bolt in summer.

Pak Choi *has large rounded leaves with excellent flavour, good eaten raw or cooked.*

'Red Giant' *mustard leaves are red-flushed with a mild, peppery, flavour. Good in salads.*

Mizuna *has mild-flavoured, serrated leaves that look attractive in salads or as a garnish.*

Tatsoi *has spoon-shaped leaves that are ideal for cutting young for use in salads.*

2 Sow inside

From midsummer onwards, and at routine intervals, fill trays or modules with seed compost, firm gently, water thoroughly, and then allow it to drain. Sow the seeds lightly across the surface and cover with compost to a depth of 1cm (½in). Firm the surface again and water in lightly. The seeds don't require additional heat and will germinate in about a week. When large enough, harden them off and transplant outside.

Plan your sowings *so that you do not end up with a glut – sow a fresh batch every fortnight.*

3 Sowing outside

Oriental greens do well sown directly. Dig over the site, remove all weeds, and apply high-nitrogen feed. Firm the soil and then rake level, before marking out 1cm (½in) deep drills 15–30cm (6–12in) apart, depending on the crop.

Water the drill, *then sow seeds 2cm (¾in) apart. Cover with soil and firm with the back of your rake.*

Seedlings *will need thinning as they appear – gently pull them so they are 10–20cm (4–8in) apart.*

4 Planting out

Prepare the soil well: dig it over to remove any weeds and apply high-nitrogen fertilizer. Once the indoor-grown seedlings are large enough to handle, harden them off by placing them outdoors during the day and bringing them indoors at night for two weeks. Some greens can become quite large, so check the spacing before planting.

These are quick-growing crops *and can be grown in the gaps left when other vegetables are harvested, making good use of the space.*

Oriental greens are thirsty plants *and will resent competition for moisture from weeds, so remove any that appear nearby by hand.*

These are ideal crops *for cut-and-come-again leaves, especially when sown in repeated batches. It can be cropped for many weeks.*

5 Routine care

Oriental greens are prone to brassica pests, such as cabbage root fly (see p.240) and flea beetle, so deter them by covering rows with a fine insect-proof mesh. Keep plants weed-free and water frequently to encourage quick growth. Doing this will also help prevent them from suddenly bolting.

6 Pick young leaves

When large enough to eat, either cut individual leaves or shoots from your crops, or shear back whole plants. Oriental crops grow quickly so it's best to sow small batches frequently during the summer. Sowing seed every fortnight will give you multiple harvests all summer, rather than one big crop.

7 Harvesting

Alternatively, allow plants to mature to their full size, gradually thinning the seedlings or transplants out as the season progresses. Cut individual heads whole at the base when a good size, or, for broccoli-type plants, pick individual shoots as they appear.

TIP	*In hot sites, sow seed slightly deeper and keep the soil moist at all times.*

Whole plants, *such as pak choi, can be cut off at the base once the heads mature.*

STEP-BY-STEP Spinach

Delicious harvested young and used in salads or allowed to mature for cooking, spinach is an easy-to-grow crop that will quickly yield armfuls of large, tender leaves. Sow seed in short drills, little and often, and you are guaranteed a constant supply all summer if you water it well. Spinach matures quickly, making it a useful crop in smaller plots as it can soon be replaced. It can also be used for a quick crop in temporary gaps and spaces.

	SPRING	SUMMER	AUTUMN	WINTER
SOW				
HARVEST				

TIME TO HARVEST: 6–12 WEEKS

SUITABLE FOR: BEDS AND CONTAINERS

3M (10FT) ROWS
Plant 7–15cm (3–6in) apart
20–45 plants

CONTAINERS
7–9 plants in each

1 Getting started

This versatile crop will tolerate cool weather and a shady site and will also grow in containers – even a small patch devoted to it will be extremely productive. Spinach needs very rich, well-drained soil, so dig in organic matter, such as well-rotted manure or compost, the season before growing.

'Bordeaux' *is both attractive and tasty. It has dark green leaves and bright red stems.*

'Medania' *produces high yields of large, succulent, dark green leaves. It is slow to bolt.*

'Toscane' *is a bolt-resistant cultivar that bears high yields of thick, tender leaves.*

'Tetona' *leaves are smooth and dark green. They resist mildew and are ideal for early crops.*

Sow directly outdoors *from mid- to late spring onwards. The last batches can be sown as late as mid-autumn if plants are covered with cloches.*

Once seedlings are large enough *to handle, thin them out, leaving the strongest to grow on every 7–15cm (3–6in) along the drill.*

2 Sowing outside

Spinach is sown directly, either into the soil or in containers and windowboxes, so there is no need to raise plants in seed trays or modules. Direct sowing makes plants less prone to bolting, which can be a problem. Dig over the soil, firm gently, and rake level. Mark out drills 2cm (¾in) deep and 20cm (8in) apart, and water the base thoroughly. Sprinkle seeds roughly 1cm (½in) apart along the drill, cover with soil, firm gently, and water in well.

TIP	*Sow in batches every few weeks if you want a constant supply of leaves.*

3 Watering

Annual spinach is a very thirsty, fast-growing crop so in order to sustain it, ensure that your plants are watered generously and regularly – this may mean watering them as frequently as once a day in very hot, dry weather. Regular weeding is also important as it will also help eliminate any competition for moisture, light, and space.

Ensure plants are kept well watered, *as annual spinach can quickly run to seed, or "bolt", if it experiences a check in growth.*

Remove any weeds *close to the plants by hand to avoid damaging the leaves. Use a hoe to remove any weeds between the rows.*

Birds may target young plants, *so net rows as a precaution. Slugs can also be a problem, so apply a light sprinkling of pellets.*

Use a pair of scissors *to harvest the young, tender leaves as a cut-and-come-again crop. Cut the outer leaves first and work inwards.*

4 Routine care

Net plants to deter birds. Downy mildew can be problematic but resistant varieties are available. Crops will benefit from either a top-dressing of a high-nitrogen granular fertilizer such as pelleted poultry manure, or regular doses of a high-nitrogen liquid feed.

5 Cutting salad leaves

Annual spinach can be harvested as a salad leaf while still small; cut individual leaves from plants as and when they become large enough. These can also be cooked as a milder-tasting, more tender leaf than those picked from mature plants.

6 Harvesting

If you prefer to allow your plants to grow larger, leave them until about 10–12 weeks after sowing and then cut all leaves off about 2.5cm (1in) above the base, discarding any yellowing ones. If the harvested row is well fed and watered, you should get a smaller flush of leaves in a fortnight which can be harvested again. It is then best to discard the plants. Alternatively, dig the plants up whole and strip the leaves.

Cut leaves as soon as they are ready, *and use them promptly to prevent them from spoiling.*

STEP-BY-STEP Swiss chard

This crop is a hardier vegetable than annual spinach (see pp.128–129) and offers the same benefits – it can also be harvested for much of the year, cropping well into autumn and winter. It is very easy to grow, and is a useful crop for small gardens as its colourful stems allow it to double-up as an ornamental in beds and pots. The foliage can be harvested as needed, either as young tender leaves for salads, or as mature leaves and crisp stems for steaming.

	SPRING	SUMMER	AUTUMN	WINTER
SOW				
HARVEST				

TIME TO HARVEST: 6–16 WEEKS

SUITABLE FOR: BEDS AND CONTAINERS

3M (10FT) ROWS
Thin to 30cm (12in) apart
11 plants

CONTAINERS
8 plants in each

1 Getting started

Swiss chard is often sold as young plants in spring, and sometimes also as a winter bedding plant. It is very easy to grow from seed however, which is the best way to raise several plants, especially to crop as baby leaves. This crop is also known as "spinach beet" and "leaf beet" but they are all the same.

'Bright Lights' *is a colourful mix of red- and yellow-stemmed plants. It is good for containers.*

'Bright Yellow' *can be harvested as baby leaves or left for its mature yellow stems.*

'Lucullus' *produces thick white stems that are delicious lightly steamed or braised.*

'Rhubarb Chard' *is grown for its purple-tinted green leaves and dark red stems.*

Swiss chard seed *are large and easy to handle. Sowing into modules, rather than pots or trays, does away with the need to prick them out later.*

Plant out the young seedlings *into prepared soil, 10cm (4in) apart, and water well. Protect them from slugs and snails with a thin scattering of pellets.*

2 Sowing under cover

Although hardy, Swiss chard can be sown under cover to give an earlier crop. Fill modular trays with seed compost, firm gently and water well. Using a dibber or pencil, make holes 2.5cm (1in) deep per cell, drop one or two seeds into each, then cover with compost and water well. The seed won't require heat and should germinate in a week or two. Thin the seedlings to one per module and grow them on under cover in a bright, frost-free place for a few weeks until large enough to handle. Harden them off for a couple of weeks to acclimatize them to outdoor conditions, then plant out, 30cm (12in) apart.

3 Sowing outside

Seeds can also be sown directly where they are to grow, and will give a later crop. Prepare the soil by digging it over and work in some granular high-nitrogen fertilizer. Rake the soil to a fine tilth and make drills 2.5cm (1in) deep, 30cm (12in) apart. Water the base well, sow seeds 5cm (2in) apart, then cover over with soil.

Space the seed carefully *to save sowing more than you need. Unused seeds can be stored for later sowings if kept somewhere cool and dry.*

Don't leave the seedlings too long *before you thin them out. They will become harder to pull and it will cause greater root disturbance.*

Swiss chard should be kept moist. *If growing it on a lighter soil, mulch around plants with some well-rotted organic matter in summer.*

4 Thinning out

Direct-sown seedlings should be initially thinned to 10cm (4in) apart, then thinned again to give an eventual spacing of 30cm (12in) as mature plants. Use the thinnings as early-season salad leaves. Water the rows after thinning to settle to the soil.

5 Routine care

Water the plants well and feed regularly with a liquid high-nitrogen fertilizer to promote leafy growth. Keep them well-weeded to prevent competition. For harvestable new leaves in winter, cover plants with a plastic or fleece tunnel cloche.

6 Harvesting

Plants can be harvested when up to 10cm (4in) tall for salad leaves. Either pick them individually or cut off whole plants near the base (they will grow back). If you want to cook the leaves like spinach, let them reach full size and cut them off as needed.

TIP	*White-stemmed varieties are the hardiest type for overwintering.*

When cutting for use in salads, *leave the base of the plant in the soil to grow back.*

STEP-BY-STEP Chicory

These robust leaves are an asset to any plot: they are highly ornamental and take up relatively little space. They can be cooked or eaten raw and have a slightly bitter but pleasant taste, which can be moderated by blanching. Witloof varieties can also be forced in winter to produce "chicons" – a unique crop of fleshy shoots packed with mild-tasting leaves. All varieties are easy to grow and most are very hardy; they are suitable for containers.

	SPRING	SUMMER	AUTUMN	WINTER
SOW				
HARVEST				

TIME TO HARVEST: 14–16 WEEKS

SUITABLE FOR: BEDS AND CONTAINERS

3M (10FT) ROWS
Plant or thin to 25–40cm (10–16in) apart
8–12 plants

CONTAINERS
3 plants in each

1 Getting started

There are three types of chicory: Witloof or Belgian types, which have a deep root and elongated, white heads – this type can be forced to produce "chicons"; red chicory, or radicchio, forms a heart, much like a lettuce; finally there are sugarloaf types, which have a loose head of green leaves.

'Treviso Precoce Mesola' *is a radicchio-type with attractive, white-ribbed, red leaves.*

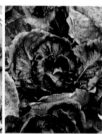

'Palla Rossa' *is a radicchio-type with bitter-tasting red leaves. Good in salads.*

'Variegata di Castelfranco' *is a late radicchio-type, with striking speckled leaves.*

'Pan di Zucchero' *is a sugarloaf-type, ideal for growing as a cut-and-come-again crop.*

Seed can be sown in trays, *although you will need to prick out the seedlings once they are large enough to handle.*

Water the seeds *using a can with a fine rose fitted to prevent washing the seeds to the edges of the tray, or into clusters.*

Prick out the seedlings *as soon as they are large enough to handle, planting them on into small pots or individual modules.*

2 Sowing seeds

Very early sowings can be started off under cover. This is also a useful technique for autumn and winter sowings for either cut-and-come-again leaves or for spring-maturing crops. Fill trays or modules with compost, water well, and allow to drain. Make holes in each cell, 1cm (½in) deep – or every 5cm (2in) – and then sow one seed in each. Cover with a little more compost and water in lightly – germination rates are usually very high.

TIP *Sow Witloof chicory between spring and summer for forcing in autumn.*

3 Sow and plant out

To sow direct, dig over the site and remove any weeds. Create drills 1cm (½in) deep, water well, then sow seeds thinly along them. Cover with soil and water in. If you have raised seedlings under cover, these can be planted outside as soon as their roots fill the individual cells. Plant at 25–40cm (10–16in) spacings. Water in well.

Seed will do well if sown direct, *as long as the soil has warmed up enough – the plants are liable to bolt if they are sown too early.*

Thin out the seedlings *as they develop, leaving the strongest to grow on 25–40cm (10–16in) apart. The thinnings can be used as salad leaves.*

Keeping plants well watered *will deter them from bolting. Chicory roots grow deeply into the soil, so make sure plants get a good soaking.*

Chicory leaves *can be harvested as cut-and-come-again crops – snip them from the plant as needed. Alternatively, lift the whole plant at once.*

4 Routine care

Keep plants well watered as they develop and weed regularly. The plants don't have high nutritional requirements but plants grown on light, sandy, or chalky soils, or those in pots, may benefit from a fortnightly dose of general purpose liquid fertilizer.

5 Harvesting

Harvest the leaves once plants reach a good size. For a second harvest, leave the stump in the ground, cut a cross in the top and remove any remaining leaves. Within a few weeks new, smaller shoots will appear – cover these with a pot to blanch them.

Forcing "chicons"

In winter, witloof chicory can be forced into producing "chicons". Lift mature roots in mid-autumn, removing the leaves, and plant them in a deep pot or box of compost. Water well, then place an upturned pot over the top to block out the light. Keep it in a warm spot. Cut the "chicons" after two or three weeks, at 10–15cm (4–6in) tall.

STEP-BY-STEP Endive

A robust, hardy grower, endive is prone to fewer pests and diseases than other salad crops, which makes it a good choice for those new to gardening. It makes an attractive addition to any vegetable plot, with a slightly bitter taste that many people find refreshing; the bitterness can be moderated by blanching the central heart to create a milder flavour. This salad leaf is similar to chicory in both its cultivation and taste (see pp.126–127).

	SPRING	SUMMER	AUTUMN	WINTER
SOW				
HARVEST				

TIME TO HARVEST: 10–12 WEEKS

SUITABLE FOR: BEDS, CONTAINERS, AND GROWING BAGS

8–12 plants

3M (10FT) ROWS
Plant 25–40cm (10–16in) apart

GROWING BAGS
5 plants in each

1 Getting started

There are two main types of endive, "curly" or "frisée" and "Batavian" or "escarole". Curly endive has narrow leaves and quite a flat habit, whereas Batavian is often hardier, broad-leaved, and the plants tend to grow more upright. Both types prefer rich, well-drained soil in a sunny or partly-shaded position.

'Frenzy' *is a compact, self-blanching frisée type with very fine leaves borne on dense heads.*

'Glory' *is a frisée type with deeply cut leaves that are especially tender when young.*

'Kentucky' *leaves are finely cut and good for blanching. It is a reliable frisée variety.*

'Natacha' *is a Batavian type, with broad, tender leaves. It shows good resistance to bolting.*

To prevent a glut of crops, *sow seed little and often, every few weeks so that you are guaranteed a steady supply.*

Harden the seedlings off *by placing the trays outside during the day and bringing them under cover at night for two weeks.*

Plant the seedlings *out 25–40cm (10–16in) apart, depending on how large you intend your plants to be.*

2 Sowing under cover

Seed can be sown in modules or seed trays under cover in spring. Fill the tray with seed compost, firm gently, water thoroughly, and stand it somewhere to drain. Sow seed 1cm (½in) deep. Make holes in the centre of every cell using a dibber or pencil, and then drop one seed into each. Firm over with a little compost and then water lightly in. Seedlings should emerge in about one week. Continue to grow on under cover until strong roots have developed.

TIP *Harvest as a cut-and-come-again crop: sow thickly in drills and cut as needed.*

3 Sowing outside

Endive can be sown directly into the ground, in growing bags, or in large containers of multipurpose compost. Dig over the soil to remove any weeds and apply a general-purpose fertilizer to light soils. Create drills 1cm (½in) deep, water well, and then sow your seeds thinly along it. Cover over, firm gently, and water in lightly.

Sow seeds directly outdoors *only once the soil has warmed up in early summer, as exposure to cold temperatures can cause the plants to suddenly bolt.*

Once seedlings are well established, *thin them out gently by hand, leaving a strong seedling to grow on every 25–40cm (10–16in).*

Keeping plants well watered *while they are developing will help reduce the risk of bolting; spray with a hose or use a can with a fine rose.*

Keep the plants well weeded, *especially when they are developing, to reduce the competition for light, nutrients, and water.*

4 Watering

Keep the area well-watered for the first few weeks after transplanting or sowing to encourage a strong root system to develop. Once established, endive is quite drought-tolerant, although it will need watering during very dry conditions.

5 Routine care

Regularly weed between plants until they become large enough to smother any competing growth. Weed by hand to avoid damaging the seedlings; weed between the rows using a hoe. Cover plants with fleece if the weather turns cold to prevent them from bolting.

6 Harvesting

Endive has a bitter flavour that can be lessened by blanching. Some varieties are described as "self-blanching" but others need intervention. The simplest method is to place a plate over the centre of the plant to block out light – first make sure the foliage is dry. Blanching takes about two to three weeks. Cut the leaves once plants reach a suitable size, and leave the stump in the ground to re-sprout for a later crop.

As soon as plants are blanched, *harvest all the leaves at once using a sharp knife.*

STEP-BY-STEP Watercress

Watercress has steadily become a must-have ingredient in salads, adding crisp texture and a fresh, peppery kick. It can also be enjoyed on its own, as well as in many other summer dishes. Although it usually grows in streams and running water, it doesn't have to, and can easily be grown in containers – providing it is kept well watered. Watercress grows quickly, and if harvested regularly, a few pots will easily meet your needs throughout summer.

	SPRING	SUMMER	AUTUMN	WINTER
SOW				
HARVEST				

TIME TO HARVEST: 8–18 WEEKS

SUITABLE FOR: GROWING BAGS AND CONTAINERS

GROWING BAGS
Plant or thin to 10cm (4in) apart
10 plants

CONTAINERS
16 plants in each

1 Sowing under cover

Watercress is hardy but can be started off under cover. Fill individual pots with seed compost, firm gently and water well. Sow seeds thinly on the surface, cover with compost 5mm (¼in) deep, and water lightly. Keep the pots on a bright windowsill or in a warm greenhouse, stood in saucers of water, 5cm (2in) deep. Thin the seedlings to leave the strongest and grow them on outside, repotting into containers at least 30cm (12in) wide.

Seed can be sown into small pots which can be thinned for small crops or potted on.

Keep the compost moist at all times. The seeds won't need additional heat to germinate.

Seedlings grow quickly once they germinate. Grow them on in a bright position under cover.

An old sink is ideal for growing watercress, sow seed across the surface and cover with compost or sow into shallow drills. Water well.

Thin seedlings as they grow and keep them well-watered at all times. Protect the young plants from slugs with a light sprinkling of pellets.

2 Sowing outside

After the risk of frost has passed, fill containers, at least 30cm (12in) wide, with multipurpose compost. Sow seed across the surface, 5mm (¼in) deep, and water in. Stand the pots outside in a sunny position in trays of water 5cm (2in) deep, and keep them topped up at all times. The seeds will germinate in about two weeks. Thin the seedlings to 10cm (4in) apart, leaving the strongest. Sow batches regularly.

TIP Use the thinned seedlings as an early crop, treating them as microgreens.

3 Taking cuttings

Instead of sowing seed, you can also easily raise your own plants by rooting cuttings. Buy fresh watercress from a supermarket, stand a few stems in water and leave them on a windowsill. The stems will develop roots after 10–14 days, when they can then be potted up into a shallow tray of moist compost. Grow them on under cover and harvest.

Stand the cuttings *in a bright position and change the water every few days to keep it fresh. Remove leaves or stems that turn yellow.*

Watercress grows quickly *but the plants soon need replacing after a few harvests. Sow more seeds every few weeks for a steady supply.*

Pick over plants *every few days and harvest the young shoots. Take only a few stems per plant and allow them to grow back.*

4 Routine care

Feed the plants with a high-nitrogen liquid fertilizer to encourage a large crop, and keep them well-weeded to prevent harvesting weeds by mistake. Plants will start to deteriorate after a few harvests and should be replaced; sow a fresh batch.

5 Harvesting

Start harvesting the plants once they have grown to 10–15cm (4–6in) in height. Begin by pinching out the main stems to encourage new sideshoots, and to prevent the plants becoming straggly. Pick over each plant lightly so that they're not over cropped.

Growing land cress

An alternative to watercress is land cress, which has similar tasting leaves and can be used in the same way. It is easier to grow than watercress because it doesn't require such wet growing conditions. It can be sown directly into the soil or grown in large containers. Plants are hardy and can be cropped through winter.

Root crops

This is an important group of vegetables in the kitchen, producing delicious, energy-packed roots – such as potatoes, parsnips, and swedes – that can be stored throughout the winter months. It is a very useful group in the garden too, and includes quick-growing roots, like radishes and turnips, that can be sown, harvested, and sown again in the same time it takes many other crops to reach maturity. In smaller plots, sweet-tasting baby roots, harvested just weeks after sowing, give a worthwhile crop even in containers, and are usually expensive to buy.

STEP-BY-STEP Radishes

In the height of summer, quick-growing radishes can be ready to harvest in as little as five weeks, which makes these tasty plants extremely handy for filling gaps in small plots. The roots are available in a range of colours and sizes, and make an attractive addition to salads. The leaves and seed pods of some varieties can also be eaten. Where space is very limited, they can also be sown direct into patio containers and windowboxes.

	SPRING	SUMMER	AUTUMN	WINTER
SOW				
HARVEST				

TIME TO HARVEST: 5–8 WEEKS

SUITABLE FOR: BEDS AND CONTAINERS

60 plants

3M (10FT) ROWS
Sow or thin to 5cm (2in) apart

CONTAINERS
32 plants in each

1 Getting started

Radishes are adaptable plants and will grow in most soils and sites, even in partial shade. Because radishes mature very quickly it is important to sow seed little and often if you want to obtain regular supplies and avoid a glut. Sow a new batch once your existing plants have reached 8cm (3in) in height.

'Cherry Belle' is a fast-growing variety. The round, cherry-red roots are ideal in salads.

'French Breakfast' has fast-growing, white-tipped, elongated roots with a sweet flavour.

'Scarlet Globe' is an easy-to-grow variety that produces attractive, round, bright red roots.

'Sparkler' is a reliable variety, known for its round red roots, which have a peppery flavour.

When sowing in larger module trays you can simply create 1cm (½in) deep planting holes with your finger, and drop the seed in.

If the clusters of seedlings are overcrowded or congested, thin them out, leaving just five or six plants to grow on in each module.

2 Sowing under cover

Radishes are hardy plants but can also be sown under cover in early spring to give an earlier start in colder areas. Fill module trays with compost to within 1cm (½in) from the top, gently firm it down, water well, then leave it to drain. Sow seed thinly on the surface in small clusters, and cover with compost. Radish seed doesn't need additional heat to grow, and come up within a few days. Harden off and plant the modules out when the frosts finish.

TIP	Grow radishes alongside slower growing crops, such as parsnips.

3 Sowing outside

Radishes mature quickly when sown directly in the ground, which is also the most straightforward way to grow them as the seedlings don't require planting out. Before sowing, prepare the soil by digging it over to remove weeds, firm it gently, then rake to a fine tilth. Avoid sowing where brassicas have been grown recently.

Mark out drills *that are about 2cm (¾in) deep. Radishes are relatively small plants, so the rows can be as close as 10cm (4in) apart.*

Water each drill *thoroughly then sow seeds 1cm (½in) apart. Cover them over with soil, firming this with the back of your rake. Water in lightly.*

Once the plants *are large enough to handle, thin them out to 5cm (2in) spacing. The thinned seedlings can be used as a peppery salad leaf.*

Flea beetles *create ragged holes in the leaves and can kill seedlings. The best way to deter them is to cover crops with fine mesh netting.*

4 Routine care

Thin out the seedlings as they grow, and keep them well watered. Radishes are quick-growing crops so will compete well with weeds. However, weeds can still harbour pests and diseases, so it is important to regularly weed your beds.

5 Protecting plants

Radishes are vulnerable to flea beetle damage, especially in hot and dry weather, and are at risk from slugs and snails. Keep plants well watered to offset any damage, and cover with fine insect netting, which will also deter cabbage root fly (see p.240).

6 Harvesting

Pull up the roots as soon as they reach a harvestable size. Do not leave them in the ground too long, however, as summer radishes can become very spicy and pithy if they are left to over-mature, and some plants are prone to bolting. Pick the radishes daily, checking along the row to find the largest roots. This will allow you to consume your harvest while each radish is young and tender.

Sow radish seed successionally *and pull the roots gently from the ground as required.*

STEP-BY-STEP Beetroots

One of the most popular crops on the vegetable plot, beetroot plants are highly productive, trouble-free, and great for small gardens – they also grow well in containers. Beetroot is very versatile, and can be harvested as baby roots a few weeks after sowing, or left to reach full size, ideal for storing. In the kitchen, gone are the days of just preserving the roots in vinegar; beetroot is also great roasted, pureed for soup, or added to cakes.

	SPRING	SUMMER	AUTUMN	WINTER
SOW				
HARVEST				

TIME TO HARVEST: 12–16 WEEKS

SUITABLE FOR: BEDS AND CONTAINERS

3M (10FT) ROWS
Sow 4cm (1½in) apart, thinning to 10cm (4in)
30 plants

CONTAINERS
12 plants in each

1 Getting started

Beetroot can be bought as plug plants in spring for a head start, but it is easily raised from seed. Most beetroot "seed" is actually a cluster of three or four true seeds, which germinate as a clump, and should be thinned out. The exceptions to this are "monogerm" varieties that produce one seedling.

'Red Ace' *produces large, dark red roots that are easy to grow and are good for storing.*

'Chioggia Pink' *has red-skinned roots with pink and white flesh. It has a sweet flavour.*

'Boltardy' *is widely grown and produces firm, round roots. It is resistant to bolting.*

'Forono' *is a reliable variety to grow for tender baby roots. It is suitable for containers.*

Beetroot seeds *are large and easy to handle, allowing you to sow one per module. Keep the soil moist after sowing.*

Thin the seedlings *as they grow to leave the strongest per module. Monogerm seed, sown singly, won't require thinning.*

Plant out the seedlings *as soon as possible so the plants develop fully in the soil. Try to avoid disturbing the roots.*

2 Sowing under cover

To give them a head start, beetroot can be sown under cover. Fill modular trays with seed compost, firm gently, water it well then allow it to drain. Make a 2cm (¾in) deep hole in each module using a dibber or pencil, and drop one seed into each. Firm the compost, water lightly, and place the tray in a propagator. As soon as roots start growing through the base of the cells, harden off the seedlings and plant them out 10cm (4in) apart.

| TIP | *Soak seeds in warm water for 30 mins before sowing to help germination.* |

3 Sowing outside

Beetroot can be sown directly in the soil, provided it is warm enough. Dig over the site to remove any weeds then rake it to a fine tilth. Along a garden line, create drills 2.5cm (1in) deep using the edge of a hoe or rake. Water the base thoroughly, then sow the seeds roughly 4cm (1½in) apart. Cover with soil, firm gently and water in lightly.

Sow the seed at regular intervals, *spacing it by hand. The soil should be at least 8°C (46°F) before sowing, otherwise germination will be slow.*

Thin the seedlings *to 10cm (4in) apart by pulling them up or pinching them off completely. The "thinnings" can be used as salad leaves.*

Carefully weeding by hand *close to the plants is safer than using a hoe, which can easily damage the top of the swelling roots.*

Water plants at the base *and avoid splashing the leaves, which can encourage disease. Plants on lighter soils should be watered more regularly.*

4 Weeding

Beetroot are fairly pest- and disease-free, but remember to regularly hand-weed around the plants to prevent weeds establishing. If left, weeds will compete against your crop for moisture and nutrients, and will slow their growth; they also attract pests.

5 Routine care

Seedlings should be watered regularly, and although mature plants are drought-resistant, the roots are more tender if the soil is kept moist. Don't overwater though, as this will encourage the production of excess leaves at the expense of roots.

6 Harvesting

Roots can be harvested as soon as they reach a usable size, or can be left to grow larger to be used as required. To harvest, carefully lift them from the ground, wash off any soil, and twist off the leaves. Surplus, undamaged roots can be stored in wooden boxes lined with newspaper. Place 2.5cm (1in) of sharp sand in the base, then a layer of roots. Add more layers to fill the box, then store in a cool, dry shed or garage.

Young roots are best enjoyed fresh, *so only harvest them on the day you intend to eat them.*

STEP-BY-STEP Carrots

This ever-popular root crop is just as happy growing in a container as it is in the soil, more so if yours is a little stoney. Carrots are a useful crop that can be enjoyed for almost 12 months of the year – with baby "pullings" in early spring and substantial maincrop roots that store well into winter. Their high sugar levels and crunchy texture make carrots a children's favourite. They are also rich in vitamin A, which promotes good eyesight.

	SPRING	SUMMER	AUTUMN	WINTER
SOW				
HARVEST				

TIME TO HARVEST: 12–20 WEEKS

SUITABLE FOR: BEDS AND CONTAINERS

24–150 plants

3M (10FT) ROWS
Depending on variety, grow 2–12cm (1¾–5in) apart

CONTAINERS
50 plants in each

1 Getting started

Carrots come in a wide variety of shapes, sizes, and even colours. They are grown from seeds, and if harvested young, they can be ready in a matter of weeks. Round varieties are the best choice for growing in containers, or in shallow or stoney soils; larger maincrop varieties need deep, moist beds.

'Carson' *is a maincrop variety that produces large tasty roots that are good for storing.*

'Parmex' *produces bite-size, sweet-tasting, round carrots. It is ideal for container growing.*

'Purple Haze' *crops early, yielding unusual purple-skinned roots with contrasting flesh.*

'Bangor' *is a maincrop carrot with large chunky roots. It has good flavour and stores very well.*

2 Sowing seeds

To sow direct, dig over the soil to remove weeds, firm it, then rake it level. Make drills with a hoe, water the base and sow the seed, then cover with soil and water in. Carrots can also be sown into short drills in deep containers.

Make seed drills *2cm (¾in) deep, 10–20cm (4–8in) apart, depending on the variety. Check the packet first.*

Sow seeds thinly, *roughly 5mm (¼in) apart. Tip them from the packet or from the palm of your hand.*

3 Growing on

Carrot seed can be notoriously slow to germinate, so be patient. It is also important to keep the soil or compost well watered until your seedlings have emerged. If sowing early crops outside in spring, these can be covered with garden fleece to provide insulation. Where space allows, seed sown in containers can be kept under cover until germinated, then moved outside to grow on. If not, cover with fleece instead.

Remove garden fleece *on milder days to let in the sunlight. Cover seedlings if hard frost is predicted.*

4 Thinning out

As they grow, thin the seedlings to the recommended distances for your particular variety. In general, maincrop varieties require much wider spacings than early carrots. Very young seedlings can be pulled but those with developing taproots should be pinched off to prevent leaving holes in the soil ideal for carrot fly eggs (see below).

Check the seed packet *before thinning the seedlings as some varieties require more space, and therefore more thinning, than others.*

Weed regularly, *as removing fully grown weeds can disturb the crop. As carrots mature, their foliage will help to suppress weeds..*

Use canes to support carrot fly netting, *and also bury the base 5cm (2in) into the soil, all the way around, to prevent flies sneaking under.*

5 Routine care

Water plants during dry spells but don't overdo it, as this promotes leafy growth at the expense of roots. Regularly weed close to plants by hand. Weeding releases the scent of the leaves, which attracts carrot fly, so it is best done at dusk, when the pests are inactive.

6 Protecting plants

Carrot fly larvae (see p.238) can be a troublesome pest, eating into the roots, especially on crops sown in late spring. To prevent the low-flying adults laying eggs at the base of plants, erect a barrier of fine insect mesh, at least 60cm (24in) high, around the beds.

7 Harvesting

Carrots are ready to pull once they reach the desired size. Early sowings are ready when they are roughly finger-thickness, and are pulled from the soil by hand. Harvest maincrop varieties when they measure about 4cm (1½in) across, easing them out with a fork.

If using a fork to lift carrots, *take care not to disturb neighbouring plants left to grow on.*

TIP	*Eat early carrots fresh; maincrop roots can be stored like beetroot (see p.143).*

STEP-BY-STEP Turnips

This vegetable is undergoing a revival, with top chefs and gardeners alike rediscovering what these sweet, tender roots have to offer. Baby crops can be harvested in as little as six weeks, or plants can be left in the ground to mature fully. Turnips can also be grown for their leaves, or turnip "tops". These can be treated like a cut-and-come-again crop and will provide several flushes of tasty leafy greens through the leaner months.

	SPRING	SUMMER	AUTUMN	WINTER
SOW				
HARVEST				

TIME TO HARVEST: 6–10 WEEKS

SUITABLE FOR: BEDS AND CONTAINERS

30 plants

3M (10FT) ROWS
Plant 10cm (4in) apart

CONTAINERS
10 plants in each

1 Getting started

Turnips prefer a site with moist, rich, well-drained soil that contains plenty of nitrogen, so dig in plenty of organic matter, such as well-rotted compost or manure, in the season before growing. Consider sowing turnips that will be harvested as baby roots alongside slow-growing crops such as parsnips or sweetcorn.

'Purple Top Milan' *should be pulled early at 5cm (2in) wide. The roots have a sweet flavour.*

'Snowball' *has pure white roots that are sweet and tender. Lift the roots at six weeks.*

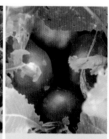

'Primera' *roots have purple tops and should be pulled small. They have sweet, tender flesh.*

'Atlantic' *produces purple and white roots that can be harvested young or left to mature.*

Hardy varieties *can be sown under cover at the beginning and end of the growing season, giving you roots during almost every month of the year.*

Harden the seedlings off *and plant them out, once their roots fill the modules. Space the plants 10cm (4in) apart, with 30cm (12in) between rows.*

2 Sowing under cover

Fill module trays with seed compost, firm gently, and water well. Let the soil drain then make a 2cm (¾in) deep hole in each cell. Sow four seeds per hole, cover over, and water in. Alternatively, fill large containers with compost and make drills 2cm (¾in) deep. Sow seed thinly along the base or sow a pinch of seeds every 10cm (4in). Thin the seedlings to one per cell, or one every 10cm (4in); harden off and plant out when they are large enough to handle.

TIP	*To prevent a glut, sow seed little and often for a small but steady supply.*

3 Sowing outside

Alternatively, you can sow turnip seed directly outside between mid-spring and late summer. Create a seedbed by digging over a patch of soil to remove any weeds and incorporating a base dressing of high nitrogen granular fertilizer. Firm gently, rake level to create a fine tilth, then create drills 2cm (¾in) deep and 23–30cm (9–12in) apart.

Water the drills well *and then sow seeds thinly along the base. Cover them back over with a thin layer of soil and then water them in lightly.*

Carefully thin the seedlings *to leave a strong specimen every 10cm (4in). Use the thinned turnip seedlings as a leafy green or in salads.*

Fine insect-proof mesh *should be used to protect crops from flying pests such as flea beetle during all stages of their growth.*

Pull out competing weeds *by hand, to avoid damaging the young turnip roots. Check the rows regularly so weeds can be pulled up when young.*

4 Routine care

Flea beetle can be a problem, especially in hot, dry weather, so cover drills with insect-proof mesh. Keep plants well watered and fed as they grow. Container plants and those on light soils can be fed periodically with a high-nitrogen liquid fertilizer to boost yields.

5 Weeding

It is important to keep the young plants weed-free, as weeds compete with the seedlings for light and nutrients and may harbour disease. Weed around the plants by hand to prevent damaging the roots, and use a hoe to remove weeds between the rows.

6 Harvesting

Pull individual "baby" roots of fast-growing summer crops once they reach the size of a golf ball – leaving them to grow any larger can result in a woody texture. Hardy winter types can be left to grow larger so that they can then be lifted in the autumn as and when they are needed. It is possible to store turnips in boxes of sand, but they are only likely to keep for a couple of weeks as they have fairly thin skins.

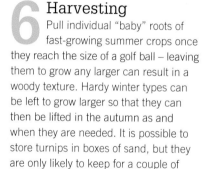

Early roots are ideal for harvesting *when they reach about 4–5cm (1½–2in) in diameter.*

STEP-BY-STEP Parsnips

A delicious staple of the winter kitchen, parsnips are a worthy addition to any vegetable plot. An impressive number can be grown on just a small patch of ground and they are very easy to cultivate – simply ensure that you give them enough water and space. Although they take a long time to grow, they are extremely hardy and can be left in the soil well into the colder months; exposure to frost is, in fact, meant to make the roots taste sweeter.

	SPRING	SUMMER	AUTUMN	WINTER
SOW				
HARVEST				

TIME TO HARVEST: 32–36 WEEKS

SUITABLE FOR: BEDS

11–15 plants

3M (10FT) ROWS
Plant 20–30cm (8–12in) apart.

1 Getting started

Parsnips grow best in light soils that are free from stones and not compacted – this reduces the risk of the roots becoming crooked or forked. Pick a site that was manured the previous autumn – do not apply manure just before sowing as it can cause root tips to become scorched, which results in forked roots.

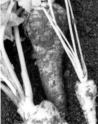

'White Gem' *has relatively short roots with white skin and excellent flavour.*

'Gladiator' *is an exhibition variety, known for its sweet, smooth-skinned roots.*

'Avon Resistor' *produces short roots that are uniform in size and have a good flavour.*

'Tender and True' *roots are large, smooth-skinned, and show some resistance to canker.*

Sow the seed in mid- to late spring, *as soon as the risk of frost has passed. Seed sown earlier than this may struggle to germinate.*

Once the seedlings *are large enough to handle, thin them by pulling out or pinching out the weakest, leaving only the strongest to grow on.*

2 Sowing seeds

Because they develop a long tap root parsnips are best sown direct. Prepare the soil then sow clumps of four or five seeds every 20–30cm (8–12in), 2cm (¾in) deep. Space rows 30cm (12in) apart. Seedlings can germinate slowly – often taking up to 10–14 days – so be patient. Save space and mark your rows by sowing fast-growing salad leaves or radishes between your parsnip seedlings – these can be harvested well before the parsnips mature.

TIP	*Buy new seed each spring because parsnip seed viability is very short.*

3 Protecting plants

As part of the carrot family, parsnips are prone to carrot fly attack. Prevent this by pinching off the surplus seedlings at soil level rather than pulling them, which can leave holes for the female fly to lay her eggs in. Also, erect a barrier of fine insect-proof mesh at least 60cm (24in) in height around your plants (see p.238).

Bury the insect-proof mesh *5cm (2in) deep in the soil, completely surrounding the plants, so that the carrot flies can't get underneath it.*

Regular watering *will encourage the roots to grow evenly – if they are allowed to become dry, later watering may cause the roots to split.*

Lift parsnips gently *to avoid damaging them. In very dry conditions, roots will emerge more readily if the soil is moistened beforehand.*

4 Routine care

Keep plants well watered as they develop to ensure good-sized, even roots. Hand-weed around the plants to avoid disturbing their roots. When the plants are established they will be better able to out-compete weeds. Parsnips do not require any additional feeding.

5 Harvesting

Early parsnip varieties will be ready to lift in early autumn; later types can be harvested during winter. Roots can grow very deep, especially on open, light soils, so insert a garden fork next to each root and use it to gently ease the root out of the soil.

Storing roots

Late-maturing parsnips can be left in the ground until required. In very cold areas, cover the plants with a mulch of straw so that when you come to dig the roots up the ground is not frozen solid. Mark plants with a cane so that they are easier to find. Roots left in the soil come spring can be stored in sand as for beetroot (see p.137).

STEP-BY-STEP Swedes

These plump, round roots are delicious roasted or mashed like potatoes, and provide welcome fresh crops in autumn and winter when the vegetable patch is pretty bare. These are slow-maturing plants, traditionally best suited to larger gardens, where they can be left to grow. However, swedes can also be sown densely to produce "baby" roots that can either be eaten within a few weeks, leaves and all, or left longer for small, sweet roots, 5cm (2in) across.

	SPRING	SUMMER	AUTUMN	WINTER
SOW				
HARVEST				

TIME TO HARVEST: 20–24 WEEKS

SUITABLE FOR: BEDS

0   1m   2m   3m

12–15 plants

3M (10FT) ROWS
Plant 20–25cm (8–10in) apart

1 Getting started

Swedes require a relatively long growing season and will take five or six months to mature fully. Dig in plenty of well-rotted organic matter, such as compost or manure, in the autumn before growing and ensure that you rotate swedes, including them in the same group as other brassica crops.

'Brora' *roots are fast-growing and have good disease-resistance. The yellow flesh is very tasty.*

'Best of All' *is a reliable variety, giving medium-sized, purple roots with yellow flesh.*

'Virtue' *is an excellent choice. It produces reddish roots that have delicious yellow flesh.*

'Marian' *produces deep purple roots that have an excellent flavour and good disease-resistance.*

Sow seed thinly along your rows *before covering it over and watering in. Multiple rows should be spaced roughly 30cm (12in) apart.*

Once seedlings begin to appear, *gradually thin them out leaving the strongest to grow on. Eventual spacing should be around 20–25cm (8–10in) apart.*

2 Sowing seeds

Because they develop a relatively long tap root, swedes are best sown direct into the ground rather than in modules or seed trays. In mid- to late spring, prepare the site for sowing by digging it over thoroughly to remove any weeds and large stones, then firm it gently and rake it level. Make a drill 2cm (¾in) deep and water it well. Sow your seeds along it, cover them over with a little more soil to level the soil surface, and then firm down gently.

TIP *For baby swedes, sow seed densely then thin to 8–10cm (3–4in) apart.*

3 Growing on

Swedes are exceptionally hardy crops, although very early sowings may need protection if there is a risk of frost. Cover them with a single or double layer of horticultural fleece, or a cloche or cold frame, to offer insulation and speed up growth. Ensure that the plants remain well watered under their protective covering.

Swedes are fully hardy *but cover early sowings with garden fleece to protect them from frost as a precaution, especially in colder regions.*

Cover plants *with wire or plastic netting to deter large pests such as pigeons. Use finer mesh to protect against flea beetles and cabbage root fly.*

Hand-weed or hoe *between the plants regularly to prevent competing weeds from checking growth; take care not to damage the roots.*

4 Protecting plants

Swedes are prone to the same pests and diseases as other members of the brassica family. Flea beetle can be very damaging to plants during hot weather; where at risk, cover over rows with fine, insect-proof mesh to prevent access to the plants.

5 Routine care

It is important that swedes don't receive a check in growth due to a lack of moisture, so keep plants well irrigated, especially during dry spells. Apply a 6–7cm (2½–3in) deep mulch of organic matter to lock in soil moisture – this is especially useful on light soils.

6 Harvesting

In early to mid-autumn, roots will become large enough to harvest. Use a garden fork alongside to gently lever each root out of the soil. If you don't have storage space, swedes can be left in the soil all winter, under a layer of straw. However, it is almost impossible to lift roots when the soil is frozen, so if you want to lift swedes in advance in autumn, they can be stored in boxes of sand or kept in a shed or garage until required.

After lifting your swedes, *clean them thoroughly and cut the stems off before storing.*

STEP-BY-STEP Potatoes

Whether you prefer yours chipped, roasted, baked, mashed, or new and slathered in butter, potatoes are a delicious must-grow crop in any garden. This extremely popular vegetable is very easy to grow, and can be grown in large containers if you don't have ample amounts of bed space. There is a huge selection of tasty varieties, classed, in order of maturity, as first earlies, second earlies, early maincrops, maincrops, and late maincrops.

	SPRING	SUMMER	AUTUMN	WINTER
SOW				
HARVEST				

TIME TO HARVEST: 12–22 WEEKS

SUITABLE FOR: BEDS AND CONTAINERS

4–6 plants

3M (10FT) ROWS
Plant 45–70cm (18–30in) apart

CONTAINERS
2 plants in each

1 Start under cover

Potatoes bought for planting are called "seed potatoes", and are available to buy in mid- to late winter. Early types may benefit from being "chitted" before planting, to give them a head start. This simply means allowing the "eyes" to sprout before the tubers are planted out. Place your seed potatoes "rose-end" – the end with the most eyes – upwards, in an egg box or tray, and position this in a cool, well-lit place such as a windowsill.

Choose seed potatoes that are certified disease-free and of good quality to maximize your chances of healthy, productive plants.

If stored in a cool, dry, frost-free place, the tubers will begin to develop "chits" within a few weeks. They are then ready to plant out.

Place the tubers into the soil, ensuring that they are planted with the rose-end facing up.

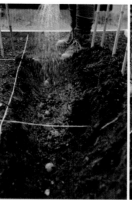

Water the chitted tubers in well before covering them to help them establish quickly.

Cover the tubers with soil, leaving the surface raised up into a slight mound.

2 Planting out

Seed potatoes can be planted in the ground or in containers. The main season to plant outside is early spring for early varieties, and mid-spring for maincrops. Dig over and weed the soil, and work in some general purpose fertilizer. Dig a drill about 15cm (6in) deep and place your potatoes along the bottom, spaced 45–70cm (18–30in) apart. Cover over with 20cm (8in) of soil to create a slight mound.

TIP The closer the potatoes are planted together, the smaller the tubers will be.

3 Container-growing

Alternatively, potatoes can be planted in containers, such as specially designed potato "barrels" or large tubs or plastic sacks. Use a 50:50 mix of multipurpose compost and good garden soil, placing a 15cm (6in) layer of this in the base. Lay the potato tubers on top and then cover with a further 10cm (4in) of soil. Water them in well.

As long as you make drainage holes *before planting, a plastic barrel makes an ideal, and space-saving, growing container for potatoes.*

Plastic sacks make good growing containers *as they can be emptied and folded away once all the potatoes have been harvested.*

Potatoes are hardy *but emerging shoots can be damaged by harsh frosts. Cover plants with garden fleece when cold weather is predicted.*

Earth up potatoes *three or four times during summer. Containers should be earthed up until the compost reaches just below the rim.*

4 Routine care

Water plants well, and feed using an all-purpose granular fertilizer. Young plants need weeding but soon develop a smothering canopy of foliage. After flowering, green, tomato-like fruits, may appear – these are poisonous and should not be eaten. Check plants regularly for potato blight (see p.246).

5 Earthing up

Plants will need "earthing up" as they grow: draw the soil up around the stem to leave the top 10cm (4in) of the plant visible. This encourages the plant to produce greater yields, and prevents the developing tubers from becoming exposed to sunlight, which makes them green and inedible.

6 Harvesting

Begin harvesting early potatoes in early summer – generally they will be ready to lift once their flowers develop; leave maincrop types until late summer or early autumn. Lift soil-grown plants gently with a fork, taking care not to damage the tubers. Container-grown plants can either be tipped out in one go, or excavated to remove the tubers as you need them – gently refirm the compost afterwards and water well.

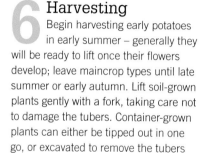

If possible, *harvest potatoes on a dry day and leave them to dry in the sun for a few hours.*

Potatoes

1 'Accent' This yellow-skinned first early potato bears reliably high yields. It has moderately good disease resistance and the tubers suffer less slug damage than other varieties.

2 'Charlotte' A second early, this yellow-skinned salad potato is reliable and has a good flavour. Higher yielding than others of this type, individual tuber-size is also impressive.

3 'Red Duke of York' This versatile first early variety can be lifted and eaten young as a new potato, or allowed to mature for baking. It has red skin and creamy-white flesh.

4 'Belle de Fontenay' This early maincrop variety is renowned for being a great salad potato. The yield of knobbly tubers is good, and the flesh is yellow and waxy.

5 'Pink Fir Apple' An heirloom maincrop variety, it produces knobbly, red-skinned tubers that have a waxy texture and a good flavour. It is widely grown as salad potato.

6 'Concorde' Renowned for its high yields, this first early variety is quick to bulk up, producing waxy tubers with yellow flesh. The tubers show some resistance to slugs.

7 'Foremost' This early variety produces high yields of tasty, firm, white-fleshed tubers, with good scab resistance. They store well under cover if kept dry and well-ventilated.

8 'Yukon Gold' A second early, it has great flavour and can be used in a variety of different ways in the kitchen: boiled as a new potato, or baked, roast, or chipped.

9 'Ratte' A good alternative to 'Pink Fir Apple', the tubers have smoother skins, making them easier to prepare in the kitchen, and mature earlier. It has a tasty salad-potato flavour.

Other varieties
'Mimi'
'Anya'
'Maris Bard'
'Maris Piper'
'Lady Christl'
'Edzell Blue'

Alliums

The unique characteristic of this group is unmistakable – no other crop has such a distinctive flavour or aroma, released from every part of the plant. These are versatile crops in the garden and highly valuable in the kitchen, too. Grow enough, and you can easily be self-sufficient in onions all year thanks to their excellent keeping qualities; likewise shallots, if you prefer something a little stronger. Leeks aren't just the mainstay of the winter plot, they can last until spring, and there are also autumn varieties to grow. The sweetness of garlic completes the group – lift it in summer for fresh cloves, or plait and store them through winter.

STEP-BY-STEP Onions

No vegetable garden is complete without onions and there are many to choose from, including red-, white-, and brown-skinned varieties. Onions need a long time to mature fully, and sizeable bulbs can be achieved by sowing seeds under cover early in the year. However, an easier method is to raise plants from "sets" that are planted in spring or autumn. Overwintered crops of hardy, often Japanese, varieties offer a useful early harvest.

	SPRING	SUMMER	AUTUMN	WINTER
SOW				
HARVEST				

TIME TO HARVEST: 20–24 WEEKS

SUITABLE FOR: BEDS

```
0          1m          2m          3m
```

30–60 plants

3M (10FT) ROWS
Sow, plant, or thin to 5–10cm (2–4in) apart

1 Sowing under cover

For larger bulbs, sow seeds under cover from midwinter to early spring. Fill module trays with seed compost, firm gently, and water well. Make a hole in each cell 1cm (½in) deep, and sow two seeds in each. The seeds don't require additional heat but should be kept moist. Germination will take a week or two. Thin the seedlings to leave the stronger per module.

TIP	For smaller, earlier bulbs, sow three or four seeds per cell and don't thin them.

Sowing seeds in modules, removes the need to prick the seedlings out as they develop.

Thin seedlings once large enough to handle. They should pull easily from the compost.

Harden off and plant out in spring – the same time when "sets" are planted out.

Spring sowings can bolt in cold weather. Don't sow too early in the year, when a cold snap may occur, and choose a bolt-resistant variety.

Thin out the seedlings gradually as they develop until they reach their final spacing. Leave only the strongest and use the thinnings in your salads.

2 Sowing outside

This method of raising onions is now less common since the introduction of "sets", which offer the crop a useful head start. Sow seeds in spring for summer crops, or in late summer for Japanese overwintering varieties. Dig over the soil to remove weeds, firm it down and rake the surface level. Prepare a drill 2cm (¾in) deep. Water the base well and then sow thinly along it. Cover and water in and, once the seedlings have emerged, thin them out to leave one every 5–10cm (2–4in).

3 Planting sets

Sets are very small onion bulbs that are planted in either autumn or spring. Each one bulks up in size to produce a larger bulb. Autumn-planted sets of winter-hardy varieties mature to produce larger bulbs than those planted in the spring. Push the sets into prepared soil, 5–10cm (2–4in) apart, positioning the tip of the set at soil level.

The space between your sets *will determine the eventual size of your onion bulbs – plant them further apart if you want larger results.*

Firm the soil gently around the sets, *leaving the tips showing above the soil surface. Water them in lightly to help settle the sets in.*

It is important *to keep crops well weeded, especially while they are young. Weed around them by hand to avoid damaging the bulbs.*

Onion bulbs are ready to harvest *once the stems and leaves have naturally died back. Lift on a dry day to help prevent the bulbs rotting.*

4 Routine Care

Onions are very sensitive to plant competition so ensure you weed regularly between your bulbs. Keep the soil evenly moist, especially if you want good-sized bulbs. Autumn sowings and plantings benefit from an application of high-nitrogen fertilizer in late winter.

5 Harvesting

Harvest onions when they reach full size, once the stems have collapsed and bent over. On a dry day, gently lift them partly out of the soil using a fork. Leave them on the ground for a week or so to dry out; dry them indoors on racks if it is wet.

Drying the bulbs

Lay the onions out on a wire rack to dry. Ensure that this is kept off the ground so that air can circulate around the bulbs. Leave them in a light, dry place such as a greenhouse or on a windowsill. Once the outer skins rustle you can either plait your bulbs and hang them up, or store them in net bags until needed.

Onions

1 'Sturon' This popular brown-skinned onion produces mid-sized bulbs with flavoursome, juicy flesh. The bulbs are resistant to bolting and keep well after harvesting.

2 'Ailsa Craig' A reliable variety, this onion develops large, globe-shaped bulbs with a mild flavour. Use them fresh, as the bulbs don't store well. Plants can be raised from seed or "sets".

3 'Senshyu' This hardy Japanese variety can be planted in autumn to harvest in early summer. It is a reliable onion and gives a good harvest of tasty, flat-bottomed bulbs.

4 'Centurion' Plant this variety in spring for an early crop of rounded, brown-skinned bulbs in summer that store well for short periods. The flesh is crisp with a good flavour.

5 'Hi Keeper' This is a Japanese variety to plant in autumn and overwinter outside, ready to harvest in early summer. It can also be sown in spring to harvest mid- to late summer.

6 'Red Baron' This variety gives a reliable crop of small to medium-sized, red-skinned bulbs in summer. It has a stronger flavour than many other red onions and stores well.

7 'Setton' Producing large, brown-skinned bulbs in late summer, these onions have a good flavour and store well. It is a reliable new variety that crops heavily. It is mainly sold as "sets".

8 'Shakespeare' Plant this variety in autumn ready to harvest the following summer. It produces brown-skinned, mid-sized bulbs that are excellent for storing. It has good flavour.

9 'Golden Bear' This variety produces large brown-skinned bulbs that mature in midsummer. It gives a good crop that stores well, and is resistant to onion white rot disease (see p.242).

Other varieties
'Bedfordshire Champion'
'Hercules'
'Hytech'
'Marco'
'Stuttgarter Giant'

STEP-BY-STEP Shallots

These small bulbs couldn't be easier to grow – simply plant sets during autumn or spring and each will divide up, producing a cluster of new bulbs. If their skins are properly dried, storage life is extremely long, giving you useful bulbs with an intense flavour for many months of the year. Shallots are delicious used whole in casseroles, when they melt in the mouth, or roasted with meat or vegetables, when they take on a caramelized sweet flavour.

	SPRING	SUMMER	AUTUMN	WINTER
SOW				
HARVEST				

TIME TO HARVEST: 20–36 WEEKS

SUITABLE FOR: BEDS

0   1m   2m   3m

15 plants

3M (10FT) ROWS
Thin and plant out to 20cm (8in) apart

1 Getting started

Shallots are most commonly grown from "sets" – small bulbs that, when planted, bulk up by splitting into numerous smaller bulbs. Alternatively, shallots can be grown from seed, either sown under cover in winter, or sown direct in mid- to late spring. Ensure that you give them rich, well-drained soil.

'Longor' *bulbs have pinkish flesh and good flavour. They are uniform in size and shape.*

'Red Sun' *is a high-yielding variety with red skins and red-flushed, crisp flesh.*

'Golden Gourmet' *is a mild-tasting variety and the large, yellow bulbs can be eaten raw.*

'Mikor' *bulbs have brownish skin and pink flesh. The large bulbs are good for cooking.*

2 Sowing under cover

Fill a module tray with seed compost, water well, and leave it to drain. Sow the seeds in small clusters and cover them with 1cm (½in) of compost. Water lightly and place the tray in a propagator; germination will take a week or two.

Plants sown from seed *under cover in winter should be ready to transplant in mid-spring.*

Once the seedlings emerge, *they will need thinning to leave the strongest seedling per cell.*

3 Planting sets

Plant your sets, either in late autumn or spring, directly outside in an open, sunny site that has been dug over to remove weeds. Push them into the soil, leaving the tip of each bulb protruding just above the surface. Plant them at their eventual spacing – leaving 20cm (8in) between sets in each direction.

TIP   *Cover sets with netting to protect against birds.*

Buy certified, virus-free sets *to boost your chances of growing successful, healthy crops.*

4 Sow and plant out

Seed can be sown direct once the soil has warmed up at the end of spring. Dig in plenty of well-rotted manure or compost. Create a drill about 2.5cm (1in) deep and sow seed thinly along it. Cover with soil and water in. Harden off your indoor-grown seedlings once their roots fill their modules and plant out 20x20cm (8x8in) apart.

Sprinkle the seed thinly *along each drill – sow plenty, as seedlings will be thinned out once they are established.*

Thin the seedlings, *pulling the weakest ones out gently by hand, leaving approximately 2cm (¾in) between them.*

If your seedlings *need transplanting to their final position, dig them up gently and re-plant them 20cm (8in) apart.*

Weed the seedlings *by hand or with an onion hoe. Keeping them well ventilated will prevent diseases such as downy mildew (see p.242).*

Leave the bulbs *to dry on the soil surface for a few days after lifting and then carefully split into individual bulbs before you store them.*

5 Routine care

Keep plants well watered and well weeded. Overwintered shallots should have a granular high nitrogen fertilizer sprinkled among the plants during spring – chicken pellets are ideal – to boost yields. There is no need to feed spring-planted shallots.

6 Harvesting

Leaves will turn yellow and wither in mid- to late summer – a sign that the bulbs are nearly mature. Stop watering at this point to encourage the bulbs to dry and set strong skins for long storage. Lift gently with a fork, taking care not to damage the individual bulbs.

Drying the bulbs

To store well, shallots should be dried fully on a raised rack in a greenhouse or a covered area for at least two weeks. After this, cut the stem off each bulb to leave a 1cm (½in) stump, rub off the loose outer skin, and store them in a net bag or cardboard box in a cool, dry, frost-free place until required.

STEP-BY-STEP Spring onions

Spring onions bring a unique flavour to salads, so make sure your plot has space for a row or two. These small plants are amazingly productive and surprisingly hardy, allowing you to extend the season with both early and late sowings. Spring onions can either form a small bulb, or grow more like a miniature leek, producing cylindrical, non-bulbing stems. There are also red-stemmed, pickling, and Japanese varieties to choose from.

	SPRING	SUMMER	AUTUMN	WINTER
SOW				
HARVEST				

TIME TO HARVEST: 10 WEEKS

SUITABLE FOR: BEDS AND CONTAINERS

150 plants

3M (10FT) ROWS
Plant out 2cm (¾in) apart

CONTAINERS
40 plants in each

1 Getting started

Spring onions are grown from seed, either sown directly in the soil or into large containers, during spring and summer. Early and late crops can also be raised under cover; sown into greenhouse borders, or into containers or growing bags. Small crops can also be grown on warm windowsills during winter.

'Guardsman' *has long, well-blanched stems and dark green leaves. It is a vigorous variety.*

'North Holland Blood Red' *produces striking red stems that deepen in colour with age.*

'White Lisbon' *is the most commonly grown spring onion and is good for container growing.*

'Summer Isle' *crops relatively late. Its mild flavour makes it ideal for eating raw.*

Seed can be sown *under cover from early spring to autumn; sow in repeat batches to provide a steady supply.*

If necessary, *encourage and protect germinating seeds by placing pots in a propagator. Keep them well ventilated.*

Seedlings in pots *will also need thinning when they reach about 8cm (3in) tall – thin to leave four or five per small pot.*

2 Sowing under cover

As certain varieties are very hardy, early- and late-season sowings can be made under cover to extend the harvesting period. Fill large containers, 30cm (12in) wide, with seed compost, firm gently, water well, and allow to drain. Mark out drills 1cm (½in) deep and 10cm (4in) apart using a trowel or short length of bamboo cane. Sow seeds 1cm (½in) apart along the base, cover over with more compost, and lightly water in. As the seedlings emerge, thin out to leave one strong plant every 2cm (¾in). Protect the young crop against slug damage with a light sprinkling of pellets.

3 Sowing outside

If sowing spring onions outside, prepare the soil thoroughly by digging it over to remove weeds and any crop debris, firm it gently, and rake it level. Mark out drills 1cm (½in) deep and 10cm (4in) apart. Water the base of the drill well and then sow seeds roughly 1cm (½in) apart along its length. Cover them over with soil and water in lightly.

A late summer or early autumn sowing *of a winter hardy variety will give crops in spring. Cover plants with fleece during harsh winter weather.*

Once seedlings are 8cm (3in) tall *thin them out to leave one every 2cm (¾in). These thinnings can be used in salads in the same way as chives.*

Watering is crucial *both indoors and out, while spring onion plants are young – drought can severely stunt the development of seedlings.*

Keep plants well weeded *– weeds will compete with the young plants for water and nutrients, and may encourage disease.*

4 Under cover crops

Crops can be grown under cover in containers to give an early or late harvest. Water them well and feed with a dilute general purpose liquid fertilizer as they mature. Keep the plants well-ventilated to deter fungal diseases, such botrytis (see p.244).

5 Routine care

Keep crops well-watered, as dry conditions can cause plants to become bulbous. Spring onions are very sensitive to weed competition, so hoe between the rows and hand-weed regularly. In cold areas, protect winter crops using garden fleece or a cloche.

6 Harvesting

Harvest individual plants when their stems are pencil-thick, gently lifting them with a hand fork and re-firming the soil so that other plants in the row can carry on growing. Spring onions don't store well, so only lift them as and when they are needed.

TIP	*Spring onions prefer an open, sunny site – they do not do well in shade.*

Spring onions reach a harvestable size *after about eight weeks. Re-sow for a constant supply.*

STEP-BY-STEP Leeks

These mildly flavoured onion relatives are an invaluable leafy alternative to brassicas during winter. Rather than producing bulbs, the long white stems or "shanks" of leeks are blanched by earthing up soil around them as they grow. Plant breeders are constantly improving leek disease resistance and length of harvest, so choose from these types where possible; some varieties can even be closely planted to give deliciously tender "baby" leeks.

	SPRING	SUMMER	AUTUMN	WINTER
SOW				
HARVEST				

TIME TO HARVEST: 30–32 WEEKS

SUITABLE FOR: BEDS AND CONTAINERS

11–15 plants

3M (10FT) ROWS
Plant out 20–30cm (8–12in) apart

CONTAINERS
5 plants in each

1 Getting started

Leeks are one member of the onion family that don't seem to mind root disturbance, so you can sow in clusters with the view to lifting the young plants "bare-root", and then planting into the crop's final position. This allows you to plant the final growing space with another crop until transplanting is required.

'Musselburgh' *is a well-established variety that reliably gives short, flavourful stems.*

'King Richard' *is a good choice for "baby" leeks, producing long, sweet, early stems.*

'Toledo' *leeks are late to crop and renowned for their uniform shape and size and good flavour.*

'Swiss Giant Zermatt' *has a mild flavour and can be pulled as "baby" leeks or left to mature.*

Seeds can be sown under cover *in midwinter as long as they are given enough heat – ensure they are kept at a minimum of 10°C (50°F).*

Biodegradable module pots *allow you to transplant seedlings straight into their planting holes without risking damage to the roots.*

2 Sowing seeds

To sow under cover fill a tall, 15cm (6in) diameter pot with seed compost, firm gently, and water well. Allow to drain and then sow your seeds thinly on top. Cover with another 1cm (½in) layer of compost, water in lightly, and place in a propagator. Alternatively, sow seed in biodegradable module trays rather than pots. Seed can also be sown direct once the soil is suitably warm and workable in spring. Prepare a seedbed and then create a short drill 2cm (¾in) deep. Water the base well and then sow your seeds thinly. Cover with a little more soil to level, firm gently, and water in lightly.

3 Transplanting

Once seedlings are 20–30cm (8–12in) tall and pencil-thick, they can be transplanted or planted out. Prepare the site then create holes using a large dibber 2–3cm (¾–1¼in) wide, 15cm (6in) deep and between 20–30cm (8–12in) apart. Lift your leeks gently, trim the roots to about 2.5cm (1in) long, and then drop one plant into each hole.

After about eight weeks, *carefully lift the seedlings from their seedbed, taking care not to break the delicate leaves.*

Use a clean pair of scissors *to trim the roots to 2.5cm (1in) before you transplant them; their roots will continue to develop.*

Drop the seedlings *into their deep holes, ready for watering. For "baby" leeks with thin stems, space plants 10cm (4in) apart.*

Water transplanted leeks *in thoroughly but don't refill the planting holes with soil. This forces the plants to produce long white, tender stems.*

Mound up soil *around the developing plants to block out the light, blanching the stems. This will also help to keep the plants stable.*

4 Watering

When the seedlings are stood in their holes, pour water around them, allowing it to drag some of the surrounding soil back around the plants. Planting them like this blanches the base of the stems. Keep plants well watered during the summer months.

5 Routine care

Crops can be vulnerable to leek moth and onion fly (see p.238), so deter these pests by covering plants with insect-proof mesh. Leek yield can suffer if weeds are allowed to develop, so keep plants well weeded. Earth up soil around the stems to blanch them.

6 Harvesting

Lift leeks using a fork. They will stand in the ground for a while but if you need the space for other crops, "heel" the leeks in: dig another hole and stand them in it, covering the roots with soil. In wintry weather, place leeks in a bucket of soil in a shed or garage.

TIP *Prevent leek rust from disrupting your crops by choosing a resistant variety.*

Leeks do not store well *so try to use them as soon as possible once they are out of the ground.*

STEP-BY-STEP Garlic

This is one of the most versatile vegetables in the kitchen and is incredibly easy to grow, even in containers. Plant out individual cloves in a sunny position between mid-autumn and early spring, when beds are often empty, and you can look forward to harvesting mature bulbs from early- to midsummer. Once lifted, these can either be used while fresh, when they have a deliciously sweet flavour, or dried to use throughout the lean winter months.

	SPRING	SUMMER	AUTUMN	WINTER
SOW				
HARVEST				

TIME TO HARVEST: 20–36 WEEKS

SUITABLE FOR: BEDS AND CONTAINERS

18–22 plants

3M (10FT) ROWS
Plant 15-18cm (6–7in) apart

CONTAINERS
4 plants in each

1 Getting started

There are two types of garlic: "hardneck", which develop flower spikes, and "softneck", which don't, and subsequently have a longer storage life. Whichever type you choose, plant the cloves in light, well-drained soil. If yours is heavy, dig in bulky, well-rotted organic matter, such as composted bark.

'Solent Wight' *is a softneck-type that produces large, white, very flavoursome bulbs.*

'Early Wight' *is a hardneck-type with early-maturing, easy-peel, chunky cloves.*

'Elephant' *is not a true garlic, but the large cloves are flavourful and ideal for roasting.*

'Mediterranean' *bulbs grow very large and taste especially good when eaten fresh.*

Final bulb size *is directly related to initial clove size, so plant the largest and dispose of any that are very small.*

Push the cloves *into the compost leaving the tip showing above the surface. Firm around them and water in well.*

Cloves will sprout *after seven to ten days. Once the roots fill the pot, plant them on outside, spaced 15–18cm (6–7in) apart.*

2 Planting indoors

If planting under cover, do so in early spring. Break the garlic bulb, or "head", into individual cloves, fill pots with compost, and plant one clove per pot. Water in well and allow to drain. Place the pots somewhere warm and bright; 10°C (50°F) is sufficient as excess warmth will cause sappy growth that will be more prone to disease. If you have a cold frame or sheltered spot outside, plants can be grown on here once their shoots reach 10cm (4in) tall.

TIP	*Plant the bulbs in autumn to overwinter for a larger harvest.*

3 Planting outside

Garlic cloves can be planted directly in the ground, any time between autumn or spring. Choose a sunny, sheltered spot and dig it over to remove any weeds. Work in a high-nitrogen granular fertilizer, gently firm the soil and rake it level. Plant the cloves with their tips facing up, deeper than those planted under cover in pots.

Space bulbs *15–18cm (6–7in) apart each way; gently push cloves into the ground, so that 2cm (¾in) of soil is above their tips. Water in well.*

Weed competition *can affect yields, so keep plants well weeded with regular hoeing or hand-weeding between the plants.*

Garlic bulbs *can be harvested during summer – those planted in the previous autumn will be ready to lift sooner than those planted in spring.*

4 Routine care

Keep young plants well watered while they develop a strong root system. Once established, garlic is quite drought-tolerant and too much water can actually impair its storage qualities, so only irrigate if there are prolonged dry periods. Keep crops well weeded.

5 Harvesting

Lift as soon as the top third of the foliage has turned yellow and begun to die – leaving plants in the soil for too long can cause them to re-sprout, which shortens their storage life. Gently ease them out of the soil with a fork, taking care not to damage the bulbs.

Drying the bulbs

In order to store well, garlic bulbs must be thoroughly dry. Lay them out on racks in a sunny, dry spot for at least a fortnight, until the skins become crisp. Then hang them up in a cool, dry, well-ventilated place, either individually or by plaiting the stems together. Garlic can be stored this way for up to ten months.

Other crops

Certain annual crops don't neatly fit into a group, but have individual qualities and characteristics of their own. Some of the most unusual flavours can be found here – the aniseed tang of fennel, the fresh sugariness from sweetcorn, and the unmistakable taste and aroma of celery and celeriac. Kohl rabi is always a talking point in the vegetable garden, looking and tasting like a turnip, held a few inches above the soil. Make room for these crops on your plot and look forward to some extraordinary treats in the kitchen.

STEP-BY-STEP Sweetcorn

Boiled and slathered in melted butter or grilled on a barbecue, sweetcorn is a delicious treat in late summer and early autumn. Pick and eat the sugary, tender cobs as soon as possible, as they are at their sweetest immediately after harvest. The flowers are pollinated by the wind, not insects, so grow them closely in blocks or groups. This is a productive crop, good for smaller plots, giving up to 32 tasty cobs from a block of plants, one metre square.

	SPRING	SUMMER	AUTUMN	WINTER
SOW				
HARVEST				

TIME TO HARVEST: 16–24 WEEKS

SUITABLE FOR: BEDS AND CONTAINERS

0   1m   2m   3m

11 plants

3M (10FT) ROWS
Plant in blocks, 30cm (12in) apart

0   50cm

CONTAINERS
4 plants in each

Cardboard "growing tubes" *are ideal for sowing sweetcorn as they are deep enough for the roots and can be planted out, tube-and-all.*

The seedlings will emerge *within a few weeks. They prefer rich, well-drained soil, so ensure that you dig in plenty of organic matter before planting out.*

1 Sowing under cover

Fill module trays or pots with seed compost, water well, and allow to drain. Sow one seed per cell or pot, 2cm (¾in) deep, water in lightly, and place in a heated propagator. Once the plants reach 10cm (4in) high, begin to harden them off. At the same time, prepare the ground by warming it with a cloche or cold frame. It is important to plant the seedlings out in a grid formation, 30x30cm (12x12in) apart.

> **TIP** *Keep different varieties separate or their flavour may be impaired.*

2 Sowing outside

If you don't have space to raise seed under cover, they can also be sown directly into their final positions. The soil needs to be at least 10°C (50°F) before sowing, and you can encourage it to warm sooner by covering the area with cloches or cold frames. Water the soil well and sow the seed in pairs into individual holes, 2cm (¾in) deep, spaced 30cm (12in) apart in a grid pattern. Keep the cloches in place until the seeds germinate in about two weeks.

Use cloches or cold frames *to warm the soil. Put them in place about two weeks before sowing.*

Sow two seeds *per hole for a greater chance of success, then thin to leave the stronger seedling.*

Plant sweetcorn in blocks *so the wind can blow the pollen from flower to flower.*

3 Routine care

Sweetcorn should be kept well-watered throughout summer, especially when the plants are in flower and the cobs are developing. It is possible to underplant sweetcorn with low-growing crops like squash, but this will demand additional watering. Protect seedlings from slugs and snails and weed young plants regularly until they establish.

Weeding is important *in the initial stages but as plants become established they are increasingly able to out-compete weeds.*

Water at the base of plants *so it soaks down to the roots. Plants are especially responsive to watering once the cobs start to fill in midsummer.*

Earth up soil at the base of plants *as they grow. This will help support the stems and prevent the roots being loosened by wind rock.*

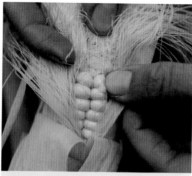

Using a finger nail, *pierce a kernel to check the colour of the sap. If it is milky, the cobs are ready to harvest, if not, give them a few days longer.*

4 Providing support

These are tall plants reaching up to 2m (6ft) and may need support, especially in more exposed gardens. Earth up soil around the base of the stems and insert canes around the edge of the blocks, joining them with string to form a flexible frame.

5 Checking cobs

In order to enjoy the cobs at their sweetest it is important to check they are ripe before harvesting. A good indication is when the tassels emerging from the cobs begin to turn brown. Gently peel back the outer leaves of the cobs to check the maturity of the kernels.

6 Harvesting

The cobs should be picked as soon as they are mature – they turn starchy and lose sweetness if left on the plant too long. Twist off the cobs when they are ready and eat them as soon as possible, as the sugar levels start falling almost immediately. Picked cobs keep best if the outer leaves are not removed, and can be kept in a fridge for a few days until needed. Surplus cobs can be frozen if necessary.

Firmly twist the ripe cobs *from the plants - you can expect each plant to produce two cobs.*

Sweetcorn

1 'Indian Summer' This heritage variety produces kernels that can be either yellow, white or brown, which gives the cobs a multi-coloured appearance. It grows best in warmer areas.

2 'Minipop' This variety is grown for its baby cobs, picked at finger-size. It is planted more closely than conventional varieties; the plants may bear more than one stem, giving a larger crop.

3 'Lark' Cropping from late summer onwards, this variety bears tender, thin-skinned kernels that can be eaten cooked or raw. It is reliable and a good choice for cooler areas.

4 'Sundance' This variety produces large cobs, 20cm (8in) long, packed with sweet-tasting kernels. It is a reliable early-maturing variety with shorter stems, suitable for cooler regions.

5 'Butterscotch' With shorter stems than many varieties, 'Butterscotch' is 1.5m (5ft) tall, and suitable for more exposed sites. It matures early, bearing sweet cobs that freeze well.

6 'Lapwing' This variety gives a large crop of well-filled cobs in late summer and early autumn. The bright yellow kernels are sweet-tasting and tender, and are carried in large cobs.

7 'Mirai 003' Producing smallish cobs, 15cm (6in) long, filled with especially sweet and tender kernels that can be eaten cooked or raw, this variety crops well even on poorer soil.

8 'Swift' This is an early variety that produces large cobs filled with sweet-tasting, thin-skinned kernels. It is a reliable variety with sturdy stems, and crops well in cooler regions.

9 'Northern Extra Sweet' This variety crops especially early, so it is ideal for areas with shorter summers. The plump kernels are sweet and tender, and are packed into cobs 20cm (8in) long.

Other varieties
'Bodacious'
'Early Xtra Sweet'
'Extra Tender Sweet'
'Mirai Bicolour'
'Prelude'

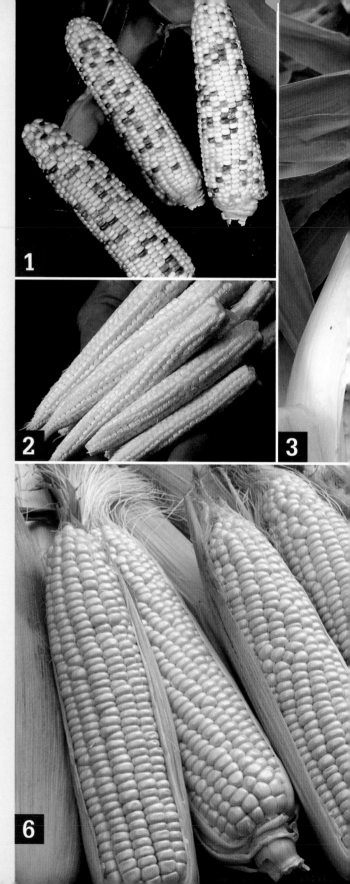

STEP-BY-STEP Kohl rabi

This unusual-looking vegetable is a type of brassica, and is closely related to the more familiar crops, cabbages and Brussels sprouts. Instead of its leaves however, it is grown for its mild-tasting "bulbs" – which are actually swollen stems – and it is growing increasingly popular with gardeners. It is very easy to grow, and is quick-maturing, and can be grown alongside slower crops to make best use of limited space. It will also crop in containers.

	SPRING	SUMMER	AUTUMN	WINTER
SOW				
HARVEST				

TIME TO HARVEST: 6–12 WEEKS

SUITABLE FOR: BEDS AND CONTAINERS

3M (10FT) ROWS
Plant 25cm (10in) apart

12 plants

CONTAINERS
3 plants in each

1 Getting started

Kohl rabi is raised from seed, which can be started off under cover in spring to give early crops a head start. Later crops can be sown directly where they will mature, and will be ready to harvest in a few weeks. As a brassica, kohl rabi is prone to club root disease, which can reduce yields (see p.242).

'Purple Danube' *bulbs are rounded with bright purple skins and crisp, white, and tender flesh.*

'Quick Star' *produces pale green bulbs that are slow to bolt and are relatively small.*

'Superschmelz' *bulbs are very large and sweet-tasting and can reach up to 20cm (8in) across.*

'Kolibri' *produces purple-skinned bulbs with sweet, juicy flesh. Good for a late harvest.*

Sow seeds under cover *until around mid-spring, after which they can then be sown directly outside. Sow into modules or small pots.*

Kohl rabi can be prone to bolting *if exposed to sudden drops in temperature, so it's important to harden off plants gradually before transplanting.*

2 Sowing under cover

Early sowings can be made under cover, ready to transplant outside later. Fill module trays with seed compost, firm, water well, and allow to drain. Then make a 1cm (½in) deep hole in each cell using a dibber or pencil, and place two seeds in each. Keep in a well-lit spot until emerged, then thin each cell to leave the stronger seedling. While hardening the seedlings off, warm the soil where they are to be planted with a plastic or fleece cloche.

TIP *Sow the seed successionally so that you don't end up with a glut.*

3 Sowing outside

During the summer months mark out drills 2cm (¾in) deep using the back of a hoe or rake, water the base well, and then sow a pinch of seed every 25cm (10in). Cover the seed over with soil and lightly water in. Germination takes a week or two; once the seedlings emerge, protect them from slugs with a light sprinkling of pellets.

Being fairly robust, *kohl rabi can be sown direct from late winter. Purple-skinned varieties are said to be more cold-tolerant than green-skinned types.*

Once the seedlings emerge, *thin them out to leave the strongest per cluster, or "station", at a final spacing of 25cm (10in) between plants.*

Kohl rabi are brassicas *and suffer with the same pests, including cabbage white butterfly caterpillars (see p.238). Net as a precaution.*

Hand-weed next to your plants *to prevent damaging the stems. Do this on warm day so that weed seedlings quickly shrivel.*

4 Routine care

Although kohl rabi is a fairly drought-tolerant crop, keeping the soil constantly moist will produce the most tender roots: growth checks result in woodier harvests. You may need to cover the plants with fine mesh to deter pigeons and cabbage white butterflies.

5 Weeding

Keeping plants weed-free is beneficial for many reasons: it will discourage competition for moisture, as well as keeping your plot tidy and discouraging the spread of disease, so pull out weeds next to the plants by hand and hoe between the rows.

6 Harvesting

Although some crops will be ready to harvest in around six weeks, the swollen stems will generally take around 12 weeks to fully develop. Kohl rabi can be harvested when they are between golf-ball and tennis-ball size – this is when they are most tender. Cut the bulb off whole, just above the root. You can store kohl rabi at the end of the season. Simply trim off the leaves and store in sand as for beetroot (see p.143).

Once the bulbs are large enough, *cut them off – the quality can deteriorate if they are left.*

STEP-BY-STEP Florence fennel

The fleshy stems of Florence fennel form a "bulb" with a mild aniseed taste, making this a unique flavour on the vegetable patch. In the kitchen, it can be used in a variety of dishes and is brilliant for braising, stir-fries, and soups. The key to successfully growing Florence fennel is to keep it growing quickly: ideally, sow it in summer and then water and feed it well. This highly ornamental vegetable is very content in small spaces.

	SPRING	SUMMER	AUTUMN	WINTER
SOW				
HARVEST				

TIME TO HARVEST: 12–22 WEEKS

SUITABLE FOR: BEDS AND CONTAINERS

3M (10FT) ROWS
Plant 30cm (8in) apart
11 plants

CONTAINERS
3 plants in each

1 Getting started

Don't be tempted to sow too early in the year as the plants may bolt: late spring should be the earliest. Florence fennel can be grown in containers of multipurpose compost but these must be large enough to provide constant moisture, so opt for a minimum diameter of 40cm (16in) for three plants.

'Zefa Fino' *produces large rounded bulbs that are slightly flattened. They have good flavour.*

'Perfection' *bears large bulbs with an excellent flavour and good bolt-resistance.*

'Finale' *bulbs are large and flattened in shape, with good bolt-resistance and excellent flavour.*

'Sirio' *produces large, rounded, slightly flattened white bulbs with an aromatic scent.*

Florence fennel seed should be sown *under cover from late spring onwards. Ensure that you keep the soil moist at all times.*

To discourage a glut, *sow Florence fennel seed little and often. Sow seed into a small number of pots each fortnight to encourage a steady supply.*

2 Sowing under cover

Sow this early crop under cover, into modules or small pots of moist seed compost. Seed can be unreliable so sow three seeds per module or pot, 1cm (½in) deep, and then thin to leave the strongest as the seedlings emerge. As soon as your module- or pot-raised plants begin filling their container with roots, start to harden them off gradually. Place them outdoors during the day and bring them back in at night for seven to ten days.

TIP *Choose a bolt-resistant variety as the plants are prone to premature flowering.*

3 Sowing outside

Seed can be sown directly later in the summer. Prepare the soil by digging it over to remove any weeds, firm it gently, and rake it level. Create drills 2.5cm (1in) deep, 30cm (12in) apart, and water thoroughly. Sow seed in clusters of three or four, cover with soil, firm gently, and water in lightly. Thin to leave the strongest seedling per cluster.

Sow clusters *of seeds every 30cm (12in). Cover the soil with newspaper to prevent it drying out: check daily and remove once seedlings appear.*

Transplant indoor-sown seedlings *30x30cm (12x12in) apart in midsummer. Enrich the soil well before planting and water plants in well.*

Plants need constant moisture *to develop good-sized "bulbs". In warm, moist conditions the plants can develop extremely rapidly.*

Earth up *around the maturing bulbs to block out sunlight and create whitened, tender crops. The mulch will also help to retain moisture.*

4 Routine care

Keep the plants well watered at all stages of growth. A dilute general-purpose liquid feed can be applied to containers or if your soil is light. Keep plants well weeded as they are quite upright in habit and so can't easily smother out weed growth.

5 Blanching stems

If you want the plants to develop to full size, water them regularly and then, when the bulb is approximately 8cm (3in) in diameter, earth them up, gently pulling soil up around the bases. This blanches the stems slightly and will give them a sweeter flavour.

6 Harvesting

You can harvest Florence fennel at all stages of growth – from "baby" bulbs that have a diameter of roughly 5cm (2in) and can be ready in as little as six weeks, to full-sized mature plants with bulbs approximately 15cm (6in) across, which will have been growing for between three and four months. The leaves can be cut in moderation at any time, or simply pull up the plants whole as they are needed.

Lift plants whole *or cut them off at the base with a knife – the cut stump will then re-sprout.*

STEP-BY-STEP Celery

While old fashioned "trenching" celery is challenging to grow, the introduction of self-blanching varieties has made this crop more manageable for gardeners. The blanched, tender stems are a key addition to summer salads, while the plants are also surprisingly hardy and will stand well into the autumn. Celery needs to be planted closely to exclude the light and blanch the stems, which makes this a highly productive crop for small spaces.

	SPRING	SUMMER	AUTUMN	WINTER
SOW				
HARVEST				

TIME TO HARVEST: 18 WEEKS

SUITABLE FOR: BEDS

0   1m   2m   3m

15 plants

3M (10FT) ROWS
Plant in a block, spacing them 20cm (8in) apart

1 Getting started

Celery requires a long growing season so seed is best started off under cover in early to mid-spring. If you don't have a suitable growing environment you can purchase plug plants later in the spring. Celery needs rich, well-drained soil, but isn't suitable for containers as it would need watering too frequently.

'Tango' *is an excellent self-blanching variety. Its tasty, long white stems resist bolting.*

'Celebrity' *stems are self-blanching with a good flavour and succulent texture.*

'Green Utah' *is a self-blanching type that produces tall, green, slightly variable stems.*

'Victoria' *produces fleshy, mid-green stems that are vigorous, tall, and self-blanching.*

To encourage germination, *seed should be kept moist and placed in a heated propagator for a couple of weeks, until they germinate.*

Celery seedlings *sown in early to mid-spring should be ready to transplant between late spring and early summer, once they are strong enough.*

2 Sowing under cover

Fill seed trays with seed compost, water well, and allow to drain. Sow the seeds thinly over the surface but don't cover them with compost, as they require light in order to germinate. Germination can be slow, so place the trays in a heated propagator set at 15°C (59°F). As soon as seedlings emerge and are large enough to handle, prick them out into individual module trays – don't let them get too big before this or they are more likely to bolt. Water the plants in well and continue to grow on in a warm position under cover – a growth check caused by cold weather can also induce bolting.

3 Planting out

When plants are about 15cm (6in) tall, harden them off ready for the move outside. Celery requires moist soil, so prepare the site before planting by digging in plenty of well-rotted organic matter, such as manure or garden compost, to improve moisture retention. Just prior to planting, work in a granular general-purpose fertilizer.

Place plants outdoors *during the day and bring them back under cover at night for a fortnight. As you begin to do so, prepare the soil for planting.*

Plant out in blocks, *20cm (8in) apart in each direction. This dense planting will encourage the celery to blanch. Water the plants in well.*

Keep the plants well weeded. *Remove any weeds that grow in and around the blocks of plants by hand to avoid damaging the stems.*

Applying an organic mulch, *5–6cm (2–2½in) deep around your plants can help to lock in soil moisture. It will also help keep down weeds.*

4 Routine care

Keep plants well watered during the growing season – plants bulk up during some of the hottest and driest months of the year and a lack of water can result in stringy, overly pungent stems. Prevent slugs attacking your plants with a thin scattering of pellets.

5 Blanching stems

If densely planted, the stems partially shade each other from the sunlight, causing them to become blanched. Plants on the outside of the bed are less shaded and will develop green stems; blanch these plants by wrapping their stems with cardboard.

6 Harvesting

You can begin harvesting celery in late summer, as soon as it is large enough. Water the plant well and then dig it up whole – stems can be broken off as needed. Cover plants with fleece or a blanket as nights become cooler, but harvest before frosty weather.

 TIP *Wash celery well before use, as soil can accumulate between the stems.*

Harvest plants whole with roots intact. They last better this way, as cut stems soon brown.

STEP-BY-STEP Celeriac

This unusual root vegetable has enjoyed something of a renaissance in recent years and has now graduated to almost gourmet status. What it lacks in looks, celeriac more than makes up for in flavour – a nutty, celery-like taste that is pleasantly mild. Roots can be grated raw, boiled and mashed, sliced and braised in milk and butter, or added to soups and casseroles. The long storage life of this crop makes it a great winter staple.

	SPRING	SUMMER	AUTUMN	WINTER
SOW				
HARVEST				

TIME TO HARVEST: 30 WEEKS

SUITABLE FOR: BEDS AND CONTAINERS

11 plants

3M (10FT) ROWS
Plant 30cm (12in) apart

CONTAINERS
3 plants in each

1 Getting started

Like other stem vegetables, celeriac prefers an open site and rich, well-drained soil, so dig in well-rotted organic matter in the season before planting. Celeriac is prone to bolting, so choose resistant varieties, plant out strong seedlings after cold weather has passed in late spring, and keep plants well watered.

'Monarch' bears strong yields of high quality white roots with good flavour that store well.

'Diamant' shows good resistance to bolting. Its medium-sized roots have excellent flavour.

'Prinz' is an exceptional variety, known for its flavour, bolt-resistance, and storage qualities.

'Mars' bears large, high-growing roots, that have dense, flavourful flesh and keep well.

Plants need a long season to mature fully, so sow seed under cover in early to mid-spring for autumn–winter crops.

After sowing, place the module trays in a propagator and ensure that they have a minimum temperature of 10°C (50°F).

Celeriac can be slow to emerge but once the seedlings are large enough to handle, thin to leave the stronger one per module.

2 Sowing seeds

For large roots it is best to sow celeriac seed under cover, to extend the growing season. Fill module trays with seed compost, firm gently, water well, and allow to drain. Make a hole in each cell 1cm (½in) deep and sow two seeds into it. Cover with compost and water lightly, then place in a propagator. Keep the compost moist to ensure germination. Grow on under cover and, once the seedlings' roots fill their modules, begin to harden them off.

TIP Plant out in late spring so celeriac can establish before the warmth of summer.

3 Planting out

Celeriac can be planted out into large containers of multi-purpose compost but the easier option is to grow the plants in the ground. Dig over the soil to remove any weeds – and add some well-rotted organic matter, such as garden compost, well before planting. Firm gently and plant seedlings 30x30cm (12x12in) apart. Water them in well.

Harden off the seedlings *by placing them outside during the day and under cover at night for a week to ten days.*

The swollen stems *will need plenty of space to develop, so ensure that seedlings are planted at least 30cm (12in) apart.*

Keep the plants *well watered. Celeriac is native to boggy areas, so these conditions need to be replicated in the garden.*

Plants can be mulched *with a 6–7cm (2½–3in) layer of compost, but do not let this come into contact with the exposed crown.*

Plants will form *small offshoots that compete with the main crown and impede its growth. Carefully remove these as you spot them.*

4 Feeding

To produce good-sized roots it is important to keep celeriac evenly watered at all stages of growth. Its food requirements are fairly low, so there is no need to apply heavy doses of fertilizer. A half-strength general-purpose liquid feed every fortnight will be sufficient.

5 Routine care

As plants develop, remove the outer leaves gradually so that the crown is exposed. Celeriac is relatively free from pests or diseases, but celery leaf miner may be a problem – it causes dry, blotchy patches on leaves. Pick off affected leaves and dispose of them.

6 Harvesting

Celeriac roots can be lifted from autumn onwards. It is best to lift the roots as and when you need them, as they will keep better in the ground than if lifted and stored. Gently insert a fork under individual plants when harvesting, and tease the root carefully out of the soil. During the winter months, cover the crowns with a mulch of straw to protect them from the worst of the weather.

Take care *not to damage the root when levering it out – insert the fork 10–15cm (4–6in) away.*

Perennial crops

For a long-term investment in the garden, dedicate some space to perennial vegetables. This group reliably emerges each spring, bears a crop, then dies back in autumn, year after year. Given an open, well-prepared site, asparagus crowns can crop for up to two decades, and the resulting spears are the ultimate in vegetable decadence. Globe artichoke hearts also deserve gourmet status and are held aloft architectural foliage that will match any garden ornamental. Add deliciously creamy Jerusalem artichokes and vibrant pink rhubarb to the group, and you complete a luxurious set of crops.

STEP-BY-STEP Asparagus

Asparagus is a luxury crop among vegetables, being available for just ten weeks of the year in a brief and uniquely delicious harvest from spring to early summer. It is easy to grow in most gardens but it takes time to establish. Be patient however, and you'll be rewarded for the next 20 years with an annual supply of succulent shoots, or "spears", fresher than any you can buy. Asparagus is a great long-term investment, but not ideal for small plots.

	SPRING	SUMMER	AUTUMN	WINTER
PLANT				
HARVEST				

PLANTING TO HARVEST: 2–3 YEARS

SUITABLE FOR: BEDS

7–8 plants

3M (10FT) ROWS
Plant out 40cm (16in) apart

1 Getting started

Asparagus can be raised from seed in spring if you want lots of plants and are happy to wait for them to grow large enough to crop. The quicker option is to buy as young plants, either bare-root to plant out from late winter, or as pot-grown specimens that you can plant at any time if you keep them well watered.

'Gijnlim' *is an early-cropping variety that gives a reliable harvest of thick green spears.*

'Connover's Colossal' *is a traditional variety, grown for its high yield and good flavour.*

'Jersey Knight' *gives a good crop of thick, flavoursome stems. It is a modern variety.*

'Purple Pacific' *bears attractive purple-flushed spears that are sweeter than many green types.*

Asparagus plants *grow in the same position for up to 20 years, so prepare the soil well before planting and remove all perennial weeds.*

Mounding the soil *at the base of the planting holes helps ensure good drainage. This isn't needed if your soil is light and sandy; the holes can be flat.*

2 Planting out

Bare-root asparagus plants are known as "crowns", and should be planted as soon they are available in spring. Before planting, prepare a hole or trench 30cm (12in) wide, 10cm (4in) deep, and mound up the base so it slightly lower than the soil surface. Spread the "crowns" out on top of the mound so that the central growing point is at soil level, with the roots below. Fill the hole with soil, firm it in gently, and water the plants in well.

TIP *Avoid berry-bearing female plants, which give a smaller crop than males.*

3 Growing on

Mulch new plants with well-rotted organic matter, such as garden compost, after planting and apply some granular general purpose fertilizer. Keep plants well-watered and weeded during their first year. The plants take time to establish and should not be harvested during their first year, then only lightly in their second.

Ferny asparagus growth *makes an attractive backdrop in the garden. If space is limited, plant it at the back of your ornamental borders.*

Mulching plants *with organic matter helps retain moisture and suppresses weeds. The mulch also releases nutrients to your plants.*

Check plants every few days *to cut the young spears at their best. These grow very quickly and soon become tough and inedible.*

4 Routine care

Established plants are drought-tolerant and only need watering in very dry spells. Mulch plants in autumn with organic matter, and apply granular general purpose fertilizer in spring and again after harvesting. The tall foliage may need support on windy sites.

5 Harvesting

Once fully established – after 3 years – plants can be harvested each spring for about ten weeks. Cut all spears, thick and thin, as this encourages more to develop. Slice them off just below soil level using a sharp knife, once they are roughly 20cm (8in) tall.

Overwintering plants

After harvesting the shoots for ten weeks, stop cutting and allow the plants to develop their "fern"– their tall, feathery top growth. Allow them to grow on all summer, giving the plants time to bulk up and recover. The "fern" will turn yellow and die back in autumn, at which point it should be cut off at the base.

STEP-BY-STEP Globe artichokes

As attractive as they are tasty, these eye-catching perennial plants produce a mass of architectural foliage before bearing tasty, thistle-like flowerheads. This makes them just as comfortable in the flower garden as the vegetable patch. Quality not quantity is the name of the game, as each plant only bears a few heads. However, the artichoke "scales" are absolutely delicious braised and then individually dipped into hollandaise sauce.

	SPRING	SUMMER	AUTUMN	WINTER
PLANT				
HARVEST				

PLANTING TO HARVEST: 64–68 WEEKS

SUITABLE FOR: BEDS

0　　　　　1m　　　　　2m　　　　　3m

2 plants

3M (10FT) ROWS
Plant 1.5m (5ft) apart

1 Getting started

Globe artichoke plants can be grown from seeds or "offsets" of existing plants (see step 3) but the simplest method is to buy pot-raised seedlings from garden centres or nurseries. You may find that this limits your selection as the varieties available are often quite restricted, so don't rule out the other two methods.

'Gros Vert de Laon' is best propagated from offsets to give flavourful, attractive round heads.

'Green Globe Improved' is a reliable, vigorous plant that bears firm, tasty heads.

'Purple Globe' yields small dark heads that are very tasty, but can be variable in quality.

'Concerto' bears attractive, spineless purple heads that have an excellent flavour.

For larger quantities of plants, sow into seed trays. Ensure that the seeds are sown at a depth of 2cm (¾in) and 2cm (¾in) apart.

Once the seedlings have their first true leaves they can be pricked out and potted on. Plant each seedling in its own pot so that it has sufficient space.

2 Sowing seeds

Raising globe artichokes from seed in early to mid-spring will provide plants that will crop in their second year – remove any heads that develop this first growing season. Fill a 9cm (3½in) diameter pot with seed compost, water it well, and allow it to drain. Make holes 2cm (¾in) apart and 2cm (¾in) deep using a pencil or dibber, and then drop a seed into each. Cover over with more compost, water lightly, and place in a heated propagator.

TIP — Dig in plenty of well-rotted manure and apply fertilizer before planting.

3 Planting out

Harden off seed-raised plants in late spring. Offsets can be propagated at this time, too: gently lift an established plant, cut off a section that is complete with roots and leaves using a sharp knife, and transplant it immediately to its new position. Plant both offsets and seed-raised plants with a spacing of about 1.5m (5ft).

Harden off globe artichoke plants *by placing them outside for seven to ten days, but bringing them back under cover overnight.*

Blackfly may be a problem, *and will swarm flower buds and stems. Wash them off by hand or apply an appropriate insecticide.*

Harvest globe artichokes whole, *while they are still young and tight. You may get a secondary crop after the main head has been cut.*

4 General care

Keep plants well watered until established, so that they develop a strong root system. Ultimately plants become extremely drought-tolerant and won't require additional irrigation, but these first two months are an exception. Remove any weeds that appear.

5 Harvesting

The largest bud will be at the tip of the spike; smaller ones often develop later on any sideshoots. Harvest each artichoke once it is a good size but before the scales begin to open and the purple flowers appear. Cut with a knife or secateurs as the stalks are very tough.

Overwintering plants

After harvesting, cut the stems back to ground level. The plants are quite hardy but severe winters can kill them, especially if the soil is wet. Apply a thick mulch of bracken, bark, or straw to protect them: cut back all the artichoke leaves and lay your mulch on top. The mulch can be dug into the soil in spring.

STEP-BY-STEP Jerusalem artichokes

Towering above other vegetables in the garden, this perennial relative of the summer sunflower bears attractive, bright yellow flowers. They are grown for their delicious knobbly tubers, which are harvested in autumn and are usually expensive to buy. Jerusalem artichokes are very easy to grow and can form a sizeable clump in a season – they are best confined or they may become invasive. Unsuitable for containers, they are best grown on larger plots.

	SPRING	SUMMER	AUTUMN	WINTER
PLANT				
HARVEST				

TIME TO HARVEST: 30–36 WEEKS

SUITABLE FOR: BEDS

11 plants

3M (10FT) ROWS
Plant 30cm (12in) apart in a grid pattern

1 Planting tubers

Jerusalem artichokes are planted as bare tubers, which can either be bought from seed suppliers – or from the supermarket if you don't want a named variety. Before planting in early spring, prepare the site by digging it over to remove weeds. Plant each tuber 15cm (6in) deep and space them 30cm (12in) apart each way. Large tubers can be cut into two or three sections, as long as each one has a distinct growing bud. Cover with soil and water the tubers in.

Plant the tubers into individual holes with the growing point, which is usually swollen and slightly pointed, facing upwards.

Tubers can be started off in pots if your soil is too wet to work in early spring. Keep them outside and plant out as soon as conditions allow.

The new shoots grow quickly in spring but protect them from slug damage with a sprinkling of pellets. Mature growth is less vulnerable.

Developing plants form dense clumps and may compete with each other for moisture. Water regularly until they reach full height - 3m (10ft).

2 Routine care

Shoots will appear after a few weeks. Once these are 20–30cm (8–12in) high, earth up soil around the plant to help support the growing stems. Keep plants well watered, especially during dry periods, otherwise tubers will become extremely knobbly and small. On lighter soils, apply a thick mulch to help retain moisture. Weed young plants until growing strongly – they will then out-compete most neighbouring plants.

TIP *If your garden is exposed, use this crop as a productive summer windbreak.*

3 Providing support

Jerusalem artichoke stems are sturdy but may need supporting as they reach full height. Insert tall canes around the edge of the clump or bed, about 1.8m (6ft) high, and tie string around them to form a flexible frame. This will also help keep plants tidy. Cut back any stems that are damaged by the wind using secateurs.

Larger clumps may withstand the wind *but it's worth providing support as a precaution. Damaged plants will still crop, but less freely.*

The flowers are attractive, *and if your plants are in a prominent position, compromise your harvest a little by leaving a few to open.*

Once they have been cut back, *the stems will act as a marker, showing you where to dig for tubers during the winter months.*

4 Removing flowers

In late summer, cut back the tall stems to 1.5m (5ft) high to prevent them rocking in the wind and loosening the tubers. At the same time, maximize the yield by removing all the flowers, which otherwise divert energy away from the developing tubers.

5 Cutting back

As the leaves begin to turn yellow in autumn, the plants start to take nutrients down the stems to store in the tubers, indicating that they are nearly ready to harvest. Once the leaves begin to yellow or fall, cut the stems to below 30cm (12in) in height.

6 Harvesting

Jerusalem artichoke tubers should be lifted as required. Since they have relatively thin skins and will not store very well, they are best left in the ground and then dug up as needed. Any tubers left in the ground will re-grow the following year, so if you plan on growing another crop in that position, thoroughly dig over the site to make sure you remove them all at the end of the winter.

Use the tubers fresh *during winter – they are cold-hardy and their flavour improves after frost.*

STEP-BY-STEP Rhubarb

Although often thought of as a fruit because it is used in desserts, this crop is actually a vegetable, and is incredibly easy to grow. The enormous leaves have their own architectural merit in the ornamental garden but the pink-flushed stems are really what rhubarb is about. Best harvested young and tender, these can be made into jams, tarts, chutneys and, of course, crumbles. Mixed with sugar and perhaps a little root ginger, the taste is just sublime.

	SPRING	SUMMER	AUTUMN	WINTER
PLANT				
HARVEST				

PLANTING TO HARVEST: 16–25 MONTHS

SUITABLE FOR: BEDS

0   1m   2m   3m

3 plants

3M (10FT) ROWS
Plant at least 1m (3ft) apart

1 Getting started

Rhubarb is best bought as a young plant and grown on – it can be raised from seed, but plants grow very large and few people want more than one. Plants are available bare-root to plant between autumn and spring. Pot-grown plants can be planted at any time providing they are kept well-watered afterwards.

'Champagne' *produces long, red-tinged stems that have a sweet, sharp flavour, ideal for cooking.*

'Timperley Early' *is an early variety that is good for forcing. It has thick, juicy red stems.*

'Victoria' *gives a later, sweet-tasting harvest, and is a good choice to grow in cooler regions.*

'Cawood Delight' *gives a smaller crop of richly-flavoured and coloured stems.*

Plant pot-grown plants *at the same depth as they were in their pots; bare-root plants should be planted with the crown level with the soil.*

Bare-root plants *are particularly susceptible to drying out during dry spells, even in autumn and spring. Keep moist and mulch as a precaution.*

2 Planting

Before planting, prepare the site thoroughly by digging in plenty of well-rotted organic matter, such as garden compost or manure, especially if your soil is light. Rhubarb is a long-lived crop, so also take care to remove any perennial weeds (see p.236). Dig a hole large enough for the roots, then plant, firm in gently and water well. Plants should be kept well-watered and weeded during their first year, until fully established.

TIP	*Rhubarb will tolerate light shade, so make use of these areas.*

3 Routine care

Mulch plants in spring with well-rotted organic matter but avoid piling it around the crown, as this can encourage decay. Older, congested plants can be divided in autumn to promote healthy new growth. Lift the plant with as much root as possible, split it into sections with a spade, and replant only one or two vigorous outer shoots.

Mulching around plants with straw *helps to retain moisture and keeps the stems clean by preventing soil from splashing up onto them.*

Forced stems *are blanched in the darkness within the forcer. Only force the earliest stems and allow later ones to develop normally.*

Harvest the stems *while young and tender but always wear gloves as the leaves are poisonous. Discard the leaves and only use the stems.*

4 Forcing stems

Rhubarb can be "forced" to give an earlier harvest by placing a "forcing pot" or an upturned bucket over the plant before it emerges. The new stems then grow up into the dark forcer, making them sweet and tender. Remove the forcer after two weeks of harvesting.

5 Harvesting

New plants can be harvested after their first year. Harvest by sliding your index finger or thumb down the curved centre of a stem until you reach the base, then gently twist to remove. Harvest until midsummer, after when stems become tough and stringy.

Growing on

The plants need time to recover after cropping, so leave them to grow from midsummer onwards. Cut out any stems that develop flowers and remove any yellowing leaves as they occur. In autumn, cut the plant to the base and mulch well with organic matter. Although poisonous to eat, the spent growth is safe to compost.

Culinary herbs

Growing fresh herbs can be very productive, even in smaller plots, giving a steady supply of leaves and stems that will add flavour to your home-grown fruits and vegetables. Grow as wide a selection as you have space for, whether in beds, baskets, or containers, and experiment with different flavour combinations. Mint is a classic partner for new potatoes and peas, but try it with broad beans or strawberries and you'll be hooked. Annual and perennial herbs are brilliant for their abundant summer leaves but also grow evergreen species, such as bay and rosemary, that will ensure a continuous supply right through winter.

STEP-BY-STEP Annual herbs

Growing annual herbs from seed is easy and rewarding and will provide you with exciting new flavours to use in the kitchen. You can obtain a good crop from even a tiny space as they don't require a dedicated bed and can be planted alongside your other crops, or in mixed beds or containers. Crops such as basil, dill, coriander, and parsley – which is grown as an annual – are ideal for pot cultivation, where the free-draining environment suits them perfectly.

	SPRING	SUMMER	AUTUMN	WINTER
SOW				
HARVEST				

TIME TO HARVEST: 10–14 WEEKS

SUITABLE FOR: BEDS, CONTAINERS, AND GROWING BAGS – UNDER COVER OR OUTSIDE

15–30 plants

3M (10FT) ROWS
Plant 10–20cm (4–8in) apart

CONTAINERS
5–7 plants in each

1 Getting started

Annual herbs generally prefer rich, well-drained soil, so if you are growing them directly in the ground, dig in some well-rotted organic matter and horticultural grit before planting. Give containers and windowboxes a warm, sunny spot – place them close to the kitchen for easy access during cooking.

Basil is excellent with tomatoes or in pesto. It is commonly green, but red forms are available.

Parsley has both flat- and curly-leaved forms. It is useful in cooking and as a garnish.

Dill produces feathery leaves with a delicious mild aniseed flavour. It makes a useful garnish.

Coriander leaves and seeds have a distinctive flavour and are used in a variety of cuisines.

Sow seed under cover from early spring, but check individual seed packets as the timings vary for different herbs.

Once the seedlings emerge, prick them out to 5cm (2in) apart, so that they have more space to grow on.

Once seedlings are 15cm (6in) tall, harden them off. Transplant directly, or plant in containers, a windowbox, or hanging basket.

2 Sowing under cover

Fill pots or trays with compost, water well, and allow to drain. Sow your herb seeds thinly on top, cover with a 0.5cm (¼in) layer of compost, water lightly, and place in a propagator. Once seedlings are large enough to handle, thin them or prick out. When larger, ease the compost out and gently split it into clumps, each containing three or four seedlings. Plant each clump in a larger pot of compost, water in well, and grow on under cover.

TIP	Pinch out the growing tips regularly to delay leafy herbs from flowering.

3 Sowing outside

Alternatively, your herbs can be sown directly into garden soil. Choose a well-drained, sunny spot and dig this over lightly to remove any weeds. Firm gently and rake level, then create drills 1cm (½in) deep, water these well and then sow seeds thinly along the base. Cover with more soil, firm gently, then lightly water in.

Herb seed can be sown *directly in the ground from spring onwards, but check the seed packets as the timings vary between different herbs.*

Once the young herb seedlings appear, *carefully thin them out to 10–20cm (4–8in) apart, depending on the variety you have sown.*

Keeping your herbs well watered *will encourage rapid, tender growth, which is ideal for eating raw or cooked, and will delay flowering.*

Keep plants well weeded *to reduce competition for nutrients, light, and water. Pull out weeds by hand when young.*

4 Watering

Keep the herbs well watered – pay particular attention to those planted in containers, as these will dry out more quickly than those planted in the ground. Annual herbs generally don't need any extra feeding, but if leaves begin to look a bit yellow, give them an dose of dilute liquid fertilizer.

5 Routine care

Keep the plants well weeded. Basil will initially create a single stem but will then naturally branch out to form a bushy habit – speed up this process by pinching out the growing tip. Parsley, coriander, and dill naturally form a rosette of leaves. Protect plants against slugs with a light scattering of pellets.

6 Harvesting

Leaves can be harvested as soon as they are large enough, although it's important not to over-crop the plants as this will impede their growth – take just a few leaves from each plant at any one time. Herbs such as basil and coriander are particularly fast-growing, so you may want to make two or three sowings throughout the spring and summer to ensure a fresh succession of tender leaves.

Treat plants as cut-and-come-again crops, *snipping the leaves for use as they are required.*

STEP-BY-STEP Perennial herbs

Perennial herbs range from low creeping plants to large shrubs, and can either be planted around the garden or given their own dedicated bed. Most also grow well in containers, allowing you to keep them within easy reach of the kitchen for handy picking. Rosemary, sage, and thyme are all valuable ingredients, and as they can be used either fresh or dried, you can enjoy them all yearlong. Grow plenty to ensure a constant supply.

	SPRING	SUMMER	AUTUMN	WINTER
PLANT				
HARVEST				

TIME TO HARVEST: 4–16 WEEKS

SUITABLE FOR: BEDS AND CONTAINERS

11 plants

3M (10FT) ROWS
Plant out 30cm (12in) apart

CONTAINERS
3–8 plants in each

1 Raising new plants

Perennial herbs are widely sold but if you want several plants they are easy to propagate yourself. For lots of new plants, sow seeds into pots or trays, following the instructions given on the packet (once established, fennel and chives will seed themselves freely). Many creeping herbs can be propagated easily as the spreading stems often have roots; these can be cut off, potted up and grown on as new plants. Established clumps of herbs, such as mint, can also be lifted and split in spring or autumn.

Sowing plants from seed *is ideal if you want lots of the same herb – maybe for a herb lawn.*

Rooted stems *provide a quick and easy way to propagate your own herbs. Just pot them up.*

New herb plants *may be large enough to divide when you buy them. Split them into clumps.*

Herb planters *are ideal for growing a mixture of plants. Plant up the side pockets first.*

Choose a mixture of plants *that creep or grow upright to make best use of the space.*

Fill with compost *to within 5cm (2in) of the rim of the pot to make watering easier.*

2 Planting a container

Most perennial herbs grow well in containers, and smaller plants can be planted together in the same pot. Many originate from the Mediterranean region and require good drainage, so plant them using a 50:50 mix of sharp grit and soil-based compost. Give them a sunny position and keep plants well watered. Feed only occasionally to avoid encouraging soft, flavourless growth.

TIP *Some perennial herbs can be short-lived, especially in cool, wet regions.*

3 Planting in beds

Most herbs prefer well-drained soil so dig in some horticultural grit if yours is heavy, and choose a sunny site. These herbs rarely require additional feeding, so don't improve the soil with compost or fertilizer, which encourages weak growth. Mint is a spreading herb, and can be invasive, so is best planted into a large container sunk into the soil.

Dig planting holes *deep enough so that new plants are at the same depth as in their pots.*

Tease the roots out *away from the root ball to encourage them to grow into the surrounding soil.*

Water plants well *until they establish fully. Pinch out the tips to encourage bushy new shoots.*

Water young plants well – *once established many herbs, such as sage, rosemary and marjoram, are relatively drought-tolerant.*

Harvest leaves and shoots *using scissors or a sharp knife. Harvest plants regularly to encourage a constant fresh crop of new growth.*

4 Routine care

Most herbs need little care once established. Stake taller plants as they grow and weed low-growing herbs so they don't become smothered. Cut back mint and marjoram in summer to encourage tasty new growth, and remove any flowers that appear, which encourage plants to become tough.

5 Harvesting

Once well established, perennial herbs can be harvested as and when required. Pinching out the growing points of mint, thyme, sage, rosemary and marjoram will not only provide you with the most tender foliage, it will also encourage plants to bush out. Individual chive leaves can be cut when needed.

Drying herbs

Perennial herbs are ideal for drying to use throughout winter. In summer, cut and bunch the stems, and hang them up somewhere warm, dry, and well-ventilated. Shorter stems, such as thyme or marjoram, can be laid out on wire racks. Dry the growth over 24–48 hours, and store it away from the light in sealed containers.

Perennial herbs

1 Parsley The leaves of this popular and useful herb are excellent used in a variety of dishes; curly types (shown) have a milder flavour than flat-leaved types. This is a biennial herb that flowers and dies after two years. Sow seed each spring to ensure a constant supply.

2 Fennel Not to be confused with Florence fennel (see pp.172–173), almost every part of this herb has a culinary use. It is also highly decorative and does not look out of place in ornamental borders, if you don't have space for a herb bed.

3 Chives If you do not have a lot of space, this attractive herb makes an excellent container plant. A member of the onion family, chives have a mild onion-like flavour. The flowers and stems can be used in a range of dishes.

4 Rosemary Both highly ornamental and extremely versatile, this is a must-have shrubby herb for any garden. The aromatic leaves are excellent for use in stews, particularly with lamb. It needs a sunny site and well-drained soil to grow well, but can be short-lived.

5 Thyme There are upright and creeping forms of this staple herb, but the former are easier to harvest for culinary use. The flavourful leaves are excellent for use in a variety of dishes and should be harvested as required. It is a good choice for pots.

6 Sage There are several varieties of this shrubby herb, including purple-leaved and variegated forms. It has many uses in the kitchen, and is easy to grow when given a sunny spot and well-drained soil. It can be short-lived in cooler areas.

7 Marjoram Closely related to oregano, this versatile, creeping herb can be used in a variety of dishes; the leaves have a spicy flavour and are often used in Mediterranean cuisine. The flavours are strongest when planted in a sunny position.

8 Mint This vigorous upright herb can be invasive when planted in borders, and is best contained to a large pot sunk into the soil. There are several varieties to grow, including peppermint and spearmint. All are easy to grow in most soils.

9 Bay Commonly seen trained into standards or as topiary, a bay tree makes a great addition to the garden. The evergreen leaves are used in many dishes. It is easy to grow but can become large, so keep plants well pruned.

Vegetable crop planner

Use this table to check when to sow and harvest your vegetable crops. The precise timings will vary slightly for each region, so adjust them to suit your own site and conditions. Sow most seeds under cover until the risk of frosts has passed.

CROPS		SPRING			SUMMER			AUTUMN			WINTER		
		EARLY	MID	LATE	EARLY	MID	LATE	EARLY	MID	LATE	EARLY	MID	LATE
TOMATOES	SOW	░	░										
	HARVEST					█	█	█	█	█			
PEPPERS	SOW	░											░
	HARVEST						█	█	█				
CHILLIES	SOW	░											░
	HARVEST					█	█	█	█				
AUBERGINES	SOW	░											
	HARVEST						█	█	█	█			
PEAS	SOW		░	░									
	HARVEST			█	█	█	█	█	█				
RUNNER BEANS	SOW			░									
	HARVEST				█	█	█	█	█				
FRENCH BEANS	SOW			░	░								
	HARVEST					█	█	█	█				
BROAD BEANS	SOW	░	░							░			
	HARVEST					█	█						
CUCUMBERS	SOW		░										
	HARVEST					█	█	█	█				
COURGETTES	SOW		░										
	HARVEST					█	█	█	█	█			
SUMMER SQUASHES	SOW		░										
	HARVEST					█	█	█	█				
WINTER SQUASHES	SOW		░										
	HARVEST							█	█	█			
PUMPKINS	SOW		░										
	HARVEST							█	█	█			
SUMMER/AUTUMN CABBAGES	SOW	░	░	░									░
	HARVEST						█	█	█	█			
WINTER/SPRING CABBAGES	SOW	░	░	░									
	HARVEST									█	█	█	█
CAULIFLOWERS	SOW	░	░	░					░	░			
	HARVEST	█	█	█	█	█	█	█	█	█	█	█	█
CALABRESE	SOW		░	░									
	HARVEST					█	█	█	█				
SPROUTING BROCCOLI	SOW	░	░										
	HARVEST	█	█	█						█	█	█	█
BRUSSELS SPROUTS	SOW	░	░	░									
	HARVEST	█	█	█						█	█	█	█
KALE	SOW		░	░									
	HARVEST	█	█							█	█	█	█
LETTUCES	SOW	░	░	░	░	░	░	░	░				
	HARVEST		█	█	█	█	█	█	█	█	█	█	█
CUT-AND-COME-AGAIN SALAD	SOW	░	░	░	░	░	░	░	░				
	HARVEST			█	█	█	█	█	█	█	█		
MICROGREENS	SOW	░	░	░	░	░	░	░	░	░	░	░	░
	HARVEST	█	█	█	█	█	█	█	█	█	█	█	█
ORIENTAL GREENS	SOW				░	░	░	░					
	HARVEST					█	█	█	█	█			

CROPS		SPRING			SUMMER			AUTUMN			WINTER		
		EARLY	MID	LATE	EARLY	MID	LATE	EARLY	MID	LATE	EARLY	MID	LATE
SPINACH	SOW												
	HARVEST												
SWISS CHARD	SOW												
	HARVEST												
CHICORY	SOW												
	HARVEST												
ENDIVE	SOW												
	HARVEST												
WATERCRESS	SOW												
	HARVEST												
RADISHES	SOW												
	HARVEST												
BEETROOTS	SOW												
	HARVEST												
CARROTS	SOW												
	HARVEST												
TURNIPS	SOW												
	HARVEST												
PARSNIPS	SOW												
	HARVEST												
SWEDES	SOW												
	HARVEST												
POTATOES	SOW												
	HARVEST												
ONIONS	SOW												
	HARVEST												
SHALLOTS	SOW												
	HARVEST												
SPRING ONIONS	SOW												
	HARVEST												
LEEKS	SOW												
	HARVEST												
GARLIC	SOW												
	HARVEST												
SWEETCORN	SOW												
	HARVEST												
KOHL RABI	SOW												
	HARVEST												
FLORENCE FENNEL	SOW												
	HARVEST												
CELERY	SOW												
	HARVEST												
CELERIAC	SOW												
	HARVEST												
ASPARAGUS	SOW												
	HARVEST												
GLOBE ARTICHOKES	SOW												
	HARVEST												
JERUSALEM ARTICHOKES	SOW												
	HARVEST												
RHUBARB	SOW												
	HARVEST												
ANNUAL HERBS	SOW												
	HARVEST												
PERENNIAL HERBS	SOW												
	HARVEST												

GROW YOUR OWN Fruit

STEP-BY-STEP Strawberries

This fruiting perennial is extremely popular, and deservedly so, with varieties that produce sweet home-grown fruit from late spring until the first frosts. Strawberries grow well in containers and growing bags, making them perfect for small spaces. They are also easy to propagate from plantlets or "runners", and can even be brought under cover to give out-of-season crops. Strawberries are delicious cooked or can be enjoyed just dipped in sugar.

	SPRING	SUMMER	AUTUMN	WINTER
PLANT				
HARVEST				

FLOWERING TO HARVEST: 2–4 WEEKS

SUITABLE FOR: BEDS, CONTAINERS, HANGING BASKETS, AND GROWING BAGS

0   1m   2m   3m

11 plants

3M (10FT) ROWS
Plant 30cm (12in) apart, 45cm (18in) between rows

GROWING BAGS
5 plants in each

1 Getting started

There are two main types of strawberries to consider. Summer-fruiting varieties are the tastiest, and crop in a single flush in early- to midsummer. "Everbearers" or "perpetual" strawberries produce their main harvest in summer, then give smaller subsequent flushes of fruit until the first frosts.

'Pegasus' is a summer-fruiting variety that freely produces large, sweet, glossy berries.

'Symphony' is a late-season, summer-fruiting variety, grown for its heavy crops.

'Konona' is a summer-fruiting variety that is easy to grow and yields huge, succulent berries.

'Flamenco' is a perpetual variety that crops heavily from midsummer to autumn.

To plant bare-root *strawberries, spread the roots out and work soil in between them. Ensure the crown of the plant sits on the soil surface.*

Planting through plastic sheeting *will suppress weeds and help conserve moisture during summer. It will also keep the developing fruit clean of soil.*

2 Planting

Strawberries are available to buy bare-root or pot-grown. They can be planted in spring, although planting in autumn gives them longer to establish before their first crop. Choose a sunny, sheltered spot, and if planting directly into the soil, fork it over to remove all weeds. Plant out leaving 30cm (12in) between plants, 45cm (18in) between rows. If planting into growing bags, space plants 20cm (8in) apart; in containers and baskets, 10cm (4in).

TIP *When planting into containers and baskets, use soil-based compost.*

3 Mulching

As plants growing in beds begin to flower, lay a mulch of straw or hay around them, so the developing fruits are held away from the soil. This keeps them clean and ensures good air movement, which deters rotting. Alternatively, use "collars" around individual plants or plant through weed-control fabric or plastic sheeting.

Straw was traditionally *used to lift the fruits from the soil, hence straw-berry. It is cheap and easy to buy, and can be composted at the end of the season.*

Ready-made strawberry collars *are ideal if you only have a few plants, and can be used from year to year. You can easily make your own.*

Support bird netting *above the plants with canes so they cannot grow through it, otherwise the fruit would be vulnerable to attack.*

Pick the fruit *when it is fully coloured but still firm to the touch. Leave the leafy crown in place until you come to eat the fruit to prevent decay.*

4 Protecting fruit

Birds will attack the fruit as soon as they start turning red; erect net tunnel cloches over rows or create small cages over single plants. Check netting regularly and keep it taut, so birds don't become entangled. Protect against slugs and snails by lightly spreading slug pellets around plants.

5 Harvesting

As soon as individual strawberries turn completely red, pick them. Do this by pinching them off at the stalk, rather than holding the fruit itself, to prevent bruising which may subsequently rot. The berries will keep fresh for a few days in a cool place, or can be frozen either cooked or raw.

6 Propagating plants

After fruiting, summer varieties send out stems or "runners", with small plantlets along their length, which can be used to propagate new plants. Plunge small pots of compost near the plantlets and peg them into it. Keep them moist until autumn, when they will be well-rooted. Cut the joining stem and grow the new plant on.

Anchor the plantlet *in place with a bent piece of thick wire, such as from an old clothes hanger.*

STEP-BY-STEP Raspberries

You could be forgiven for thinking that raspberries demand a lot of space – visit any allotment and you'll see vast rows of canes. However, for the majority of people this actually yields too much fruit, and a smaller plot can easily meet your needs. Both summer- and autumn-fruiting varieties are available, allowing you to enjoy sweet, tart berries from midsummer right through to the first frosts. Raspberries are also very easy to grow.

	SPRING	SUMMER	AUTUMN	WINTER
PLANT				
HARVEST				

FLOWERING TO HARVEST: 6–8 WEEKS

SUITABLE FOR: BEDS AND CONTAINERS

11 plants

3M (10FT) ROWS
Plant 30cm (12in) apart, with 1m (3ft) between rows

CONTAINERS
3 plants in each

1 Getting started

Summer-fruiting raspberries crop from mid- to late summer; autumn varieties fruit late summer to mid-autumn, so plant both for the longest harvest. Summer raspberries should be planted against horizontal wires held 40cm (16in) and 80cm (32in) above the soil. Autumn-fruiting varieties can be grown free-standing.

'Joan J' *is a spine-free, autumn-fruiting variety that stays compact, and is suitable for containers.*

'Cascade Delight' *is a free-fruiting summer raspberry, with large, rich-tasting berries.*

'Tulameen' *fruits in summer over several weeks, and is a good choice for cooler areas.*

'All Gold' *crops in autumn, producing tasty yellow fruits that won't stain your fingers.*

Plant new canes *in evenly spaced rows and provide suitable support for summer-fruiting varieties. Water and mulch after planting.*

New shoots develop in spring *after which the original woody cane can be cut to the ground. This will encourge further new canes to develop.*

2 Planting

New canes are best planted in late autumn, although winter and early spring are also an option, and are generally sold bare-root or root-wrapped – lifted from the ground and bundled together loosely in compost. They prefer moist, free-draining soil, and will tolerate a little shade. Dig well-rotted organic matter into the soil in autumn, allowing it to settle for two weeks before planting. Space the canes 30cm (12in) apart in rows at least 1m (3ft) apart.

TIP *Plant new canes to the same depth as the original soil mark on their stems.*

3 Routine care

Keep plants well watered during summer and apply a tomato feed to promote a good harvest. Mulch near the base of the canes with composted organic matter to help retain moisture. As soon as the fruit starts to ripen, protect it from birds. Cover plants with a cage or using netting, held taut using canes to prevent snaring birds.

Water the plants *once or twice a week during summer, even daily on light soils during dry spells. Avoid splashing the stems, which spreads disease.*

Birds soon attack summer raspberries *but are less interested in autumn-fruiting varieties, which can even be grown without protection.*

Handle the berries *carefully when picking as they are easily damaged. Squashed fruits quickly spoil so are best eaten straightaway.*

After pruning in summer *tie the new shoots onto the horizontal wires. These will fruit the following year, then be replaced by new growth.*

4 Harvesting

The berries are ready as soon as they turn fully red or yellow, depending on variety, and pull easily from the plant leaving the central "plug" behind. Avoid picking on rainy days as wet fruit does not store well. Check your plants daily to ensure you harvest them at the perfect point of ripeness.

5 Summer pruning

Summer-fruiting raspberries are pruned straight after the last fruits have been harvested, cutting the fruited canes to the base. Younger, unfruited stems, produced that summer, should be tied to the wires in their place. Keep only the strongest and tie them in 10cm (4in) apart, to fruit next year.

6 Winter pruning

Autumn raspberries are pruned in winter by cutting all the canes down to the ground. Alternatively, to encourage a staggered harvest the following year, cut a few canes down by only half their height in winter. The half-height canes will then produce an earlier crop in early to midsummer. These fruited canes can then be pruned out completely after harvesting.

Cut autumn-fruiting canes *closely to the ground. New shoots will appear in late spring.*

STEP-BY-STEP Blackberries and hybrids

Gone are the days of small berries, carried on large, vicious plants – modern blackberries have been bred to have fewer thorns, often none, and to give generous harvests of plump, tasty fruit. They are also easier to look after, being more disease resistant, and some new varieties fruit on new growth, making them easier to prune. Plant one of the blackberry hybrids as well, like a loganberry or a tayberry, and you've a jam-maker's dream.

	SPRING	SUMMER	AUTUMN	WINTER
PLANT				
HARVEST				

FLOWERING TO HARVEST: 6–8 WEEKS

SUITABLE FOR: BEDS AND BORDERS

0	1m	2m	3m

1–2 plants

3M (10FT) ROWS
Plant 1.5–3m (5–10ft) apart, according to variety

1 Getting started

There are many blackberry varieties to choose from, with different qualities to suit your garden, including thornless plants. Hybrid berries are more distinct and result from cross-breeding blackberries with raspberries, or with other related hybrids. For the largest selection, try mail order specialist fruit nurseries.

Blackberries *fruit from mid- to late summer, and there are many varieties, some being thornless.*

Loganberries *are best cooked with plenty of sugar and taste like sharp raspberries.*

Boysenberries *are a hybrid of a loganberry and blackberry, but taste much like the latter.*

Tayberries *are a cross between a raspberry and a blackberry, and have delicious fruit.*

Make a hole *slightly wider than the root ball so you can firm the soil in after planting. Lower the plant in to check the depth.*

Remove the plant *from its container and tease out the roots to help them establish. Spread out the those of bare-root plants.*

Pot-grown plants *are planted level with the soil surface; bare-root plants to the depth of the soil mark on their stems.*

2 Planting

Blackberries and hybrid berries are clambering shrubs, so plant them against a wall or trellis, or a system of posts and wires, where their stems can be trained. To help them establish quickly, they are best planted in autumn, while the soil is still warm and moist, although they can be planted through winter into spring. Choose a sunny site, dig over the soil to remove weeds, and mix in organic matter and granular, general purpose fertilizer. Water well after planting.

TIP *Blackberries can be very thorny, so wear gloves when handling the plants.*

3 Routine care

Keep plants well watered during summer and mulch them using well-rotted organic matter. If you use manure for this, no additional fertilizer is needed, otherwise apply a balanced granular fertilizer in spring. Net the fruits as they ripen, but ensure it's held taut to prevent birds becoming snagged. Check the netting regularly for gaps.

A fruit cage is ideal *for protecting plants from birds, if you have space. If not, make a temporary structure using nets and canes until harvest.*

Unlike raspberries, *blackberries and the hybrid fruits pull off whole when picked, and don't leave behind a white core. The juice can stain fingers.*

To help prune out fruited canes, *untie them from their supports first. This will make the cut stems easier to untangle and remove.*

4 Harvesting

Depending on variety or hybrid, the fruit ripens from mid- to late summer. For maximum sweetness, wait until the berries are fully coloured when it should be easy to pull them from the plant. Unless the fruit is to be eaten straightaway, pick the fruit while it is still firm and only during dry weather.

5 Pruning

Most blackberries and hybrids fruit on canes in their second year. These should be cut to the base in autumn after fruiting, while new unfruited canes that fruit in their first year of growth are tied in. New varieties that fruit on new summer growth can be cut completely to the ground in winter.

6 Training

Although these plants can be left to ramble, they are more manageable, and take up less space, when trained against horizontal wires. In winter or early spring, train unfruited stems produced the previous summer to form a fan either side of the crown. This will encourage flower and fruit formation. Also tie in new season stems during summer to fruit next year.

Supporting wires *can be attached to walls and fences, or stretched between two upright posts.*

STEP-BY-STEP Red- and whitecurrants

If you've ever seen a well-grown red- or whitecurrant bush, you'll know how bountiful they are – they can literally drip with fruit. Combine this with the fact that they are easy to grow, even in moderate shade, that the fruits freeze well and have a high pectin content (making them good for jams and jellies), and you can understand their value. They can also be planted against walls if space is limited, making them ideal for smaller gardens.

	SPRING	SUMMER	AUTUMN	WINTER
PLANT				
HARVEST				

FLOWERING TO HARVEST: 10–12 WEEKS

SUITABLE FOR: BEDS AND CONTAINERS

3M (10FT) ROWS
Plant bushes 80cm (32in) apart
4 plants

CONTAINERS
1 plant in each

1 Getting started

Red- and whitecurrants grow best in acid soil but will tolerate alkaline conditions. Plants are widely available grown in pots throughout the year, or can be bought bare-root during autumn. If deciding between the two types, redcurrants generally have a sharper, more acidic flavour; whitecurrants are sweeter tasting.

'Jonkheer van Tets' *is an early variety that produces a large crop of rich, bright red fruit.*

'Red Lake' *produces long "strigs" of berries from midsummer. It is a large, vigorous shrub.*

'Blanka' *bears masses of sweet-tasting, pale yellow berries from mid- to late summer.*

'Versailles Blanche' *fruits in midsummer, giving a plentiful harvest of sweet-tasting berries.*

Plant redcurrants *so that all growth emerges from a short stem, or "leg", growing just above the soil surface.*

Fill in between the roots *of bare-root plants with soil; lightly tease out the roots of pot-grown bushes before planting them.*

Firm the soil after planting *to remove air pockets, ensuring the "leg" remains above the soil surface. Water in well.*

2 Planting

Currants establish best when planted between autumn and spring, although container-raised plants can be planted at any time if kept moist. They can be planted in sun but also don't mind a shady spot, and can be grown against north- or east-facing walls. Prepare the site by digging it over, space plants 80cm (32in) apart, then water well and mulch after planting. In smaller plots, plant into 30cm (12in) wide pots filled with soil-based compost.

TIP *Plant pot-grown currants so the compost is level with the soil surface.*

3 Routine care

Plants will require regular watering in their first summer to encourage root establishment. After this time they become more drought-tolerant, but yields will be improved by regular watering in spring and summer. Mulch plants with rich, well-rotted organic matter, and apply a dressing of high-potash fertilizer every spring.

Organic mulch retains moisture, *reducing the need for watering during summer. It also degrades, providing nutrients for your plants.*

Birds love berries *and will repeatedly raid your plants. Net individual bushes or consider buying a fruit cage if you have several plants.*

Harvest the fruit *as whole strigs rather than as individual berries, as they are small and easily squashed. Eat the berries fresh or freeze them.*

4 Protecting fruit

Birds will quickly strip plants of berries, so erect a cage of netting over your bushes as soon as the fruits begin to ripen. (Whitecurrants turn from green to translucent white as they near maturity). Ensure all netting is pulled taut to prevent birds becoming trapped. Remove the net after harvesting.

5 Harvesting

The berries are carried on trailing stems or "strigs", which should be picked whole once all the berries along them have ripened. Pull the strig from the stem using your fingers, or carefully snip them with scissors. Check your bushes every three or four days to harvest the berries at their best.

6 Pruning

Currants fruit at the base of stems that are at least a year old. In early- to midsummer, prune the new stems back to 10–15cm (4–6in) to encourage more fruiting spurs, which will also help the fruit ripen and improve airflow. In winter, cut the pruned stems back to two buds above the cluster of buds at the base of the stem; also remove any dead or diseased growth.

Pruning encourages fruiting spurs *that develop in clusters at the base of cut stems.*

STEP-BY-STEP Blackcurrants

These robust bushes fruit in summer, producing long stems or "strigs" of intensely flavoured berries that are excellent when eaten fresh, and even more so when cooked and made into preserves, pies, and summer cordials. Blackcurrants are easy to grow and very reliable, even in colder areas, making them a good choice for beginner growers. They are also easy to prune, and modern varieties are prone to few pests or diseases.

	SPRING	SUMMER	AUTUMN	WINTER
PLANT				
HARVEST				

FLOWERING TO HARVEST: 10–12 WEEKS

SUITABLE FOR: BEDS AND CONTAINERS

3 plants

3M (10FT) ROWS
Plant bushes 1m (3ft) apart

CONTAINERS
1 plant in each

1 Getting started

Blackcurrants are widely sold throughout the year growing in containers, but they can also be bought and planted bare-root in autumn. Bare-root plants are cheaper than pot-grown, which is helpful if you want several. Look out for modern, disease-resistant varieties, which have 'Ben' in their names.

'Ben Sarek' *is a free-fruiting variety, with a compact habit, and is ideal for smaller plots.*

'Ben Connan' *fruits from midsummer, and gives a good harvest of sweet, juicy berries.*

'Ebony' *is an early variety that crops from early summer. Its sweet fruit are especially large.*

'Ben Lomond' *crops freely from midsummer onwards, producing large, sweet berries.*

Using a guide, *plant slightly deeper than the soil mark on the stem, or deeper than the level of the compost if pot-grown.*

Backfill the hole *with soil, making sure you don't leave large air pockets, and that the plant is upright.*

Firm in gently *and water in well. New blackcurrant bushes should be pruned immediately after planting.*

2 Planting

The best time to plant is between autumn and spring, when the soil is warm and moist, although currants can also be planted in summer if watered well. Choose a sunny, sheltered site and weed it thoroughly. In smaller plots, plant into 30cm (12in) pots, filled with soil-based compost. Water plants in, mulch well, then cut back all the stems to soil level to promote sturdy new growth. If planting more than one bush, space them at least 1m (3ft) apart.

TIP *Plant blackcurrants deeply, so all the stems emerge directly from the soil.*

3 Routine care

Keep young plants well watered throughout their first summer; established plants are more drought tolerant but will crop better if watered during dry spells. Mulch plants in spring with well-rotted organic matter, such as garden compost, and apply a granular high-nitrogen fertilizer. Use canes to support fruit-laden stems.

Mulch plants *to help retain moisture in summer and to suppress weeds. As the mulch slowly breaks down, it releases nutrients to your plants.*

Support stems *using a simple frame of string and canes to prevent them collapsing and snapping under the weight of summer fruit.*

Use netting *to prevent birds from targetting your berries. Keep it as taut as possible.*

Ripe berries *pull easily from the bush but handle them carefully as they are easily bruised.*

4 Protecting fruit

Birds can strip plants of berries in a matter of days. As soon as fruit begins to ripen, protect your plants with netting, secured at the base to prevent birds sneaking in underneath. Check the nets regularly for gaps.

5 Harvesting

Older blackcurrant varieties ripen as individual berries and can be picked one-by-one when ready. Modern types are only picked when the whole stem, or "strig", is ripe. The strigs should pull easily from the bush.

6 Pruning

Blackcurrants fruit mainly on one-year-old stems, and can be pruned and picked at the same time. Cut stems that have fruited to the base, leaving the new growth to crop next summer. Plants pruned this way must be fed well in spring with a high-nitrogen fertilizer. An alternative method is to allow the stems to fruit for three years, then prune them to the base in winter. This leads to larger plants, less suited to smaller gardens.

Pruned growth

STEP-BY-STEP Gooseberries

This easy-to-grow fruit gives its main crop in early summer, but by using the tart fruitlets thinned in late spring in your kitchen, you can enjoy an even earlier harvest. There are culinary or dessert varieties to grow, while a few are dual-purpose and give you the best of both worlds. Gooseberries are reliable plants, and breeders are continually developing varieties with improved disease resistance, yield, and thankfully, fewer thorns.

	SPRING	SUMMER	AUTUMN	WINTER
PLANT	■		■	■
HARVEST		■		

FLOWERING TO HARVEST: 10 WEEKS

SUITABLE FOR: BEDS AND CONTAINERS

0   1m   2m   3m   0   30cm

3 plants

3M (10FT) ROWS
Plant bushes 1m (3ft) apart

CONTAINERS
1 plant in each

1 Getting started

Young plants are widely sold pot-grown throughout the year, or bare-root during autumn. There are many varieties to choose from, with fruit that varies in size, shape, taste, and colour. However, some have sharp thorns, which you may want to avoid, especially in smaller gardens or if you have children.

'Careless' *is suitable for eating fresh or cooking, and gives an early crop of tasty green fruits.*

'Invicta' *fruits from early- to midsummer, giving a heavy crop to cook or enjoy fresh.*

'Lancashire Lad' *needs good soil to crop well. It bears rich red fruit from mid- to late summer.*

'Hinnonmäki Röd' *is easy to grow and ideal for beginners. Its sweet-tasting fruit mature red.*

Dig a planting hole that is wide enough *so the roots of bare-root plants can be spread out fully, and to fit the root ball of pot-grown bushes.*

Plant bare-root bushes *at the same depth as the soil mark on their stem; plant pot-grown plants so the compost is level with the soil surface.*

2 Planting

Pot-grown gooseberries can be planted throughout the year if watered well, although they establish best between autumn and spring. Unlike many fruits they tolerate shade, so can be planted in north- or east-facing spots. Dig the soil over to remove all weeds, mix in some general purpose fertilizer, and water well after planting. Space plants 1m (3ft) apart. They can also be planted in 30cm (12in) wide containers, filled with soil-based compost.

TIP *Keep plants in pots well watered, especially when in flower or fruit.*

3 Routine care

Water new plants well in their first year, and water established plants during dry spells. In spring, mulch plants with rich organic matter, and add granular balanced fertilizer on sandy or chalky soils. Protect the fruit from birds with fruit cages, or use netting held taut to stop birds becoming caught up. Check regularly for gaps.

Wire hoops and bent canes *are ideal for supporting bird netting. The structure can be left in place all year or removed after fruiting.*

4 Harvesting

To encourage larger fruits, thin the developing gooseberries in late spring, and rather than waste them, use the sharp-tasting "thinnings" for cooking. Aim to take no more than half the berries and, if your bush has yet to establish a regular heavy cropping pattern, only take one quarter. Once the remaining berries are fully ripe they can be harvested. Hold the berry by the stalk when picking, not the fruit, to avoid bruising and subsequent decay. Pick over your bushes regularly as they ripen to enjoy the fruit at its best.

Picked gooseberries keep in the fridge *for about a week. For longer-term storage, they also freeze well and can be made into preserves.*

5 Pruning

Gooseberries fruit at the base of stems that are at least one-year-old, and are pruned twice a year. In midsummer, cut back all of the growth produced this year to 15–20cm (6–8in) long. In winter, these pruned stems should be cut back further to leave only two or three buds each, which will then bear fruit next year. At the same time, remove any dead, diseased, or damaged growth, as well as any thinner stems that look likely to droop on the ground once laden with fruit.

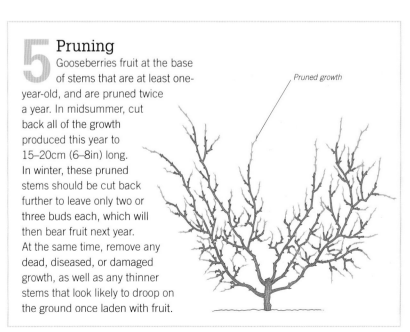

Pruned growth

STEP-BY-STEP Blueberries

Incredibly popular with gardeners, blueberries were one of the first crops to be crowned with "superfruit" status, thanks to their naturally high levels of health-giving antioxidants and vitamins. Give them an acid or "ericaceous" soil and plenty of water during the growing season, and blueberries yield abundantly. Even if you don't have an acid soil, they crop very successfully in pots, which also makes them an ideal choice for smaller gardens.

	SPRING	SUMMER	AUTUMN	WINTER
PLANT				
HARVEST				

FLOWERING TO HARVEST: 8–10 WEEKS

SUITABLE FOR: BEDS AND CONTAINERS

4 plants

3M (10FT) ROWS
Plant bushes 75cm (30in) apart

CONTAINERS
1 plant in each

1 Getting started

Blueberries are usually sold growing in pots and can be bought throughout the year. The plants are self-fertile, so you only need one in order to produce a crop. However, they fruit more freely when cross-pollinated, so if you have space, grow two or more varieties that flower at the same time.

'Spartan' produces a generous crop of large, richly-flavoured berries in midsummer.

'Bluetta' is a compact variety, ideal for smaller gardens or for growing in containers.

'Jersey' is a tough variety for cooler areas. It must be grown near another variety to fruit.

'Herbert' fruits in late summer, giving a good crop of sweet, intensely flavoured berries.

Ease the plant from its pot and lightly tease the roots away from the root ball to encourage them to grow into the surrounding soil.

Plant the blueberry so the surface of the compost is level with the surrounding soil. Firm it in gently and water well.

Mulch with organic matter, such as composted pine bark, that will help provide and maintain acid soil conditions.

2 Planting

Blueberries prefer boggy growing conditions, and are best planted between autumn and spring when the soil is moist. They also require acid soil with a pH below 6 (use a soil testing kit if you are unsure), otherwise they must be grown in containers filled with lime-free, ericaceous compost. Before planting, incorporate composted bark into the soil and add sulphur chips to help maintain a low pH. Water plants in well and keep moist.

TIP To help retain moisture, line porous pots with pierced plastic sheeting.

3 Routine care

Mulch plants in containers and borders in spring with well-rotted organic matter, such as leaf mould or composted bark. Water plants well throughout the year, especially when in flower and fruit, particularly those in pots. Feed plants every fortnight from early- to midsummer with a liquid fertilizer suitable for ericaceous plants.

Use rainwater to water *blueberries to help maintain the soil acidity. Tap water commonly contains lime, especially in hard-water areas.*

Acid-loving plants *require specific fertilizers, which are widely available as liquid or granular feeds. Don't use conventional fertilizers.*

Handle bird nets carefully when picking, *as the ripening fruit is easily knocked off.*

Blueberries ripen over a long period, *and each shrub can be in fruit for several weeks.*

4 Protecting fruit

Blueberries flower in early spring and it's worth protecting them against frost damage in cold areas with garden fleece. The ripening fruit should also be protected in summer from birds using taut netting or a fruit cage.

5 Harvesting

Check your plants every few days to ensure you pick the berries at their best. Ripe fruits pull easily from the plants but are also easy to squash, so take care. The berries are best enjoyed fresh but any surpluses can be frozen.

6 Pruning

Blueberries are usually grown as freestanding bushes, whether in containers or beds, and are pruned just before they come into leaf in spring. Remove lower branches and weak growth, along with any dead, diseased, or damaged shoots. The fruit is predominantly produced on one-, two- and three-year-old wood. Using sharp loppers or a pruning saw, remove less productive, older stems completely at the base.

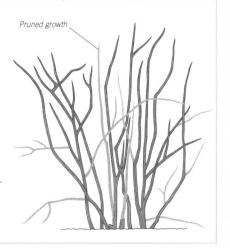

Pruned growth

STEP-BY-STEP Apples

Apples are the classic garden fruit and the availability of dwarfing rootstocks means even those with limited space can embrace apple growing. There are hundreds of different varieties to try. Many are widely available, each with individual flavours, disease-resistance, and cropping potential. Many can also be grown in containers, and for those with more time and experience, apples can be trained into neat, space-saving shapes, such as cordons.

	SPRING	SUMMER	AUTUMN	WINTER
PLANT				
HARVEST				

FLOWERING TO HARVEST: 14–20 WEEKS

SUITABLE FOR: BEDS AND CONTAINERS

4 plants

3M (10FT) ROWS
Plant trees 75cm (30in) apart, depending on rootstock

CONTAINERS
1 plant in each

1 Getting started

Container-grown apples are available all year, whereas bare-root trees can be bought between autumn and early spring. In order to produce fruit, apple flowers must be pollinated and you will need at least two compatible trees unless there is already one growing nearby. Seek advice before deciding what to buy.

'Cox's Orange Pippin' *is a well-known dessert variety that bears richly flavoured fruit.*

'Greensleeves' *fruits freely in early autumn, bearing sweet, sharp-tasting dessert apples.*

'James Grieve' *is a dessert apple that fruits in early autumn. It grows well in cool, dry areas.*

'Bramley's Seedling' *is a renowned culinary apple. It requires another variety for pollination.*

Lay a guide *across the hole and plant at the same depth as the soil mark on the tree, or the top of the compost if pot-grown.*

Backfill the hole *with soil, improved with organic matter, and firm it gently with your foot. Water the plant in well.*

Stake the tree, *before or after planting, and attach it using an adjustable tree tie. Nail the tie to the stake to hold it in place.*

2 Planting

Apple trees establish better if planted while dormant from autumn to spring, although pot-grown trees can be planted at any time if kept moist. Choose a sunny, sheltered site, dig over the area to remove weeds, and fork in organic matter if the soil is sandy or heavy clay. Pot-grown and bare-root trees are planted using the same technique (see left). Apples on dwarfing rootstocks can also be planted into large containers of soil-based compost.

TIP	*Trees should be established after two years, when the stake can be removed.*

3 Routine care

Water trees well, especially in their first year, to help them establish. Trees in pots will always require regular watering; those in the ground will need less water once fully rooted. Mulch trees in spring with organic matter and apply a high-potash granular fertilizer. Apply liquid high-potash feed to pot-grown trees in spring and early summer.

Regular watering is vital *for new apple trees. Watering mature apples during dry periods will also help to prevent the disease bitter pit (see p.244).*

Rich organic mulch *helps suppress weeds, retains moisture, and keeps the roots cool. It also releases nutrients as it degrades, feeding the tree.*

To help new trees establish, *remove any fruit that sets during its first year. Later crops can be allowed to develop once thinned.*

Harvest apples *regularly to enjoy them at their best. Early varieties are best eaten fresh, later varieties can be stored if you have a surplus.*

4 Thinning out

To encourage full-sized apples, thin the developing fruits in early summer, once they reach walnut-size. Thin dessert apples to one or two fruits per 15cm (6in); culinary types to one every 15cm (6in). Always thin out the central fruit, which can grow abnormally.

5 Harvesting

When fruits are ready to harvest, gently cup them in your hand, lift and twist. The fruit should come away without pulling, if it doesn't, try again in a day or so. Pick over the tree regularly as the fruit ripens, and handle the apples carefully to avoid bruising them.

6 Pruning

Established apples are pruned in winter. Prune out congested growth from the centre to maintain an open shape, and remove dead, diseased, damaged, and weak growth. Cut back new stems by half to encourage fruit-bearing spurs at their base. Older fruit spurs should be thinned if they are congested.

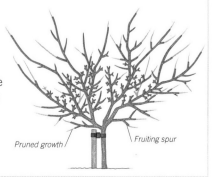

Pruned growth

Fruiting spur

STEP-BY-STEP Pears

A perfectly ripe pear is a real indulgence, but picked fruits can go past their peak in a matter of days, so it's something you're unlikely to fully appreciate until you grow your own. Pears are as easy to grow as apples, and there are culinary and dessert varieties to choose, offering different flavours, textures, and storing qualities. The trees prefer a sheltered spot, and where space is limited, they can be planted and trained against walls and fences.

	SPRING	SUMMER	AUTUMN	WINTER
PLANT				
HARVEST				

FLOWERING TO HARVEST: 16–20 WEEKS

SUITABLE FOR: BEDS AND CONTAINERS

0   1m   2m   3m

4 plants

3M (10FT) ROWS
Plant trees 75cm (30in) apart, depending on rootstock

0   30cm

CONTAINERS
1 plant in each

1 Getting started

Pears are available in pots all year, or bare-root in autumn to early spring. You can also buy pre-trained trees to plant against walls. Most varieties must be pollinated before they will set fruit, so unless there are pear trees growing nearby, you will need to plant more than one. Seek advice for compatible varieties.

'Concorde' is easy to grow, has a good flavour, and stays compact. It is ideal for smaller plots.

'Doyenné du Comice' need a sunny spot but produces delicious fruit in mid-autumn.

'Beurré Superfin' crops in early autumn, bearing richly aromatic fruit. It is ideal for wall-training.

'Packham's Triumph' has richly flavoured fruit in mid-autumn. It grows best in a sheltered site.

To plant a pear tree in a pot, fill the bottom with soil-based compost and incorporate some slow-release fertilizer.

Tease out the roots of pot-grown trees and spread out those of bare-root plants. Fill around the roots with compost.

Make sure the tree is planted to the depth of the soil mark on the stem. Insert a stake for support and water it in well.

2 Planting

Pear trees flower in early spring and need plenty of sun to ripen the fruit, so choose a warm, sheltered site. Prepare the soil before planting by digging it over to remove weeds, and work in some granular general purpose fertilizer and organic matter. Once planted and staked, firm the soil gently, and water in well. Pears grown on dwarf rootstocks can also be planted in large containers, 60cm (24in) wide, filled with soil-based, John Innes No.3 compost.

TIP Protect the blossom with garden fleece at night; remove it during the day.

3 Routine care

Pears prefer to be kept moist, so water them well during their first year and during prolonged dry spells in the future. To help retain moisture and shade the roots, mulch around the trunk in spring with well-rotted organic matter, such as garden compost. Apply general purpose fertilizer in spring, followed by a high-potash feed in summer.

Water well *in summer, especially trees growing in containers. Don't allow trees to become dry while in flower or fruit, or the crop may be lost.*

High-potash feeds, *such as tomato fertilizer, encourage plants to flower and produce more fruit. Apply it as a liquid as the fruit develops.*

Pears naturally shed *some excess fruitlets in early summer, which is called "June drop". Wait until it has passed before thinning them further.*

Early varieties *are picked underripe, while still hard, to ripen indoors. Pick later varieties only when they are completely ripe.*

4 Thinning out

Trees can set a heavy crop, which should be thinned to promote full-size fruit. In midsummer, thin the fruitlets leaving one per cluster. As fruits swell, support heavily laden branches to stop them snapping.

5 Harvesting

Fruits will begin ripening from late summer, depending on variety. The best way to pick them is to cup a fruit in your hand, lift and twist. It should come away easily, without pulling, otherwise leave it a little longer.

6 Pruning

Established freestanding pear trees are pruned in winter. Prune out congested stems in the middle of the tree to maintain an open shape. Also remove any dead, diseased, damaged, and crossing growth. Cut back stems produced in summer by half their length to encourage spurs to develop at their base – these will fruit next year.

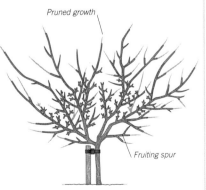

Pruned growth

Fruiting spur

STEP-BY-STEP Plums

Plums are deliciously sweet and juicy, and the trees fruit so freely that you're almost certain of a glut, providing ample material for jams, bottling, and freezing. Modern varieties grafted on dwarfing rootstocks are ideal for smaller gardens and can even be grown in containers. Plums, which includes damsons, gages, and bullaces, are very easy to grow and need little pruning. If you choose a self-fertile variety you will only need one tree to produce a crop.

	SPRING	SUMMER	AUTUMN	WINTER
PLANT				
HARVEST				

FLOWERING TO HARVEST: 14–16 WEEKS

SUITABLE FOR: BEDS AND CONTAINERS

3M (10FT) ROWS
Plant trees 1.5m (5ft) apart, depending on rootstock

2 plants

CONTAINERS
1 plant in each

1 Getting started

Bare-root trees can be bought and planted from autumn to mid-spring; those sold in pots can be planted at any time. Most varieties need to be cross-pollinated to set fruit, so you will need to plant two or more. Self-fertile varieties can be grown alone although crop better when pollinated by a suitable variety.

'Victoria' is the classic plum and gives a heavy crop of tasty purple-red fruit in late summer.

'Shropshire Damson' is self-fertile, so you only need one tree. It crops in early autumn.

'Oullins Gage' bears sweet, golden fruits in late summer that are good eaten fresh or cooked.

'Langley Bullace' crops freely in early autumn, producing sharp fruit for cooking.

Place a guide across the hole and plant at the same depth as the soil mark on the tree, or the top of the compost if pot-grown.

Backfill the hole working the soil in well between the roots of bare-root trees. Firm it gently as you go. Water the tree in well.

Attach the stake to the tree with an adjustable tie. Check all ties occasionally and remove the stake after two years.

2 Planting

Choose a sheltered, sunny site, dig it over to remove weeds, and work in well-rotted organic matter, such as garden compost, and add some high-nitrogen granular fertilizer. When planting, stake the tree, firm it in gently, and water it well. Plums can also be planted in containers, although they must be kept well-watered as they are sensitive to drought. Use a container at least 60cm (24in) wide, and fill it with soil-based, John Innes compost.

TIP Plums and gages can be eaten raw; use bullaces and damsons for cooking.

3 Routine care

Water trees well in the first year, and during dry spells in later years. Plums have relatively shallow roots and benefit from a thick mulch of organic matter in spring. They are especially hungry for nitrogen, which you can provide by mulching with well-rotted farmyard manure, which is rich in nitrogen, or apply a granular fertilizer.

New plum trees *need regular watering until well-rooted. Established trees can fend for themselves, except in dry spells or on sandy soils.*

Mulch trees *but leave the base of the trunk clear to prevent decay. Use well-rotted material that will release nutrients to the tree.*

Leave the developing fruitlets *into early summer, in case any drop from the tree naturally. Then thin them out to promote larger fruits.*

Harvest the fruits *regularly when they are ripe to enjoy them at their best. If necessary, underripe plums can be stored for a few days.*

4 Thinning out

Plum crops can be variable as frost can kill the early flowers. In milder years when the crop is good, thin the fruit to 5–8cm (2–3in) apart to encourage full-size plums. It will also help stop over-laden branches snapping.

5 Harvesting

Leave plums and gages to ripen fully so they are as sweet as possible; bullaces and damsons can be picked while quite sour. Watch out for wasps when picking and cover trees with muslin if they become a problem.

6 Pruning

Plums are pruned as little as possible to protect the trees from the fungal disease, silver leaf (see p.244). As soon as fruit is harvested, use a clean saw or loppers to remove any dead, diseased, or damaged growth, along with spindly or crossing stems. Then thin out the remaining branches, if necessary, to reduce congested growth.

Pruned growth

STEP-BY-STEP Cherries

Sweet cherries are a real treat when eaten fresh in summer, whereas sharp-tasting acid varieties are excellent for pies and preserves. Whichever you prefer, recent progress with dwarfing rootstocks and self-fertile varieties means that these are now exciting times for cherry lovers. Modern compact trees are easy to grow and are ideal for smaller gardens. Their small size also makes it easier to protect them against the fruit's traditional enemy – birds.

	SPRING	SUMMER	AUTUMN	WINTER
PLANT				
HARVEST				

FLOWERING TO HARVEST: 10–14 WEEKS

SUITABLE FOR: BEDS

0   1m   2m   3m

2 plants

3M (10FT) ROWS
Plant trees 1.5m (5ft) apart, depending on rootstock

1 Getting started

Pot-grown cherries are sold all year and can be planted at any time; bare-root trees are available to plant between mid-autumn and mid-spring. Self-fertile varieties set fruit if grown alone, so you only need one tree. Conventional varieties don't, and you'll need to plant two or more that flower at the same time for a crop.

'Lapins' *is a self-fertile sweet cherry that bears large fruit in midsummer that ripen almost black.*

'Morello' *is an acid cherry that crops from late summer into early autumn. It is self-fertile.*

'Sweetheart' *is a sweet cherry with dark berries. It must be grown near a second variety to fruit.*

'May Duke' *is a sweet cherry with the sharper taste of an acid variety. It crops in midsummer.*

Place a guide *across the hole and plant at the same depth as the soil mark on the tree, or the top of the compost if pot-grown.*

Backfill the hole *with soil, which should be improved with organic matter, firm it in gently with your foot, and water in well.*

Insert a wooden stake *and attach it to the tree using an adjustable tree tie; nail the tie to the stake to keep it in place.*

2 Planting

Sweet cherries require a sunny, sheltered site to grow well, acid types are less demanding and will even tolerate shade. To prepare the site before planting, dig over the soil to remove weeds, and fork in sharp grit or composted bark to improve heavier soils. Insert a stake alongside your tree, then firm the soil gently and water in well while planting. Although there are dwarf rootstocks available, cherries aren't ideal for growing in containers.

TIP *When choosing varieties, acid cherries are easier to grow in cooler regions.*

3 Routine care

Keep new trees well-watered during their first year, and water established trees in dry spells. Mulch in spring with well-rotted organic matter, ideally manure (if mulching with another material, provide additional feed by also applying general purpose fertilizer). To encourage a good harvest, feed the trees regularly in summer with a liquid high-potash feed, such as tomato fertilizer.

Cherries flower *in early spring when the blooms can be killed by frost. Cover with garden fleece but remove on mild days to allow pollination.*

Protect trees with netting, *securing it at ground level to prevent birds sneaking in underneath. Wasps also like cherries; take care when picking.*

Handle ripe fruits *gently to avoid bruising them. Cherries can be stored for up to a week if kept in an open plastic bag in the fridge.*

4 Protecting fruit

Cherries are notoriously favoured by birds and it is essential to net trees as soon as fruits show the first signs of colour – a cage of netting over individual trees is ideal. Keep nets taut and check them regularly for gaps.

5 Harvesting

Once the first fruits begin to ripen fully, cover the tree with a sheet of clear plastic to stop rain getting to the cherries. Ripe fruits can absorb moisture through their skins which encourages splitting and decay.

6 Pruning

To avoid the fungal disease silver leaf (see p.244), prune after fruiting, while the tree is still in leaf, but keep pruning to a minimum. To prune sweet cherries, only shorten over-long stems to keep the tree within bounds. To prune an acid cherry, cut one quarter of the fruited shoots back to the next branch, and remove any dead, weak, or damaged growth.

Pruned growth

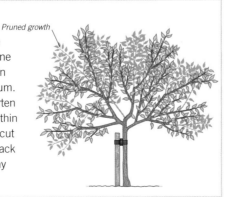

STEP-BY-STEP Peaches and nectarines

If given a sunny, sheltered spot, peach and nectarine trees make delicious talking points in the garden. One tree can yield a sizeable harvest of sugar-packed fruits, which have a characteristically heady perfume when ripe. Many modern varieties are extremely compact, which makes them ideal for smaller gardens, and also means they are easier to maintain. They also grow well in containers, allowing you to move them to the best spot possible.

	SPRING	SUMMER	AUTUMN	WINTER
PLANT				
HARVEST				

FLOWERING TO HARVEST: 16–20 WEEKS

SUITABLE FOR: BEDS AND CONTAINERS

1–4 plants

3M (10FT) ROW
Plant 75cm–3m (2½–10ft) apart, according to variety

CONTAINERS
1 plant in each

1 Getting started

Trees are available bare-root to buy and plant between mid-autumn and mid-spring; pot-grown trees can be bought and planted at any time. Dwarf forms are sold pot-grown, and are the only types suitable for growing on in containers. All trees are self-fertile, meaning you only need to grow one to set a crop.

'Peregrine' is a great peach variety for cooler areas and bears large fruit in midsummer.

'Garden Lady' is a dwarf peach, ideal for containers. It crops mid- to late summer.

'Fantasia' crops in late summer, producing large, delicious nectarines. It grows well in cool areas.

'Lord Napier' is a good nectarine for cooler sites. It bears large, tasty fruit in midsummer.

2 Planting

If planting in the ground, choose a sunny, sheltered site, such as near a south-facing wall or fence. Dig over the soil to remove weeds and incorporate some well-rotted organic matter. To plant in a container, use a pot 10cm (4in) wider than the original one, and plant into soil-based compost.

Use a cane to check the planting depth. Plant bare-root trees level with the soil mark on the stem.

Backfill the hole, holding the tree upright, and support it with a stake and adjustable tie. Water in well.

3 Routine care

Water trees during dry spells, mulch well, and apply high-potash fertilizer in spring. To prevent the flowers being killed by spring frosts, cover trees with garden fleece on cold nights, removing it on mild days so the blooms can be pollinated. To prevent peach leaf curl, shield trees from the rain until late spring with clear plastic sheeting. Move container-grown trees under cover to protect them from frost damage and rainfall.

Ensure insects can reach the flowers or use a soft paintbrush to pollinate them yourself by hand.

4 Thinning out

Trees often set a very heavy crop, which is best thinned to encourage fewer, but larger, fruits. Thin conventional varieties to about 15–20cm (6–8 in) apart once the fruits are the size of walnuts; fruit on dwarf trees should be thinned to 10cm (4in) apart. As the fruit ripens it often attracts wasps, so hang sugary traps among the branches.

Homemade wasp traps *filled with a sugary liquid are easy to make. Hang them in the trees near to developing fruits to lure wasps away.*

Thinning the fruit *helps concentrate the tree's energy so that the remaining fruit grow larger and are more likely to develop fully.*

5 Harvesting

Begin harvesting fruits as they ripen from midsummer onwards. Mature fruits will feel slightly soft to the touch and will release their characteristic scent. Ideally, leave the fruit on the tree to ripen as fully as possible, although you may find that wasp damage warrants picking earlier. To pick, cup the fruits in your hand and twist gently.

TIP *If necessary, underripe fruits will ripen indoors on a sunny windowsill.*

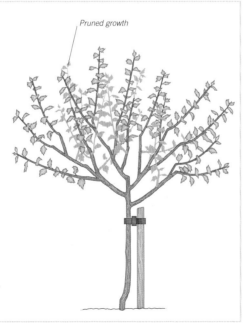

Peaches and nectarines *are the same species, and are grown and eaten the same way. The only difference is that peaches have fuzzy skins.*

6 Pruning

Peach and nectarine trees mainly fruit along the length of stems produced during the previous summer, and should be pruned annually to promote new growth. Immediately after harvesting the fruit in summer, remove one third of the fruited stems from established trees to leave a framework of healthy, well-spaced, branches. To help avoid the disease silver leaf (see p.244), avoid pruning peach and nectarine trees at any other time of year and use sterilized tools.

Pruned growth

STEP-BY-STEP Figs

Figs are a true taste of the Mediterranean, and although they need a sunny spot and take a long season to ripen fully, they give a good crop in most gardens. Left to their own devices, figs are large trees but they can be kept to a more manageable size by restricting their roots, which also encourages them to fruit more freely. In colder areas, figs can be grown in containers and protected during winter. They can also be wall-trained where space is tight.

	SPRING	SUMMER	AUTUMN	WINTER
PLANT				
HARVEST				

FLOWERING TO HARVEST: 32–40 WEEKS

SUITABLE FOR: BEDS AND CONTAINERS

3M (10FT) ROWS
Plant trees 1.5–3m (5–10ft) apart

1–2 plants

CONTAINERS
1 plant in each

1 Getting started

Figs are generally sold as container-grown plants, and establish best when planted in mid-spring. There are several varieties to grow although few are widely sold, so you may need to contact a specialist supplier. Fig flowers don't need to be pollinated in order to set fruit, so you only need to grow one tree.

'Brunswick' needs a mild site to crop well, and bears large, sweet figs in late summer.

'Panachee' produces unusual-looking striped fruit. It is best trained against a warm wall.

'Brown Turkey' is widely available and grows well in cool areas. It crops in late summer.

'Rouge de Bordeaux' produces delicious figs but needs a sheltered, warm spot to grow well.

Dig a hole and line the sides with stone slabs. To ensure good drainage, line the base with broken pots or stones to a depth of 20cm (8in).

Plant the tree at the same depth as it was in its pot, then backfill the hole with soil. Water the tree in well and hammer in a suitable tree stake.

2 Planting

If growing the tree directly in the soil, dig over the site to remove weeds, and incorporate sharp grit or composted bark (not manure) to ensure good drainage. To restrict the roots, create a planting pit, 60cmx60cm (24inx24in), and plant the tree into it (see left). To plant into a container, choose one at least 60cm (24in) wide and deep, place stones or pieces of broken pot in the base for drainage, and fill it with soil-based compost.

TIP Fig trees become more drought-tolerant once they establish fully.

3 Routine care

New figs should be watered in their first year but otherwise they thrive on neglect. Although the trees are fully hardy, the tiny fruitlets that overwinter from one year to the next (see below) can be damaged by frost. Cover freestanding and wall-trained trees with garden fleece if practical. The trees will benefit from annual pruning.

Fig trees grow well in pots *and can be brought under cover during winter in colder regions to protect the developing fruitlets.*

Remove any larger fruitlets in autumn. *Thinning them prevents the tree from wasting energy on fruits that won't reach maturity.*

Ripe figs soon spoil, *so eat them as quickly as possible to enjoy them at their best. Surplus fruit can be preserved or dried to eat later in the year.*

4 Thinning out

Our summers are too short for figs to ripen in one year. Instead, tiny fruitlets produced in late summer overwinter on the tree and mature the following summer. Any fruitlets larger than pea-size won't survive the winter however, and should be removed in late autumn by snapping them off.

5 Harvesting

It is important to let figs mature as fully as possible before picking them, as they won't ripen much further indoors. Ripe fruits hang downwards from the branch, sticky sap appears at their bases, and they soften and emit a slight scent; they will pull easily from the tree. Birds may target the soft, ripe fruits.

6 Pruning

Young trees only need pruning to keep them in shape. Older trees are pruned twice in spring to promote fruiting and a healthy shape. In early spring, cut out some of the older stems to encourage new growth. Then, in late spring, pinch out the tips of this new growth to promote the formation of new fruits.

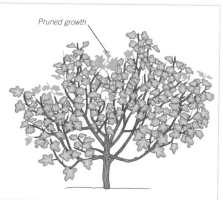

Pruned growth

Fruit crop planner

Use this table to check when to plant, prune, and harvest your fruit crops. Timings will vary for different regions so adjust accordingly to suit your own site and conditions. When planting bare-root trees and shrubs, water them well afterwards, even during winter.

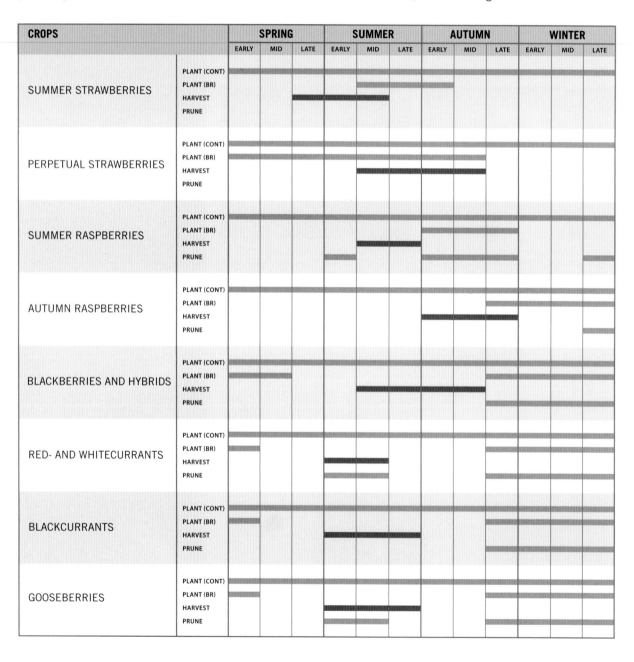

CROPS		SPRING			SUMMER			AUTUMN			WINTER		
		EARLY	MID	LATE	EARLY	MID	LATE	EARLY	MID	LATE	EARLY	MID	LATE
SUMMER STRAWBERRIES	PLANT (CONT) PLANT (BR) HARVEST PRUNE												
PERPETUAL STRAWBERRIES	PLANT (CONT) PLANT (BR) HARVEST PRUNE												
SUMMER RASPBERRIES	PLANT (CONT) PLANT (BR) HARVEST PRUNE												
AUTUMN RASPBERRIES	PLANT (CONT) PLANT (BR) HARVEST PRUNE												
BLACKBERRIES AND HYBRIDS	PLANT (CONT) PLANT (BR) HARVEST PRUNE												
RED- AND WHITECURRANTS	PLANT (CONT) PLANT (BR) HARVEST PRUNE												
BLACKCURRANTS	PLANT (CONT) PLANT (BR) HARVEST PRUNE												
GOOSEBERRIES	PLANT (CONT) PLANT (BR) HARVEST PRUNE												

KEY	CONT: CONTAINER-GROWN PLANTS
	BR: BARE-ROOT PLANTS

CROPS		SPRING			SUMMER			AUTUMN			WINTER		
		EARLY	MID	LATE	EARLY	MID	LATE	EARLY	MID	LATE	EARLY	MID	LATE
BLUEBERRIES	PLANT (CONT)	██	██	██	██	██	██	██	██	██	██	██	██
	PLANT (BR)	██									██	██	██
	HARVEST				██	██	██						
	PRUNE										██	██	██
APPLES	PLANT (CONT)	██	██	██	██	██	██	██	██	██	██	██	██
	PLANT (BR)	██									██	██	██
	HARVEST					██	██	██	██	██			
	PRUNE					██							
PEARS	PLANT (CONT)	██	██	██	██	██	██	██	██	██	██	██	██
	PLANT (BR)	██									██	██	██
	HARVEST					██	██	██	██	██			
	PRUNE					██	██	██					
PLUMS	PLANT (CONT)	██	██	██	██	██	██	██	██	██	██	██	██
	PLANT (BR)	██									██	██	██
	HARVEST					██	██						
	PRUNE			██									
CHERRIES	PLANT (CONT)	██	██	██	██	██	██	██	██	██	██	██	██
	PLANT (BR)	██									██	██	██
	HARVEST				██	██							
	PRUNE	██				██							
PEACHES	PLANT (CONT)	██	██	██	██	██	██	██	██	██	██	██	██
	PLANT (BR)	██									██	██	██
	HARVEST				██	██	██						
	PRUNE			██									
NECTARINES	PLANT (CONT)	██	██	██	██	██	██	██	██	██	██	██	██
	PLANT (BR)	██									██	██	██
	HARVEST				██	██	██						
	PRUNE			██									
FIGS	PLANT (CONT)		██										
	PLANT (BR)												
	HARVEST					██	██	██					
	PRUNE	██			██								██

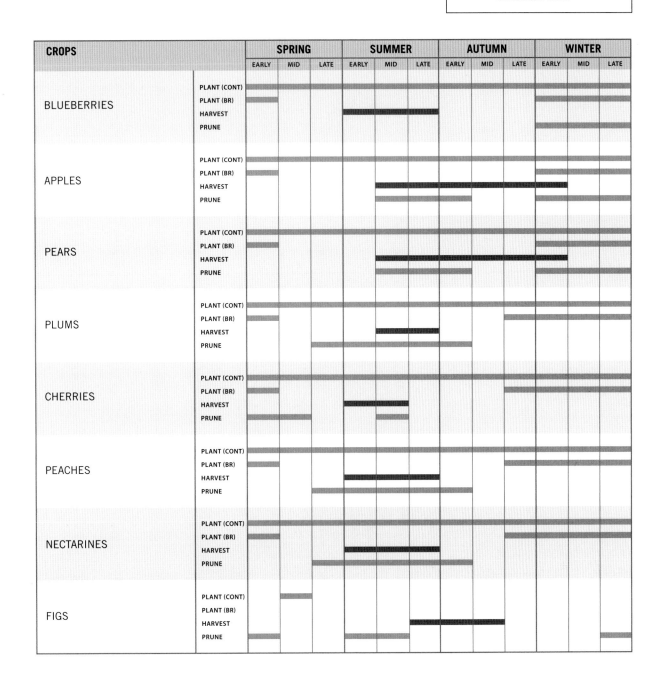

Problem solver

The organic approach

One of the best things about growing your own fruit and vegetables is that you can choose whether you want organic produce or not. Both organic and non-organic approaches have their pros and cons, so weigh these up carefully. You may find yourself compromising and using a bit of both – hand-weeding here and applying weedkillers there, for example – when making decisions about your garden's management.

Different approaches

In simple terms, taking a non-organic approach means using man-made fertilizers and pesticides to manage your garden. Organic gardening, on the other hand, involves using natural, non-artificial methods. The essence of organic gardening is to harness nature for your benefit, creating a balance between predators and prey, and using natural resources sensibly and sustainably, with as little impact on the environment as possible.

Feeding

There is a range of organic and non-organic fertilizers available, but you can't beat organic matter such as well-rotted manure or compost for mulching and improving the soil.

Tackling pests and diseases

For non-organic gardeners there is a variety of chemical sprays for targeting pests and diseases. Organic gardening requires more planning, and you may need to use a few methods to keep problems at bay. Sowing marigolds to draw aphids away from crops – known as companion planting – is one such pest control method, while biological control is another and is especially useful for undercover crops. Here, natural predators are used to prey on the pests. Another option is to plant sacrificial plants to shield valuable crops from damage. However, if these techniques fail to solve the problem, there are also organic sprays that can be used to target specific pests.

Plant diseases can often be difficult to control organically so it is best to aim for prevention rather than cure.

Weed management

For the non-organic gardener there is a range of highly effective weedkillers, but if you've chosen to go organic, or simply don't want to use chemicals near your crops, weeding manually is the best option. The saying that "one year's weed is seven years' seed" is a useful reminder to try to remove weeds before they can set seed.

(left) **Nasturtiums** *are good companion plants, and are said to draw blackfly away from crops. Their edible leaves, flowers, and seeds have a peppery flavour.*

(right) **Apply a mulch** *of bark chippings between plants as this will helps to suppress weeds. Grow a mix of crops to discourage attack from pests.*

Preventing problems

Whether you decide to go organic or not, your primary aim should be to encourage resilient, healthy plants, as these are best able to withstand competition from weeds. Make sure your site and soil are suitable for your crops: improve any compacted areas by digging in plenty of bulky organic matter; ensure that plants are well ventilated and not too crowded; and enrich nutrient-deficient plots with an appropriate fertilizer.

Common problems

Plants are affected by a number of factors, including nutrition, soil, and climate. If your plants look sickly, you may need to do some detective work to make an accurate diagnosis. For example, if your soil is sandy, or very acidic or alkaline, it may be prone to nutrient deficiencies (see p.246), while an over-cropped site can be exhausted of a specific nutrient. Bear in mind that blindly applying fertilizers in an attempt to solve the problem can be just as harmful to plants, not to mention environmentally unsound.

Soils may also contain pockets of compaction that impede root growth, or waterlogged areas that can cause roots to rot; "rainshadows" against walls or fences can cause dry spots. Digging in organic matter to improve the soil structure will help. Weather-related damage, such as scorching of foliage by frost, sun, or wind, can often look very dramatic, but this damage is often superficial and, because the root system is unharmed, plants will often re-sprout and recover (see p.244).

Preventing weeds

In an ideal gardening world we would prevent weeds appearing rather than simply controlling them once they've established. Realistically, this doesn't always happen, but luckily there are ways to tackle both situations.

Weed-suppressing mulches are good at preventing unwanted growth, as weeds will quickly exploit bare soil if you let them. Your options include man-made materials, such as weed control fabric or black plastic sheeting, flattened cardboard boxes, or recycled sheets of polythene – laying these on your plot in autumn will save you a vast amount of weeding come the spring. Alternatively, an 8cm (3in) thick layer of organic matter, such as weed-free garden compost or well-rotted manure, can also be effective and also has the benefit of releasing

Mature courgette plants and other trailing crops suppress weeds naturally. Other plants that are good at this include potatoes, pumpkins, and vigorous leafy plants such as Swiss chard.

Preparation is key, *so dig over the soil well at the beginning of the season, and remove any weeds that may have developed.*

valuable nutrients as it decomposes.

Crops are most vulnerable to weed competition when they are young, so try a nifty technique known as the "stale seedbed" to trick weed seeds into germinating before this. Simply prepare your bed, water well, and keep moist. After one week a flush of weed seedlings will appear – remove these then sow your chosen seed.

Dealing with weeds

There are a number of organic tactics to try when removing weeds. Manually digging them out with a hoe or hand fork is often the best method, but be aware that shallow-rooted crops such as cherries and raspberries can sucker profusely if their roots are damaged. Flame guns can be used to scorch annual weeds, and perennials can be smothered with a mulch and then dug out completely. You can also choose from a number of highly effective non-organic weedkillers – follow the manufacturer's guidelines with care.

Weeding tips

It is vital to do all you can to prevent and remove weeds from your plot, as they will compete with your crops for water, nutrition, and space, and may also harbour pests and diseases. Try to do so before weeds have a chance to flower and produce more seeds.

1 Hoeing and hand-weeding Using a hoe to weed between rows of plants will help you to cover large areas with relative speed. If possible, weed on a dry day and leave the weeds on the soil surface to shrivel and die. If you are removing perennial weeds, do so with a garden or hand fork, and try to ensure that you remove the entire root so the weeds do not regenerate.

2 Feeding Strong, healthy plants are best able to compete with weeds, so prepare the soil in advance, and apply fertilizer to the soil if necessary. Dig in plenty of well-rotted manure or compost before planting as well.

3 Mulching with straw Even vigorous, leafy plants like potatoes will benefit from a mulch of material, such as straw, to prevent competing weeds from growing nearby.

4 Planting through plastic Many crops benefit from being planted through black plastic sheeting, which not only suppresses weeds but has the added benefits of keeping the soil warm and helping to prevent it drying out. This method is especially useful for crops that don't produce weed-suppressing foliage, like strawberries and onions.

Common weeds

1 Stinging nettle These tall-growing weeds can establish a deep network of roots and their leaves deliver a painful sting. Dig them out completely to get rid of them.

2 Dock The broad, unattractive leaves of this perennial weed look unsightly in a vegetable patch. The plants have a long tap root, which should be entirely removed from the ground.

3 Creeping buttercup This common perennial weed is found in many gardens. It uses horizontal runners to creep across the ground – dig out its whole root system or it will regenerate.

4 Shepherd's purse This annual weed produces characteristic purple heart-shaped seed pods – to prevent it spreading, dig the plants up and compost them before the seed pods form.

5 Groundsel This annual weed produces fluffy white seedheads from yellow, daisy-like flowers. Dig the plants out before the seeds have a chance to disperse.

6 Goosegrass Also known as "cleavers", this sticky, clinging weed is covered with tiny hooks and can rapidly spread throughout a vegetable patch. It can be pulled up by hand.

7 Dandelion A common perennial weed, dandelions must be dug out before the seeds are released. Remove the tap root completely as any pieces left behind will regenerate.

8 Hairy bittercress Target this fast-growing annual while it is young and easiest to pull up. Do not allow the delicate seed pods to form as they split easily and will spread seed far and wide.

9 Creeping thistle This tough perennial is difficult to eradicate so you may need to consider using a chemical weedkiller.

10 Bindweed This perennial weed can be very difficult to eradicate. Ensure that you remove the entire root before destroying it. Consider applying a systemic weedkiller.

11 Annual meadow grass This common lawn grass is considered a weed in the vegetable patch – the best way to deal with it is to hoe it regularly to prevent it flowering and setting seed.

12 Ragwort This rosette-forming annual weed has attractive yellow flowers but can produce a prolific amount of seeds; dig the plants out before these have a chance to form.

Avoiding pests and diseases

No garden is immune to attack from pests and diseases, but there are measures you can take to reduce the risk, and methods you can use to deal with problems as they arise, both organic and non-organic. Maintaining good garden hygiene and encouraging strong crops, by keeping plants well fed, well watered, and well ventilated, is a good start. Keep in mind that it is easier to prevent pests and diseases rather than cure them.

Removal of infected crops *is, in some cases, virtually fundamental for the next year's success. Removing diseased plants will significantly reduce the risk of infection the following year.*

copper tape to containers to deter slugs; or try companion planting. A classic partnership is marigolds with tomatoes – the marigolds are believed to deter whitefly. Moving crops to a new location is useful for disrupting the lifecycle of soil-borne problems. And you can always remove larger pests, such as caterpillars, by hand.

Of course, pesticides are useful too – if the population of a pest is utterly out of control, they can offer a quick, effective solution. Choose from fatty acid-based organic sprays, or artificial pesticides with man-made active ingredients. As with weedkillers, it's important to follow the instructions on the packaging very carefully.

Dealing with pests

Building up a population of beneficial creatures is a useful organic method for keeping pests at bay. Encourage them by providing habitats, such as ponds for frogs and suitable flowers for hoverflies. This can also attract other useful wildlife such as bees and butterflies. You may also want to use biological controls, such as parasitic wasps to target whitefly, predatory mites to feed on red spider mite, and microscopic eelworms to infect slugs. Introducing the predator before the pests become too numerous is crucial, but the results can be very effective.

There are many other organic methods to try: create a barrier against pests by covering crops with insect-proof mesh or a tunnel cloche; attach

Dealing with diseases

The limited number of fungicides available to amateur gardeners means that avoiding or preventing plant diseases is a far better option than controlling them once they arrive. There is a range of organic and non-organic methods to try but one of the most fundamental goals should be good garden hygiene:

keep pruning and digging tools sterilized. It also helps to keep plants well watered and well ventilated.

For non-organic gardeners, fungicides are also an option, but always follow the manufacturer's guidelines and, if plants are severely affected, consider consigning them to the compost heap as a lost cause.

Resistant varieties

Choosing resistant varieties and planting them in uncontaminated soil will also help to avoid infection. For some crops this can be very important: 'Kilaxy' cabbage shows good resistance to clubroot, which is useful as there is no fungicidal cure for this root disease and its spores can survive in the soil for up to 20 years. There are resistant varieties within many crops, so keep on the lookout. Remember though, that resistance doesn't mean immunity and plants may still succumb.

To prevent the risk of further contamination, *do not compost any infected plant material. As a precaution, remove any diseased plants from your site or burn them.*

Natural measures

Be pro-active in your garden and try to discourage pests from attacking. Daily walks among your crops will allow you to spot problems early, and once you spot the symptoms of a specific problem, you'll be well armed with the tools to make an informed plan of attack. For further, more specific pests and diseases information, see pages 238–247.

1 Pollinating Planting nectar-rich flowering annuals and perennials will attract hoverflies, whose larvae have a voracious appetite for aphids. As well as looking beautiful, these flowers will also attract pollinating bees and butterflies to the garden. Provide hibernation sites for them.

2 Beneficial wildlife Consider making your garden amphibian-friendly. A wildlife pond, log pile, or shady, damp corner will entice frogs and toads, which love to eat one of the garden's most common pests: slugs.

3 Insect-proof mesh Fine mesh is good for protecting crops such as brassicas, as it will deter their common pest: cabbage white butterflies. Support the mesh on sticks and bury it in the soil, all the way around the plants, to stop the pests getting underneath.

4 Companion planting Rows of nasturtiums or marigolds planted around the plot not only look beautiful but may help to draw marauding pests, such as aphids, away from valuable crops.

Common pests

1 Wasps These common pests target the sweet flesh of ripe fruits, especially apples, pears, and plums. Hang jam and water traps from the branches of the trees to lure them away.

2 Cabbage caterpillars Nibbling the leaves and boring into the heart of the cabbages, these pests cause considerable damage. Pick them off, use netting, or apply an appropriate insecticide.

3 Onion fly These maggots attack the roots of onions and leeks and bore into the base of the vegetables, causing them to rot. Destroy infested plants. Rotate crops and cover with fleece.

4 Leek moth There is no insecticide for these caterpillars, which mine the leaves and flesh of leeks and onions. Kill any that you find, and cover crops with horticultural fleece to deter them.

5 Colorado beetle Not established in the UK, this is a serious pest, so report any sightings to DEFRA. The yellow- and black-striped beetles eat the foliage of potatoes and tomatoes.

6 Pea moth Eggs are laid on plants in summer; the caterpillars hatch and burrow into the pods to eat the peas. Sow early or late types to avoid the adult moths, or protect plants with netting.

7 Carrot fly The maggots tunnel into carrots and parsnips. Use horticultural fleece to deter them or grow resistant varieties.

8 Codling moth The caterpillars of this pest tunnel into apples and pears and feed on the cores. Use pheromone traps and spray the fruits with an appropriate insecticide in summer.

9 Wireworms This pest is the larvae of the click beetle and will kill seedlings and feed on potatoes and onions. There is no available insecticide, so remove the larvae as you spot them.

10 Mealy cabbage aphids Massed on underside of brassica leaves and sucking the sap out, this pest turns the foliage yellowish-white. Control it using an appropriate insecticide.

11 Whitefly The pest sucks sap from the underside of leaves and excretes honeydew, encouraging sooty mould to form. Use a biological control in greenhouses or use insecticide.

12 Raspberry beetle Feeding on raspberries, blackberries, and other hybrids, this pest causes grey-brown patches to form on the fruits. Spray with insecticide; this pest is hard to control.

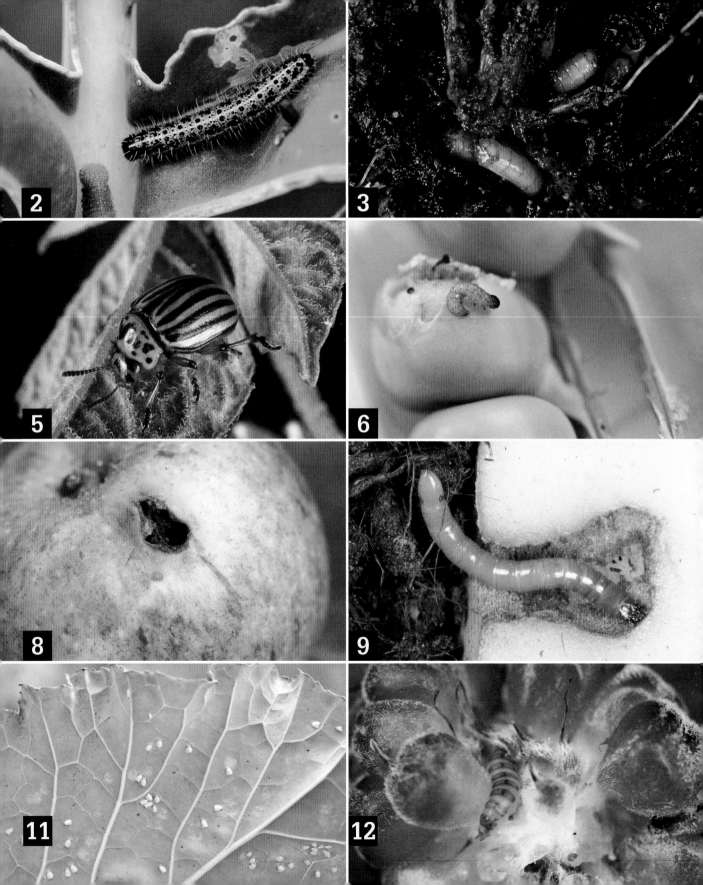

13 Pea and bean weevil This pest targets the leaves of peas and beans, eating neat "U" shapes out of the margins. As the majority of the leaf is unharmed, attacks are rarely fatal, but raise plants in pots if necessary or spray with an insecticide.

14 Gooseberry sawfly Causing severe damage to gooseberries and redcurrants, this pest can completely strip plants of their leaves. Pick insects off or use a biological or chemical control.

15 Plum fruit moth The pale pink caterpillars feed on the flesh of plums, damsons, and greengages. Hang pheromone traps in early summer to catch adult males – this can reduce damage.

16 Pear midge This pest lays its eggs in pear blossom; the maggots hatch and then feed inside the fruits, causing them to turn black and shrivel. Remove infested fruits as you spot them.

17 Capsid bugs Sucking the sap from apples and currants, this pest creates corky, brown patches on the skin of fruits. Chemical controls are available but affected fruit is still edible.

18 Cabbage root fly The white larvae of this common brassica pest feed on roots and will severely damage young plants. There is no insecticide; the best defence is brassica collars.

19 Aphids Greenfly or blackfly are tiny, swarming, sap-sucking insects common on many plants and can distort new growth. Encourage natural predators or apply an appropriate insecticide.

20 Red spider mite Common in greenhouses, this pest causes the leaves of a range of plants to become mottled, turn yellow, and then drop. Use a biological control or a fatty acid spray.

21 Cutworms These brownish white caterpillars target the roots of seedlings and eat holes in root vegetables. There is no effective cure, so remove the pest by hand if you spot it.

22 Slugs and snails These very common pests will target leafy crops and seedlings, causing rapid damage. Deter them using gritty barriers or copper tape, set up beer traps, or use pellets.

23 Root aphids Carrots and lettuces are vulnerable to this pest, which suck sap from roots, causing the plants to wilt. There is no cure so practise crop rotation and keep plants well watered.

24 Asparagus beetles The adults and their larvae target the leaves and bark of asparagus plants and can rapidly defoliate them, causing the stems to die. Pick off any that you find, or apply an appropriate insecticide.

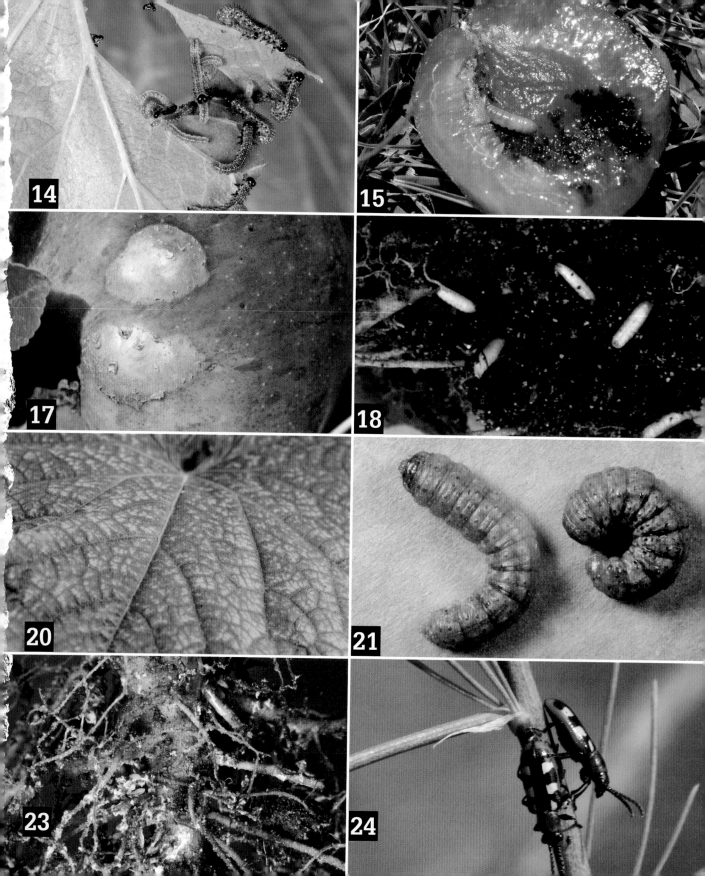

Common diseases

1 Scab This disease causes brown patches on the skins of apples and pears and can spread to leaves and branches. Rake up fallen leaves in autumn, as it can overwinter.

2 American gooseberry mildew Powdery fungal patches on leaves, fruits, and stems are a symptom of this disease. Keep plants pruned and well watered to reduce the risk of attack.

3 Rusts These fungi cause disease on many plants. They cause bright orange pustules to form on leaves or stems; remove infected material and rotate crops.

4 Bacterial leaf spot Yellow-ringed dead patches form on the leaves of crops such as brassicas and cucumbers. Remove and destroy affected leaves and rotate crops in future years.

5 Clubroot This slime mould affects brassica crops. It causes roots to swell and foliage to wilt, and can be fatal. Reduce the soil acidity with lime and improve drainage.

6 Downy mildew This disease causes brown patches on the leaves of lettuces and brassicas, with mouldy growth beneath. Destroy infected leaves and keep plants well ventilated.

7 Tomato blight Affecting mainly outdoor types, this disease causes stems, leaves, and fruits to discolour and rot: remove and destroy them. Spray with copper before symptoms are seen.

8 Cucumber mosaic virus Causing leaves to become mottled and distorted and stunting fruit growth, this disease affects a range of crops so destroy infected plants if symptoms are spotted.

9 Onion neck rot Onions, shallots, and garlic bulbs will become soft and coated with a fluffy grey mould. Rotate crops.

10 Onion white rot Able to survive in the soil for many years, it causes bulbs to rot and foliage to become yellow and wilt. Destroy infected plants carefully to avoid contamination.

11 Brown rot Affecting a range of tree fruits including pears and apples, the fungus rots the flesh and causes brown pustules to appear on the skin. Remove infected fruits promptly.

12 Fungal leaf spot This disease affects a range of crops, such as celery and strawberries, and causes grey, brown-ringed spots on leaves. Remove infected leaves and destroy them.

13 Sclerotinia This disease causes crops such as celery to turn yellow and suddenly wilt, with mouldy stems often containing black structures called sclerotia. It can persist in the soil for years so it is vital to remove and destroy infected plants promptly.

14 Strawberry viruses These cause a number of problems, such as yellowing leaves and stunted growth. Remove and destroy infected plants; rotate crops to deter future occurrences.

15 Canker This disease causes existing wounds in tree trunks to grow or distort, often causing resin to ooze from the bark. Prune the infected growth out and apply a copper fungicide.

16 Blossom end rot The result of a calcium deficiency, this disorder creates dark, mouldy patches on crops such as tomatoes and peppers. Remove affected fruits and water well.

17 Bitter pit Black spots or indentations will appear on the skins of apples, which can also develop bitter-tasting flesh. Keep any affected fruit trees mulched and well watered as the disorder is a result of drought-induced calcium deficiency.

18 Potato common scab Common in dry soils that lack organic matter, this disease causes unattractive corky, brown patches on the skin. Choose a resistant variety and water plants well.

19 Scorch Caused by either hot sun or cold, dry winds; both can strip the plant of its moisture and cause it to become brown and crisp. Shelter plants and water in the cool of the evening.

20 Raspberry cane blight This disease results in split, brittle canes and withered foliage. Cut any diseased wood out and destroy it. Prune the plants to encourage good ventilation.

21 Powdery mildew Affecting a range of crops, from courgettes to currants, this host-specific disease causes a white coating on leaves and fruits; remove these and water plants well.

22 Honey fungus This root disease can be fatal to trees; its honey-coloured toadstools may appear in the autumn. Any plant with white fungal growth should be dug up and destroyed.

23 Silver leaf Plum, cherry, apricot, and peach trees are at risk, developing a silvery appearance on the leaves; branches may die back too. Prune in summer to reduce the risk of infection.

24 Botrytis Grey mould is a common fungus that causes fluffy greyish mould on crops, which will rot and die back. Any infected material should be removed promptly and destroyed.

25 Chocolate spot This disease affects broad beans, resulting in dark brown or greyish spreading spots on the foliage, stem, and pods. Remove any infected plants and destroy them.

26 Potato black leg Leaves become yellow and stems rot and become black at the base; remove any infected plants and destroy them. Rotate potato crops in future seasons.

27 Tomato ghost spot Although fruits do not become inedible, they develop faint yellow or green rings on the skin.

28 Damping off Deterred by growing crops in clean pots and watering them with mains water, damping off causes greenhouse seedlings to collapse and can affect their roots.

29 Parsnip canker This disease targets damaged roots, resulting in orange-brown growth at the top; spots can also appear on the leaves. Rotate crops and choose resistant varieties.

30 Potato blight This disease causes patchy, rotten foliage and later spreads to the tubers – destroy infected foliage. Spray with copper before symptoms are seen. Choose a resistant variety.

Common nutrient deficiencies

1 Iron Yellowing leaves which later brown at the edges can indicate a lack of iron. Add chelated iron to the soil.

2 Calcium A lack of water or an acidic soil can inhibit a plant's uptake of calcium, resulting in disorders such as blossom end rot (pictured). Keep plants well watered and lime the soil.

3 Magnesium Plants develop yellowing foliage that turns brown between the veins. Spray a solution of epsom salts on the leaves.

4 Boron This deficiency affects a variety of crops, causing roots to split and preventing sweetcorn from developing properly. Apply borax to the soil or use as a foliar spray for fruit trees.

5 Potassium A lack of this nutrient causes leaves to turn brown and plants to flower and set fruit poorly. This nutrient is easily leached from the soil, so apply tomato feed to plants.

6 Nitrogen The foliage of plants becomes yellow and overall growth is weak. Dig in well-rotted manure or apply fertilizer.

25

28

1

4

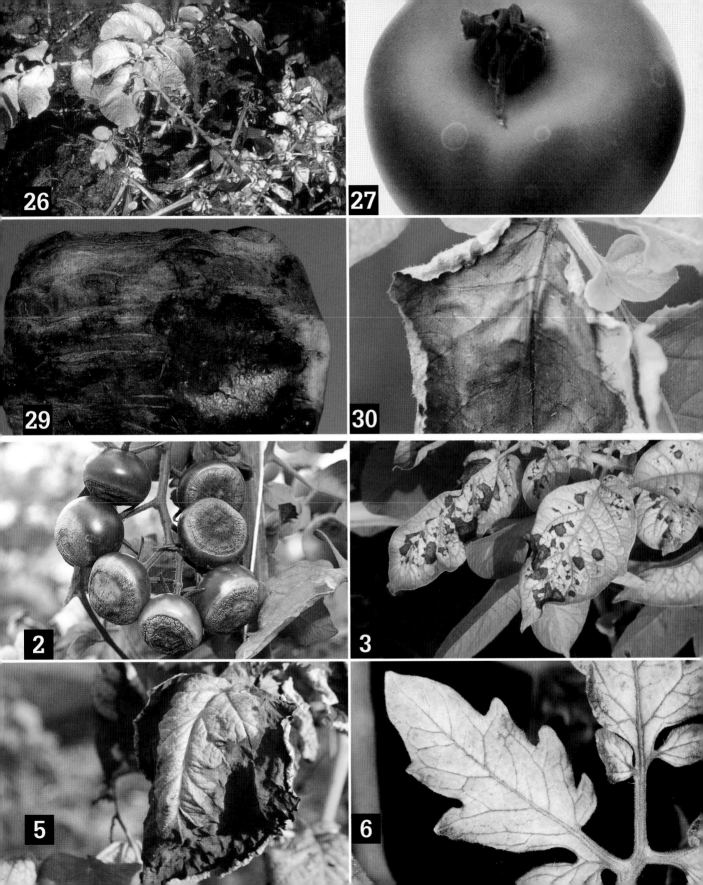

Useful resources

Seeds and plug plants

Chiltern Seeds
Bortree Stile
Ulverston
Cumbria
LA12 7PB
01229 581137
www.chilternseeds.co.uk

Dobies of Devon
Long Road
Paignton
Devon
TQ4 7SX
0844 701 7625
www.dobies.co.uk

D.T Brown
Bury Road
Newmarket
CB8 7PQ
0845 3710532
www.dtbrownseeds.co.uk

Edwin Tucker
Brewery Meadow
Stonepark
Ashburton
Newton Abbot
Devon
TQ13 7DG
01364 652233
www.edwintucker.com

Marshalls Seeds
Alconbury Hill
Huntingdon
Cambs
PE28 4HY
01480 443390
www.marshalls-seeds.co.uk

Mr Fothergill's
Kentford
Suffolk
CB8 7QB
0845 3710518
www.mr-fothergills.co.uk

Nicky's Nursery
Fairfield Road
Broadstairs
Kent
CT10 2JU
01843 600972
www.nickys-nursery.co.uk

Plant World Seeds
St Marychurch Road
Newton Abbot
Devon
TQ12 4SE
01803 872939
www.plant-world-seeds.com

Seeds of Italy
A1 Phoenix Industrial Estate
Rosslyn Cresent
Harrow
Middlesex
HA1 2SP
0208 427 5020
www.seedsofitaly.co.uk

Simpsons Seeds
The Walled Garden Nursery
Horningsham
Warminster
Wiltshire
BA12 7NQ
01985 845004
www.simpsonsseeds.co.uk

Suttons Seeds
Woodview Road
Paignton
Devon
TQ4 7NG
0844 922 0606
www.suttons.co.uk

The Real Seed Catalogue
PO Box 18
Newport
Pembrokeshire
SA65 0AA
01239 821107
www.realseeds.co.uk

The Organic Gardening Catalogue
Riverdene Business Park
Molesey Road
Hersham
Surrey
KT12 4RG
01932 253666
www.organiccatalogue.com

Thompson & Morgan
Poplar Lane
Ipswich
Suffolk
IP8 3BU
0844 248 5383
www.thompson-morgan.com

Victoriana Nursery Gardens
Buck Street
Challock
Ashford
Kent
TN25 4DG
01233 740529
www.victoriananursery.co.uk

Fruit trees and shrubs

Blackmoor Nurseries
Blackmoor
Hampshire
GU33 6BS
01420 477978
www.blackmoor.co.uk

Chris Bowers and Sons
Whispering Trees Nurseries
Wimbotsham
Norfolk
PE34 3QB
01366 388752
www.chrisbowers.co.uk

Keepers Nursery
Gallants Court
East Farleigh
Maidstone
Kent
ME15 0LE
01622 726465
www.keepers-nursery.co.uk

Ken Muir Ltd
Honeypot Farm
Rectory Road
Weeley Heath
Clacton-on-Sea
Essex
CO16 9BJ
01255 830181
www.kenmuir.co.uk

Reads Nursery
Douglas Farm
Falcon Lane
Ditchingham
Suffolk
NR35 2DY
01986 895555
www.readsnursery.co.uk

Biological pest control

Biowise
Hoyle Depot
Graffham
West Sussex
GU28 0LR
01798 867574
www.biowise-biocontrol.co.uk

Buzz Organics
PO Box 18
Pontefract
West Yorkshire
WF9 5WZ
08450 509409
www.buzzorganics.co.uk

Defenders
Coldharbour Farm
Amage Road
Wye
Ashford
TN25 5DB
01233 813121
www.defenders.co.uk

Green Gardener
Chandlers End
Mill Road
Stokesby
Great Yarmouth
NR29 3EY
01493 750061
www.greengardener.co.uk

Ladybird Plant Care
The Glasshouses
Fletching Common
Lewes
East Sussex
BN8 4JJ
0845 0945 499
www.ladybirdplantcare.co.uk

Sundries and equipment

Garden Direct
The Garden Centre
Birchall Lane
Cole Green
Hertford
SG14 2NR
0845 217 0788
www.gardendirect.co.uk

Gardeners' Heaven
2nd Floor
76–80 Southwark Street
London
SE1 0PN
0203 103 9310
www.gardenersheaven.co.uk

Greenfingers
10 Lindsay Square
Deans Industrial Estate
Livingston
West Lothian
EH54 8RL
0845 345 0728
www.greenfingers.com

Harrod Horticultural
Pinbush Road
Lowestoft
Suffolk
NR33 7NL
0845 402 5300
www.harrodhorticultural.com

Two Wests and Elliot
Unit 4, Carrwood Road
Sheepbridge Industrial Estate
Chesterfield
Derbyshire
S41 9RH
01246 451077
www.twowests.co.uk

Index

Main entries are indicated by **bold** page numbers. Main entries for crops include full details for sowing, growing, feeding, watering, cultivation, and harvesting. These details are not indexed separately.

Acknowledgments

The publisher would like to thank the following for their kind permission to reproduce their photographs:

(Key: a-above; b-below/bottom; c-centre; f-far; l-left; r-right; t-top)

Alamy Images: ableimages 118br, Andrea Jones Images 184bc, Bon Appetit 225c, Brigette Sullivan / Outer Focus Photos 178tl, 180fcr, Karen Cairns 203tr, 209cl, Nigel Cattlin 239crb, CJG 213c, Elena Elisseeva 221c, foodimagecollection 209ca, funkyfood London - Paul Williams 169br, Trish Gant 211tc, Anne Gilbert 118fbr, 163cla, Brian Hoffman 64cl, Marvin Dembinsky Photo Associates 223c, Peter Titmuss 181c, Rob Walls 118fcr; **Blackmoor Nurseries:** 222cr; **Corbis:** Klaus Hackenberg 210fcr, Jacqui Hurst 240br, Image Source 201ca, Ocean 120fcr, Emma Shervington 219c; **Dobies of Devon:** 44br, 58c, 58cr, 70cr, 75, 169c, 186cl, 186c, 202c; **Dorling Kindersley:** Alan Buckingham 13bc, 47crb, 47br, 49crb, 49br, 145crb, 200cr, 201br, 202cl, 202bc, 203tc, 203c, 203br, 204c, 205tc, 205fcr, 206cl, 206c, 206fcr, 207cla, 207ca, 207bc, 208cr, 208fcr, 210cl, 210c, 210cr, 211fcr, 212cl, 212c, 212cr, 212fcr, 214cl, 214c, 214cr, 214bl, 214fcr, 215tr, 215cla, 216c, 216cr, 216fcr, 216-217cl, 217cl, 218c, 218cr, 218bl, 218fcr, 219tr, 219cla, 219br, 220cl, 220c, 220cr, 221cla, 222cl, 222c, 222fcr, 224cl, 241cla, Caroline Reed 31tr, 213tr; Chauney Dunford 23br, 23fcra, 237ftr; Emma Callery 241tr; Jan Van Der Voort 237cra; Jo Whittingham 179ca, 185ca; Mel Shackleton 185cl; **DT Brown Seeds:** 76c, 76cr, 84c, 98cl, 108fcr, 158cl, 158c; **FLPA:** Nigel Cattlin 241tl, 243cra, 243clb, 243br, 246cra, 247br; **Fothergills:** 100fcr, 138c, 138cr, 140cl, 154c, 168tr; **GAP Photos:** Maxine Adcock 8cr, 155ca, Thomas Alamy 193c, Lee Avison 146c, BBC Magazines Ltd 129cla, 163c, Dave Bevan 126cr, 140bc, 247cra, Richard Bloom 27tr, Christina Bollen 187ca, Mark Bolton 231c, Elke Borkowski 26clb, 48bc, 170fcr, Jonathan Buckley 84cr, 142-143cr, 198-199, Chris Burrows 144cr, Simon Colmer 228-229, Sarah Cuttle 48bl, 131fcr, Lydia Evans 28bl, FhF Greenmedia 27br, 46cla, 130bc, 141fcrb, 145tc, Victoria Firmston 193bc, Suzie Gibbons 18clb, 24cr, Marcus Harpur 19cla, 155br, Michael Howes 99bc, Martin Hughes-Jones 176fcr, Lynn Keddie 63br, 131cla, Geoff Kidd 126fcr, 244crb, Michael King 27bc, 159bc, 186bl, 186bc, Fiona Lea 9br, Jenny Lilly 155bl, Howard Rice 168br, 185fcr, Gary Smith 11tl, 145cl, Friedrich Strauss 25tr, 27cr, 29tc, John Swithinbank 175bc, 193cla, Visions 128ca, Juliette Wade 19c, 88-89tc, 118bl, 177bc, Jo Whitworth 16-17ca, Mark Winwood 118c, 130fcr, 143c, 144bc; **Garden World Images:** Dave Bevan 239br, 242cra, 245, Sine Chesterman 225fcr, Francoise Davis 225tc, Giles DelaCroix 122c, Glenn Harper 224fcr, Martin Hughes-Jones 128fcr, Andrea Jones 224c, Trevor Sims 29bc, 64cr, 90-91cr, 122cl; **The Garden Collection:** Torie Chugg 64c, Liz Eddison 25tl, 27tc, Nicola Stocken Tomkins 25cra; **Getty Images:** Ben Bloom 223br, Richard Bloom 181cl, Brian Carter 244br, Sarah Cuttle 131ca, Michael Davis 170cr, FhF Greenmedia 118cr, Jan Tove Johansson 239tl, Photos Lamontagne 184c, Cora Niele 176cl, Howard Rice 187fcr, Gary K Smith 48, Mark Turner 118bc, Juliette Wade 182bc, Jo Whitworth 129fcrb; **iStockphoto.com:** 179clb; **Marshalls Seeds:** 62tr, 75bl, 80cl, 82cl, 97tr, 97bl, 97br, 104fcr; **Photolibrary:** 144fcr, 184bl, 184fcr; **Photoshot:** Photos Horticultural 80fcr; **RHS The Garden:** Tim Sandall 10bl; **Ron Ludekens:** 224cr; **Royal Horticultural Society:** 240tr, 245bl, 247tr, P. Becker 238br, 241crb, Andrew Halstead 241cra, Horticultural Science 243crb, 246tr, 247tl, 247cla, Joyce Maynard 239tr, 239cla, 240cra, 241bl, Pathology 242tr, 245clb; **Science Photo Library:** Dr Jeremy Burgess 245tl; **Suttons Seeds:** 48fbl, 76cl, 104cl, 104cr, 108c, 140c, 142fcr, 144cl, 160cl, 160cr, 168cra, 170cl; **Thompson & Morgan:** 45bc, 64fcr, 90cl, 98c, 99fbr, 100c, 100cr, 102cr, 122fcr, 142c, 154-155c, 155cr, 156c, 158c, 160c, 169tr, 200fcr; **Tozer Seeds:** 56tr; **Victoriana Nursery Gardens/Stephen Shirley:** 46cb, 68c, 70fcr, 89tr, 89ca, 89bl, 89fcrb, 89fbr, 90c, 169crb, 172cl, 176cr, 186cr, 202cr, 220-221fcr

All other images © Dorling Kindersley
For further information see:
www.dkimages.com

Author's acknowledgements:
Chauney Dunford for politely and patiently answering all my queries and tolerating my 'green pen moments'; Alison Shackleton for sending an early cover design to motivate me during the late hours; and to my parents for their never-ending support.

Dorling Kindersley would like to thank:
Mark Winwood for his exceptional work growing and photographing most of the vegetables featured in this book; and his wife, Lizzie, for her help and patience.

Louise Furnival, Steve Hernandez, Alan Crick, Lucie Pendred and James Perkins for their kind help.

Becky Tennant for additional design assistance; Fiona Wild for proofreading; and Susan Bosanko for indexing.

Robin and Brenda Beresford-Evans, and the growers at Cannizaro Allotments, Wimbledon, London.

Dobies/Suttons, D.T Brown, Floranova, Marshalls/Unwins, Mr Fothergill's, Thompson & Morgan, and Victoriana Nursery Gardens for their kind permission to reproduce their images.